To Susan,

Your friendship
helped me to do this.
Lots of love,

Wendy
(the <u>author</u>)

2005

CONSENSUAL FICTIONS: WOMEN, LIBERALISM,
AND THE ENGLISH NOVEL

WENDY S. JONES

Consensual Fictions:
Women, Liberalism, and
the English Novel

UNIVERSITY OF TORONTO PRESS
Toronto Buffalo London

© University of Toronto Press Incorporated 2005
Toronto Buffalo London
Printed in Canada

ISBN 0-8020-8717-5

Printed on acid-free paper

Library and Archives Canada Cataloguing in Publication

Jones, Wendy S.
  Consensual fictions : women, liberalism, and the English
novel / Wendy S. Jones.

  Includes bibliographical references and index.
  ISBN 0-8020-8717-5

  1. English fiction – 19th century – History and criticism.   2. English
fiction – 18th century – History and criticism.   3. Women in literature.
4. Liberalism in literature.   5. Marriage in literature.   I. Title.

PR830.M36J65 2005   823'.8093522   C2004-905805-3

University of Toronto Press acknowledges the financial assistance to
its publishing program of the Canada Council for the Arts and the
Ontario Arts Council.

University of Toronto Press acknowledges the financial support for its
publishing activities of the Government of Canada through the Book
Publishing Industry Development Program (BPIDP).

For Jos and Maggie

Contents

Acknowledgments

I have many people to thank for their intellectual and moral support as I worked on this project throughout the years. Susan Bruce, Walter Cohen, J. Ellen Gainor, Deborah Harrison, John Kucich, Shawn Maurer, Yona Zeldis McDonough, Kathryn Temple, Stuart Davis, Reeve Parker, and Martin Wechselblatt helped me to think through ideas at various times. Alison Case and Harry Shaw, fellow Richardson enthusiasts, were astute readers of my work on this favorite author. I am particularly grateful to Rick Bogel for his guidance, friendship, and loyalty. Gordon Teskey gave me vital feedback on my manuscript; even more important, our many conversations have challenged my assumptions and enriched my thinking. Chandra Talpade Mohanty has been a helpful friend and an inspirational scholar, and I have tried to emulate her example of dedicated scholarship that never forgets the practicality of ideas or the idealism of practice. From my first day as a graduate student, Laura Brown has been a steadfast advisor and advocate; I have often benefited from her clarity and wisdom. To Dorothy Mermin, I am indebted for rigorous attention to my work, sound advice of many kinds, and the pleasure of seeing a mentor become a friend.

Allyson May at University of Toronto Press offered excellent and substantial suggestions – and a touch of elegance – well beyond the mandate for copy-editing. The guidance and dedication of my editors, Jill McConkey and Barbara Porter, forwarded this project in gratifying ways. I thank my first proofreader, Maggie Vandermeer, for her careful reading of the manuscript. An earlier, shorter version of chapter 2 was published as 'The Dialectic of Love in *Sir Charles Grandison*,' in *Eighteenth-Century Fiction* 8, no. 1 (October 1995): 15–34; this was reprinted in slightly modified form in *Passion and Virtue: Essays on the Novels of*

Samuel Richardson, ed. David Blewett (Toronto: University of Toronto Press, 2001), 295–316. Chapter 4 also appeared in an earlier, shorter form as 'Feminism, Fiction, and Contract Theory: Trollope's *He Knew He Was Right*,' *Criticism* (Summer 1994): 401–14. I thank the University of Toronto Press and Wayne State University Press for permission to incorporate this work in *Consensual Fictions*. I gratefully acknowledge the generous financial contribution of the Hull Fund of Cornell University towards publication.

To my family, I owe the nurture that only the best of families can provide. My parents, Vicki and Iz Singer, have been sustaining influences. My daughters, Jocelyn and Maggie Sawyer, provided companionship and fun; it has been wonderful to observe them become increasingly able to understand my work. My husband, Paul Sawyer, has given advice, tolerance, and empathy. I could not have completed this project without his consistent and dedicated support.

The competing claims of public and private selves continue to pose dilemmas for women, no matter how factitious and reactionary this distinction. In the following pages, I follow the logic of this conflict within the English novel; I have lived it as well. Even within the academy, and even within the humanities, women still make difficult choices that they should not have to make. Because of this, in addition to my gratitude to colleagues and family for their help with various aspects of my work, I also thank them for never ceasing to think of me as a scholar, even when some of my personal decisions left me with significantly fewer prospects for an academic career. Their continued faith and respect was in the end their most important contribution.

With the hope that in our policies, laws, and institutions, as well as in our private lives, we will realize the value as well as the price of motherhood, I lovingly dedicate this book to my daughters.

CONSENSUAL FICTIONS

Introduction

'Witty was that young Gentlewoman's answer to an inconsiderate suitor: who with much instancy solicited the father for the affection of his daughter; whereto having at last consented, and the covenants of marriage concluded, this indiscreet wooer unseasonably imparts his mind to the daughter; who made strange of with, saying, *she never heard of any such matter: Yea but*, replied he, *I have made your father herewith acquainted, and he hath already consented: And you may marry him too*, answered she, *for you must hold me excused.*'[1]

This clever anecdote from an early conduct book, *The English Gentlewoman, drawne out to the full Body* (1641), testifies to the rise of the marriage for love, the expectation that children – even daughters – will have a say in choosing their spouses and will not be forced into repugnant matches. At the same time, it dramatizes the conflicts in authority engendered by this shift in attitude from an earlier time, when arranged marriages were the norm among the propertied classes. It is therefore as much a story about the clash between emergent and residual beliefs as it is the story of a confrontation among a father, a daughter, and a lover. The suitor is confident that he can manipulate a match without the daughter's knowledge because he rightly assumes that the father has authority over her marriage choice. Indeed, the father feels entitled to negotiate on his own. But he does so only after the persistent urging of the suitor; such reluctance betrays his awareness that his methods are not entirely scrupulous. In the current day and age, his daughter's consent would be considered a vital part of the engagement. For this reason, the wooer is naively tactless in announcing his engagement as a *fait accompli* to his betrothed: whatever bargaining has gone on behind the scenes, mores as well as morality demand that he should have attempted an exchange of a more romantic sort. It is therefore not surprising that the daughter finds such bargaining 'strange' and rejects it altogether, implicitly claiming responsibility for her decision to marry. The abrupt switch from narration to dialogue formally replicates the shift in responsibility for the match from father to daughter: third person narration encodes the daughter's lack of agency, while the shift to dialogue makes it clear that lovers, not parents, must plot their own course. It is significant that this challenge to the father's authority comes from a daughter rather than a son, for this suggests that changing attitudes towards love and marriage ruptured the seamless transfer of patriarchal authority from father to husband.

Although the young woman's rejoinder appears to settle the issue of authority over the marriage choice in this instance, it fails to resolve the fundamental conflict in obligations. However wrongly the father has behaved, filial obedience and respect for a father's wishes were cherished values, especially on the part of daughters: 'a strong sense of duty is no bad part of a woman's portion,' says Anne Elliot,' the heroine of *Persuasion*.[2] Yet if women were to choose their husbands, they were obviously excused from unwavering deference to their fathers.

By epitomizing the conflicts engendered by a broad shift in belief about marriage, the witty gentlewoman's anecdote encapsulates the history of the rise of married love and the consequences of this ideal for women. In the pages that follow I hope to demonstrate that the novel helped to ratify love as both the moral prerequisite to Christian marriage and the emotional basis for individual happiness, and that this project was inextricable from exploring the implications for women of the basic 'right' to choose a spouse. Yet this story does not begin with the novel. Although the novel was instrumental in asserting modern ideals of marriage, the moral imperative to marry for love predated the establishment of the genre as a respectable literary form in the mid-eighteenth century. This new ethic had its origins in classic liberalism, in particular the writings of John Locke, whose account of the contractual origins of civil society epitomized an emergent 'structure of feeling' – a fundamental way of conceptualizing one's place in and relation to the world – within collective belief.[3] Following from the premise that the civil society originated in a social contract, legitimate relationships of various kinds, including marriage, began to be seen as based on consent rather than force. It is no accident that the rise of married love and the cultural hegemony of liberal theory coincide, or that

consensual married love, with its emphasis on the individual's significance, identity, and right to self-fulfilment, articulates the very characteristics that liberal theory grants to its citizen-subjects.

Changing ideas about marriage therefore created an important theoretical ground for conceptualizing women's rights. Consensual married love implied what I call a 'contractual subjectivity' for women that
was seen by many, whether in positive or negative terms, as ultimately
incompatible with women's subjection. If men and women entered
marriage voluntarily out of mutual regard, this implied that a woman
should not be subordinate to her husband, or considered his inferior,
for if she were capable of choosing her spouse, she was presumably
capable of other important choices and of taking responsibility for her
life. Married love also undermined rigid conceptions of sexual difference, a crucial theoretical justification of women's subordination. If
women were the companions rather than the servants of men, the
sexes necessarily had much in common, and therefore ought to have
equal laws and opportunities. Or, to put it in terms of the liberal theory
that informed this logic, once love rather than status or wealth was
supposed to be the basis for marriage, the lovers rather than their parents became parties to the marriage contract. Since women as well as
men were independent agents in this important transaction, wives
were entitled to the same protections and liberties that civil society
theoretically accorded to their husbands. Determining the proper place
of women in society was therefore very much a part of the novel's persistent thematic focus on the virtues of married love.

The ideal of consensual married love and the liberal version of
women's subjectivity it generated were inextricable from the politics of
class. Initially embraced by the 'middling sort' in the seventeenth century, an ethic of married love gradually supplanted the older, primarily
aristocratic, ideal of marriage for interest. This displacement of aristocratic beliefs and traditions was an important means by which the middle classes would secure their legitimation as part of England's elite.
By asserting the principle that marriage should be motivated by love
rather than status or money, an economically successful middle class
designated their own social group as eligible to enter England's ruling
elite through family connections. Even more important, they appropriated enormous symbolic capital by assuming responsibility for generating England's ethical and representational codes with respect to marriage and other subjects. In the course of the following two centuries,
middle-class ideals of love and marriage were accepted by disparate

social groups: the love match came to be viewed generally not as an exception restricted to a lucky few, but as a moral imperative for all.

As marriage for love gained acceptance, it became necessary to rede-fine 'love' in ways that were appropriate for the people most affected by new ways of negotiating marriage – those who owned money or property. Love had to be conceptualized in such a way as to safeguard English society from the destabilizing consequences of affective indi-vidualism, most notably, class miscegenation. It was feared that if per-sonal desires were allowed to dictate decisions about marriage, there was nothing to prevent people from marrying vastly beneath their sta-tion, and upsetting the hierarchical structure of English society. Love had to encode good judgment so that young people, particularly young women, would make appropriate choices. The novel responded to this mandate. In the eighteenth century, novels distinguished legiti-mate kinds of love from unstable and corrupted, primarily aristocratic, forms of passion with which love had been previously identified, rep-resenting both virtuous passion and warm friendship as normative, acceptable options that led to good marriages.[4]

In the nineteenth century, while these definitions remained intact, other cultural imperatives led to the elevation of love over companion-ship as a marital motive, a view we still accept. Nineteenth-century writers, responding to a fear of widespread materialism and selfish-ness rather than to the need to maintain social and economic bound-aries, shifted the terms of valorization towards passionate love, al-though they never completely rejected companionship as an acceptable basis for marriage. In this period, the dangers of individualism were associated with economic rather than libidinal desire: the unbridled greed of *homo oeconomicus* was a greater threat than his errant sexuality. In the Victorian novel, as in novels of the previous century, married love is identified as virtuous, but in contradistinction to a commercial rather than an aristocratic ethos.

The elevation of passion over friendship as the most important fac-tor in the marriage choice strengthened the argument for women's autonomy that had been implicit in an ideal of consensual married love from the start. For if eighteenth-century constructions of love encoded the social control of desire to fix on appropriate subjects, such safeguards also delimited women's independence by bonding paren-tal-paternal criteria and authority to desire itself, since strategies for the social and economic advancement of individual families, such as marrying 'up,' often advanced the classes to which they belonged. The cultural endorsement of strong feeling also meant a more cogent emphasis on women's desiring and autonomous selfhood.

The ideal of consensual marriage thus threatened the status quo of English society in the eighteenth and nineteenth centuries with respect to its established hierarchies of gender and socio-economic status. The typologizing of love provided a way of disarming the threat of individual desire to social stability, at least in theory. But the progressive implications for women of new 'liberal' and liberating ways of thinking about marriage proved harder to undermine, even in the earlier part of this period. For even when acceptable forms of passion appeared to guarantee a woman's proper choice, the threat of her autonomy was inherent in the fact of choice itself. For this reason, despite the prevalence of an ethic of married love, cultural allegiance divided between two co-existing versions of marriage, both of which remained influential models for thinking about heterosexual relationships. A traditional, patriarchal view of marriage in which women were subordinate conflicted with a progressive, consensual ideal that could potentially reorganize relationships between men and women in revolutionary ways. Novels clearly show the tension between cultural ideals: many attempt to reconcile both versions of marriage by representing marriage as a loving friendship between spouses where the husband is nevertheless lord and master.

Forms of discourse other than the novel were certainly instrumental in asserting new beliefs about marriage, and they also provide material for analysing cultural attitudes. *The Spectator* in particular repeatedly articulates the middle-class ideology of marriage that predominates in the novel. And much of eighteenth-century women's poetry concerns marriage, particularly its oppressive aspects for women. Nevertheless, marriage and related topics do not receive the kind of sustained attention in other genres that they do in the novel. Dramatic comedy, for instance, in which the marriage choice is a central and recurring theme, does not explore this topic with the depth and seriousness that the novel devotes to it. Even a suggestive statement such as that made by Congreve's Mirabell, that she will 'dwindle into a wife' – a statement that openly signals the relationship between marriage *comme il faut* and women's restrictions – is no more than a semaphore.[5] But exploring the implications of marriage for love became the novel's 'repetition compulsion,' as novel after novel attempted to anticipate and resolve the possibilities and problems associated with this new ethic. As Ruth

Perry observes, by the second half of the eighteenth century, 'it is difficult to think of a single novel in which no woman is pressured to
marry against her will – or not to marry where she wishes to – because
of some family exigency that creates an unresolvable dilemma between
duty and desire.'[6] This focus remained consistent throughout the following century, and the novel was so bound up with these issues that
when Elizabeth Barrett Browning speculated on writing a poem that
would confront sexual mores and expectations, 'running into the midst
of our conventions, and rushing into drawing rooms and the like,
"where angels fear to tread"; and so, meeting face to face and without
mask the Humanity of the age and speaking the truth as I conceive of it
out plainly,' she thought of her work as 'a sort of novel-poem.'[7] Later,
when she had written this 'novel-poem,' which was of course *Aurora
Leigh*, she compared it to *Clarissa*.[8]

A particular conjuncture of literary and social history caused the
novel to focus on courtship and marriage almost exclusively, revising
earlier attitudes in specific, consistent, and highly legible ways. Love
had traditionally been the subject of prose fiction; by reforming the
representation of love in accordance with new ideals of marriage, novelists also reformed the genre itself, in the process becoming the self-
appointed sages of everyday life. In a quest for legitimacy, they rein-
vented their fictions in the image of a largely middle-class audience
who characterized themselves as guardians of virtue, as opposed to
the morally lax upper and lower classes.[9] Two mandates therefore
guided the representation of marriage and related issues in the novel:
dissociating the genre from aristocratic beliefs and asserting the
novel's moral and didactic nature. In the traditional romance, love is a
pervasive trope for expressing the aristocratic identification of worth
with birth: true love is repeatedly shown to be inspired by noble character, for which the prerequisite is always noble blood. The novel represents desire as constituted by a different kind of value: moral
worth.[10] This revision of representational codes undermines aristocratic ideals in the process of asserting middle-class beliefs about the
value of individual morality, which is acquired rather than inherited.
The rise of married love thus proved to be foundational for the establishment of the novel as a serious literary form; by defining ideals of
love and marriage, novelists distinguished their 'new Species of Writing'[11] from other types of prose fiction such as romances and scandalous novels, many of which had been published relatively recently or
were contemporaneous.

The novel's moralization of love and marriage had much to do with its presumed audience. As anti-novelistic discourse through the nineteenth century reveals, many feared that the consumers of novels were women, who were prone to confuse truth with fiction in dangerous ways.[12] Fiction's deleterious effects were likely to be registered in the areas which concerned a woman most: courtship, marriage, and family, as we see from novels which thematize the dangers of reading and writing. It was widely believed that a young lady was likely to glean unrealistic expectations about her prospective spouse and the process of courtship from her reading, as happens in two well-known works, Charlotte Lennox's *The Female Quixote* and Jane Austen's *Sense and Sensibility*. The novel's revision of romance addressed the dangers of fiction by adhering to the twin imperatives of ethics and realism, offering, in eighteenth-century critical terminology, 'a *faithfull* and *chaste* copy of Real Lives and Manners.'[13] Indeed, the injunction to realism added special urgency to the mandate for ethical representation. As Samuel Johnson argues in *Rambler* 4, the novel's realism renders it more influential, and therefore novelists have a responsibility to 'convey the knowledge of vice and virtue.'[14]

Literary history thus tells us why the novel is preoccupied with marriage; individual narratives show us how the genre provided what William Warner calls 'replacement fictions' for earlier representations of the subject.[15] But an equally compelling reason for looking at novels as opposed to other forms of writing is that, through the workings of literary form, we can trace the trajectory of the specific cultural logic that followed from the new ideal of consensual marriage. Novelistic form reveals the working through of ideological problems associated with a liberal ideal of married love. For whether individual novelists accepted or undermined the progressive implications of consensual marriage for women, they necessarily responded to its challenge.[16] They shaped their responses primarily through the formal device of the multiple plot.

It is a commonplace in novel criticism that multiple plots revolve around similar themes and topics within a given work. In his study of the Victorian multiplot novel, Peter Garrett complicates this basic insight by viewing the multiple plot in terms of Mikhail Bakhtin's concept of dialogism. Multiple plots evince a 'tension between [the] structuring principles' of unity and multiplicity that enables a play of meaning: 'The devices of analogical and causal connection, metaphoric and metonymic links between the novel's double plots ... produce a high degree of formal coherence, but they are all subject to the play of shifting perspectives, a movement of continual substitution which exceeds and resists any monological formulation.'[17] I would argue, however, that in eighteenth- and nineteenth-century novels, the use of the multiplot form does not stem from an abstract allegiance to multiplicity, as Garrett would suggest, nor do the majority of novels employ multiple narratives to consider a wide or eclectic range of issues. Rather, multiplot novels of this period address a specific set of cultural problems associated with the ways in which liberalism influenced conceptualizations of marriage, love, and gender. Multiplot structure facilitates the exploration of this subject, as different story lines can be used to suggest alternatives with respect to values and choices. The multiple plot also frequently serves to resolve contradictions that re-emerge when they are seen outside the mechanism of narrative, such as the desire to reconcile patriarchal and liberal conceptualizations of marriage.

Reading novels for what they tell us about cultural ideals of love and marriage has led me to engage with scholarship in several areas. I intend first to contribute to the branch of cultural and literary studies that explores the cultural construction of desire. In this field, heterosexual desire is largely neglected by scholars of literature, culture, and history, who in recent years have tended to treat heterosexuality as the norm which, in contradistinction to alternative modes of feeling and identity,[18] has no need to speak its name. I hope that my account of the novel's role in defining modes of love opens further discussion of this important subject.

This study also draws upon political theory. Histories of the novel since Ian Watt's groundbreaking study have relied on the assumption that characterization in the novel depends on notions of liberal subjectivity. But the implications of liberal definitions of selfhood for women have not been closely examined.[19] Utilizing political theory proper, that of earlier times as well as our own, to address this omission, I hope to extend the focus of feminist historicist literary scholarship that examines the role and place of women in English society in the past. Literary scholars in recent years have argued that Englishwomen had considerable influence, despite the many laws and institutions that curtailed their freedoms and opportunities. For instance, Elizabeth Langland has convincingly demonstrated that middle-class wives in nineteenth-century England were influential participants in their social and economic milieu because they negotiated 'networks of representa-

tions' in daily life.[20] While the Victorian middle-class husband provided the money necessary to the running of the household, the wife
displayed the signs of middle-class status that ratified the family's
socio-economic position, a contribution that was equally important. Langland concludes that the inherent contradiction between a
woman's two identities, one openly acknowledged (the domestic angel
unpolluted by issues of money or class), the other tacitly assumed
(the domestic manager who conspires to produce both money and
position), ultimately undermined Victorian domestic ideology. While
Langland's conclusions are convincing without reference to liberal theory proper, such theory nevertheless subtends her argument in important ways. The very function of marriage as a partnership, which
underlies Langland's argument, depends on a liberal notion of marriage as a contractual relationship. It was only because this notion was
so widely accepted that John Stuart Mill could argue for women's
rights by pointing out that marriage was the only partnership that
robbed one of its associates of all autonomy.[21] Moreover, Victorian culture's fundamental endorsement of married love, which was ultimately a belief in a liberal, consensual ideal of marriage, proved a
powerful theoretical tool for feminist activism. Discourses of Victorian
feminism show that the conflict between liberal and patriarchal ideals
of marriage was the paradigmatic contradiction for women within Victorian society, one which began the process of unravelling other widely
held but ultimately inconsistent beliefs about gender and domesticity.
In short, the power and autonomy that Langland argues Victorian
middle-class women possessed, as well as the economic and legal
autonomy that they obtained in the late nineteenth century, were
authorized by political theories that underwrote their society's ideal of
married love. Novels repeatedly reveal the connection between liberalism and feminism; because the consensual ideal of marriage articulated the basic principles of liberalism, liberal theory is central to
representations of love, marriage, and women in the novel.

If attention to political theory yields insights for the novel, literature
conversely provides insights for political theory. My exploration of the
novel's role in transforming notions of women's place and nature has
involved me in debates about the value of liberal theory for feminism,
an area of study that has largely been the provenance of political theorists. Their discussions often focus on characterizing liberalism as a
progressive or reactionary force vis-à-vis feminism. Although I argue
that liberalism enabled a conceptualization of women's subjectivity

that authorized the historical struggle for women's rights, I do not choose sides in the contemporary debate among feminist scholars. Rather, I contend that the very terms of that debate need to be reframed. Discussions of liberalism couched in abstract terms – a pitfall even for those critics of liberal theory who accuse defenders of failing to consider cultural specificity – neglect to assess its value with respect to history.

The yoking of the history of marriage with feminism might appear to be paradoxical. Marriage has traditionally been used as a justification for women's subordination within Anglo-American culture: because the family is a single unit, it requires only one leader, the husband. Until the late nineteenth century, marriage laws placed a wife almost entirely in the power of her husband, both financially and legally. So unjust was marriage as an institution that ameliorating its inequities was a primary goal for early feminists. In addition, scholarly assessments of the history of the family have shown that we should not rush to associate consensual marriage with improved circumstances for women.

In his influential study of married love, *The Family, Sex and Marriage in England 1500–1800*, Lawrence Stone argued that the expectation that love should be a factor in the marriage choice eroded the patriarchal nature of English marriage. In *The Rise of the Egalitarian Family*, published at roughly the same time, Randolph Trumbach contended along similar lines that the new 'affective' family of the eighteenth century was a relatively egalitarian institution.[22] Both studies cite evidence of changes in married women's property settlements in support of their claims: because families began to settle 'separate property' beyond the control of husbands on their daughters, these scholars assumed that women had greater independence and parity with men. Yet other scholars have taken issue with this line of argument. In a review of both books, Susan Moller Okin argued that the companionate ideal was retrograde rather than progressive. The 'sentimental family,' held together by affection, 'provided a new rationale for the subordination of women' by constituting a 'special sphere of life ... held to depend for its life on the total dedication of women, suited for these special tasks [of domestic work and childrearing] on account of the very qualities that made them unsuited for the harsh world of commerce, learning, and power.'[23] The rise of companionate marriage authorized women's ineluctable and essential difference from men, which necessitated their exclusion from political power and public life. Okin thus locates the origin of the notion of separate spheres, which was so crucial in justifying restrictions on women's lives throughout the eighteenth and nineteenth centuries, in the supposedly liberating discourse of love and affection: sometimes bonds of love are simply bonds.[24] In comprehensive study of eighteenth-century marriage law, Susan Staves further demonstrates that the changes in financial practice cited by Stone and Shorter in support of their optimistic view of marriage neither reflected nor contributed to equitable relationships between men and women. The practice of settling property on women under the legal system of equity did not lead to an increase in women's autonomy or power: on the contrary, an array of legal practices emerged in the period that ensured wives' dependence on and subjection to their husbands.[25] Women rarely had control over 'their' separate property. And in any case, changes in marriage law to grant women separate property had already come about by the time ideals of love and marriage had begun to change, so that the law could not have been influenced by the new ethos. The increase in separate property for wives in the early modern period was designed to protect the property of families rather than to grant women independence.[26]

Invoking liberalism as an ally of feminism is also problematic, as the very different evaluations of liberalism by two distinguished scholars, Wendy Brown and Martha Nussbaum, demonstrate.[27] According to Brown, liberalism is essentially and fundamentally masculinist. It does not allow for true equality between men and women because it is premised on a set of oppositions that are inextricable from the way it constructs the liberal subject: 'he ... bears an array of attributes that confer his specifically masculine status' (149). Such a gendered division of personality is premised on the opposition between the family and civil society: In 'liberal doctrine ... the family is ... rendered *opposite and subordinate* to civil society ... state and civil society stand in opposition to the family – its values, concerns, activities, and putative ethos' (151). Hence the liberal subject, who is always male in terms of his subject position, 'moves about freely in civil society. He is not encumbered by conflicting responsibilities or demands elsewhere; he does not have dependents attached to him in civil society, making claims on him, ... This dimension of autonomy refers to the absence of immediate constraints on one's entry into and movement within civil society, and it contrasts directly with women's encumbrance by familial responsibilities that limit her movement into and within civil society' (156). The only reason men have the liberty to function as autonomous subjects within civil society is that women do not. Someone must nurture children and ensure the continuity of daily life. If the liberal subject is to be given the degree of freedom accorded by liberal discourse, then the encumbered work of reproducing both daily life and the human race must devolve upon women. Brown writes, 'The liberal formulation of liberty is thus not merely opposed to but premised upon encumbrance; it is achieved by displacing the embodied, encumbered, and limited nature of existence onto women, a displacement that occurs discursively and practically through a set of assigned activities, responsibilities, and emotional attributes' (156). The very terms of personhood in liberal philosophy therefore contain women's subordination. And when women 'become' men in terms of subject position by entering politics and the workplace on these male terms, they must hire other 'women' to do their work at home: 'Insofar as this formulation of liberty *requires* the existence of ... those without liberty, it can never be fully universalized' (156). Thus, when feminists argue for women's rights within the terms of liberal theory, they cannot possibly achieve equity. They must either struggle for equality by 'becoming' male, or argue for recognition as women, an ineluctably subordinate position. Either way, they must play according to rules that cast them as losers from the start.

Martha Nussbaum, in contrast, argues for a liberal feminism. Nussbaum observes that liberalism has been criticized first for being too 'individualistic,' because 'by encouraging self-sufficiency as a goal, liberalism subverts the values of family and community, ends that feminists rightly prize' (61). She maintains that this is a misreading of liberal thought, and that on the contrary, liberal thinkers do not ignore such connectivity; rather, individualism, 'the view that the primary focus of ethical and political thought should be the individual, understood as a separate unit' does not assert that 'our most basic desires can be satisfied independently of relationships to others' (61). Thus where Brown sees dissociation, Nussbaum sees individualism. Similarly, where Brown maintains that a gendered and differential identity (whether biological or not), which grants total autonomy to the liberal (always 'male') subject, is constitutive of liberalism, Nussbaum contends that freedom and individualism can be extended to women. In fact, liberalism has not been individualistic enough where women are concerned: thinking of women as individuals is actually invaluable for feminism, considering that women's subordination stems in large part from neglect of such individuality, from their having been 'treated as parts of a larger unit, especially the family, and valued primarily for their contribution as reproducers and caregivers rather than as sources of agency and worth in their own right' (63).

Nussbaum also defends liberalism from its critics' claim that it espouses a formal conception of equality that ignores the realities of social and other differences. According to her reading of liberalism, many liberal theorists have rejected the formal notion of equality, aiming not at formal abstract equality, but at equality of capabilities: 'the aim [of liberal philosophers] is not just to distribute some resources around but also to see that they truly go to work in promoting the capacity of people to choose a life in accordance with their own thinking' (68). Finally, she defends liberalism against the charges of some feminists that its designation of reason as the ground of equality emphasizes a trait that men have traditionally valued, ignoring such 'female' characteristics as emotion and imagination. Liberalism, she argues, views this very opposition as false, and many liberal philosophers have insisted on the impossibility of divorcing reason from emotion by claiming that 'the capacity for sympathy is a central mark of both private and public rationality, and indeed of humanity as such' (73).[28]

How can the same body of discourse yield such different conclusions? Nussbaum's reading of liberalism might be seen as so selective and subtle that it leads us to question whether she is still talking about liberalism at all, and indeed, she claims to be discussing 'liberalism of a kind' (56). For instance, when addressing the feminist charge that by elevating reason as the defining human trait, liberalism denigrates womanly characteristics, she draws on writings of Rousseau to support her contention that liberalism creates no such dichotomy. But she fails to mention that Rousseau insists throughout his work that women lack reason, nor does she tell us that this is the basis on which he excludes them from civil society and denies their right to education and other male entitlements. But one might equally ask if Brown's account disposes of the good with the bad. Her criticism of the injustices of liberalism, that is to say, of what liberalism denies to women, suggests that she agrees with Nussbaum's characterization of the fundamental tenets of this philosophy: '[A]ll, just by being human, are of equal dignity and worth, no matter where they are situated in society ... the primary source of this worth is a power of moral choice within them, a power that consists in the ability to plan a life in accordance with one's own evaluations of ends and ... the moral equality of persons gives them a fair claim to certain types of treatment at the hands of society and politics' (57). At the end of her essay, Brown admits that she has been analysing an 'unreconstructed liberal discourse' (164). What then would a rehabilitated liberal discourse look like? Has Nussbaum given us this? If not, what alternative to liberal values will be most helpful to women?

One drawback to both of these analyses is that they neglect to ask 'when' – they do not consider history in assessing whether liberalism is good or bad for women. Although Brown admits that liberalism is 'subject to historical change and local variation,' she invokes history only to dismiss it, maintaining that there is a core of meaning inherent in liberalism that remains constant: 'insofar as liberalism takes its definitional shape from an ensemble of relatively abstract ontological and political claims, it is ... possible to speak of liberalism in a generic fashion, unnuanced by time or cultural inflection (141). Even if we agree that there is a body of theory that defines liberalism transhistorically, the issue of how liberalism has functioned differently within different times with respect to feminist activism, of how articulations of liberalism have played themselves out within particular histories, remains. Despite Brown's disclaimer, her conclusion makes it clear that she is cognizant of this second issue and that it is important. She queries the effect that liberalism will have on the future for women: 'Are the lives of men as well as women likely to be more pervasively regulated by the unreconstructed discourses of rights, autonomy, formal equality, and liberty, not only in the domains of civil and entrepreneurial life but in the domains of childrearing, health, sexuality, and so forth? Or are the social forces such that the sovereign, rights-bearing subject of liberalism is likely to be increasingly challenged both as an empirical fiction and a normative ideal, a challenge that could signify the breakdown of historically masculinist norms governing political life?' (165).

Such speculation unmasks the presence of history in Brown's analysis. Despite her claim that history is irrelevant in evaluating liberalism as a theory, and regardless of her discussion of what we might well agree to be ontological truths about liberalism, she directs her speculation to the effects of liberal theory on the lives of men and women in the immediate future. If we read the remainder of her analysis with this concern in mind, we see that her insights apply to the lives of men and women in Western culture today, as (mainly) women attempt to balance the claims of work and family, fight for reproductive rights, and attempt to institute equity in the workplace. That is not to say that Brown's analysis is untrue, but rather that it is meaningful now because of the particular set of problems confronting contemporary Western women.

Nussbaum rejects historical specificity in a somewhat different way. Rather than making the usual error of mainstream Western feminism and failing to take cultural difference sufficiently into account, Nussbaum does not account adequately for the ways in which liberal theory has underwritten practices in her own day and age, within her own culture; she does not acknowledge the extent to which liberal theory has had negative repercussions for women in law and the civil sphere. We have seen that a nuanced reading of liberal theory enables Nussbaum to conclude that liberalism abjures formal equality and its injustices. She contextualizes this claim by alluding to several instances in which liberal theory, as she interprets it, has formed the basis of legal decisions. These examples demonstrate judicial sensitivity to the inequities of power, and grant justice to women. But she does not acknowledge that this version of liberalism (if indeed it is still liberalism) has not predominated in Anglo-American societies today with respect to women. As Anne Crittenden's important book, *The Price of Motherhood*, demonstrates, the assumption of a formal equality, one that is necessarily grounded in liberal subjectivity as Brown defines it – autonomous, public, and free of dependents or dependency – has prevailed in law and the workplace, exacting a huge financial sacrifice from women and other 'mothers' who reject or cannot fully inhabit this subjectivity because of familial responsibilities.[29] Whatever the positive implications of liberal theory for women, especially in its more recent articulations, classical liberalism in our own time more often than not has justified laws and practices that are detrimental to women and opposed to the goals of most feminists.

Yet this was not always the case. Whether or not liberalism has a radical future, it has certainly had a radical past.[30] Those who fought to extend rights and liberties for women in the eighteenth and nineteenth centuries invoked liberalism; indeed, it was the fundamental theoretical force behind this earlier discourse and activism. Not only was liberalism uncontroversial for these early feminists, it was also effective. Many of women's advances in the nineteenth century, such as married women's separate property laws, were argued in terms of liberal principles. And this is true despite the fact that the classic liberal texts used to support feminist discourse were decidedly 'unreconstructed.' It did not take a sophisticated reader to detect the misogyny of writers such as Rousseau and Locke.

Earlier feminists could glean the good and ignore the bad in a way that has become difficult, if not impossible, for many feminists today for two reasons. The first has to do with the inconsistencies of liberalism itself. If we ignore the openly misogynist statements by liberal writers, the remainder of their discourse ostensibly promises equality and justice unilaterally. This positive reading of liberal theory was indeed the one that prevailed. Such progressive tendencies appear to be especially true of Locke, the most influential liberal thinker for early English feminism. Even apart from specific statements which support women's equality with men, statements which render his *Two Treatises of Government* self-contradictory, many of Locke's arguments about inherent rights of 'man' appear to be gender-neutral, applicable to both men and women. The second reason explains the first: liberalism could be allied with feminism so easily because the feminism of past centuries was a different feminism from ours. For instance, to return to the problem of formal equality, it is only because women now work outside the home that we can see how the workplace in general assumes that all workers are male and that no workers are 'mothers.' When wives were fighting for the basic right to be considered as separate persons by the law rather than against discrimination in the workplace, the liberal promise of autonomy seemed unproblemmatic. The victories of feminism, and the transformation of women's legal and social status since the nineteenth century, have put pressure on the liberal ideal, showing that it is, at the very least, necessary to interpret and rearticulate liberal principles in new ways, or perhaps to divorce feminism from liberalism altogether. In short, while many theorists now argue that liberal discourse is inherently masculinist, liberalism underpins those very feminisms of the past which have placed us in a position to criticize it. It is only recently that both feminist advocates and critics of liberalism have achieved the necessary critical distance to be nuanced rather than naive readers of liberal theory. This explains why meticulous scholars such as Stone and Trumbach could be so mistaken, despite their contributions to feminist scholarship (both scholars helped to change the nature of what we consider history by assuming that women and private life are as much a part of political history as the reign of kings). If they reached overly optimistic conclusions about the liberating power of married love for women, it is because they took for granted the premises of liberal contract theory, assuming that it theoretically confers a benefit to women, and concluding that this benefit must have translated into empirical improvement.

The chapters that follow trace the relationship between changing ideas of love and marriage and the emergence of modern feminist thought and activism. While I focus for the most part on the ways in which the multiplot novel articulates these connections, chapter 1 turns to a variety of extra-novelistic texts from the seventeenth through the nineteenth centuries, as well as to the work of historians and cultural theorists who draw on these materials, on the assumption that an analysis of the novel's intervention in the ideology of marriage and related issues depends on recognizing its place in ongoing cultural dialogues about love and identity. These non-fiction texts show how the transformation in beliefs about marriage implied 'liberal' rights for women (the rights of a contracting agent), while also challenging and even shifting cultural definitions of 'woman' and 'man.'

In chapter 2, I explore the ways in which *Sir Charles Grandison* champions married love while undermining its threat to paternal/patriarchal power. Through its various plots, which display the Byzantine, perhaps Machievellian, logic that critics have long associated with *Clarissa*, it defines appropriate, non-subversive forms of love that guarantee that a woman's/daughter's choice will not contradict the monetary and dynastic interests of the family – that is, the will of fathers. As long as women love correctly, they will choose correctly. *Grandison*'s stories also dissociate women's rights from women's passion, thereby safeguarding the marriage choice from its complicity with liberal ideals: contradicting precisely the logic of contract that I argue can be traced in the ideology of marriage, these stories assert that allowing a woman to choose her spouse will not lead to other entitlements. Finally, the narratives defend the ethical Christian male – the 'new' kind of husband who participates in 'new' ideals of marriage – from the taint of effeminacy.

Just as a woman's right to choose her husband suggests a contractual subjectivity that is incompatible with complete subjection to her husband, it also suggests that she does not owe total obedience to her father or, in the case of *Persuasion*, the subject of chapter 3, to someone who represents his interests. Conduct books reveal the inherent conflict in advocating both married love and patriarchal control by maintaining that a daughter is supposed to marry for love but also to obey her parents, whose judgment of a suitable spouse might differ from her own. *Persuasion* registers this impasse within prevailing ideals about love and marriage, duty and authority. Using a version of the double plot, the novel literalizes this problem by structurally dividing between its opposing points of view. Although in the end it privileges the desires of daughters over fathers, this novel also calls into question the efficacy of a discourse of rights to guarantee justice for all, especially for those, like daughters, who are almost always (relative to fathers) economically and psychologically unempowered.

By the mid-Victorian period, married love had become an overdetermined concept, signalling the ethical quality not only of individual relationships but of society as a whole. In novels by Dickens, Eliot, Thackeray, and Trollope, among others, marriage for love was thematized as an expression and affirmation of a Christian ethic, both individual and collective, that was in danger of being overpowered by an anti-ethic of materialism and capital. This stance continues to intersect with the 'woman question,' which was by now a familiar topical issue. In chapter 4 I show that Trollope, while no friend to feminist causes in his day, nevertheless confronts the conflict between parity and hierarchy that marriage evoked. I read *He Knew He Was Right* against John Stuart Mill's *The Subjection of Women*, the most thorough formulation of the relationship between contract and women's rights in the period. This novel foregrounds rather than denies the relationship between married love and the contractual subjectivity it implies, even though it suggests paternal and oppressive solutions to the dilemma of advocating both married love and patriarchy.

Mill viewed his society's belief in married love as evidence of its best character; its failure to enact the progressive, contractual ethic that this relationship evoked would inevitably be overcome. But the pessimistic obverse of this view, which emerges intermittently in *The Subjection*, is that marriage in his own time did not measure up to the ideal of a loving partnership. Margaret Oliphant's work, the subject of chapter 5, narrativizes this pessimism. Oliphant's works announce the irreconcilability of contract theory and the rhetoric of choice on the one hand, and traditional, patriarchal understandings of marriage on the other. Rather than regarding married love as a reality that authorizes changes in law and society – the assumption that underpins Richardson's need to put women in their place – Oliphant suggests instead that the legal and social limitations that women face make a good marriage hard to find. Women of limited intellect, drive, and vision might be happy with marriage as it was, with its assumption of woman's inferiority, and of complementary roles for husband and wife. But this can never be enough for women of ability. Oliphant's novels, *Phoebe Junior*, *Hester*, and *Kirsteen*, express progressively somber views of marriage. In these works, Oliphant re-envisions cultural expectations about marriage and the gendering of personality through a radical revision of novelistic convention and form. Even more important than the multiple plot (which is also a feature of her work) is a variation that we might call the 'shadow plot': in each of these novels, Oliphant invokes a conventional courtship story only to radically rework it in terms of her views on marriage and women.

What follows is by no means a complete history of the novel. I look closely at a limited number of exemplary texts which articulate some of the major discourses of married love – that is, in which married love and its consequences are addressed most fully and specifically. Some of these texts remain familiar to readers while others have fallen into relative obscurity. But we could look at almost any novel of the eighteenth and nineteenth centuries and find the same questions being asked: Why should people marry? What kind of love is best? How do the ways we think about love and marriage influence the ways we think about women and men?

I focus on a particular segment of English society, primarily the middle classes, and, to a lesser extent, the upper classes. Since class is such a prominent category in my analysis, I want to be clear that I use it in a broad sense to refer to affiliations of groups who had economic interests and social and cultural characteristics in common.[31] My use of class in this way, however, especially with reference to the eighteenth century, brings up the vexed issue of whether it is appropriate to talk about class at all before class consciousness proper emerged in the nineteenth century. Does a group need to be homogeneous, internally self-consistent, and conscious of a collective identity to be labelled with an inclusive term such as 'middle-' or 'upper-class'? Does it need to be economically homogeneous as well, deriving income from similar enterprises? Approaching this question from the perspective of literary analysis leads to a less definitive answer than might satisfy those who quest for unequivocal precision.[32] Defining class too narrowly leaves us without a way of theorizing or historicizing many of the ideological and thematic elements of the early novel, for novels written before the nineteenth century repeatedly assert a cluster of values, among them married love, that are marked within these narratives as either opposed to an aristocratic ethos or identified with what Robinson Crusoe calls 'the middle station' of life, 'in the middle of the two extremes, between the mean and the great.'[33] Defoe's terminology, echoed in writing throughout the period, supports Harold Perkin's contention that self-definition for the middling ranks depended on knowing who they were not, rather than who they were; this was true well into the nineteenth century.[34] Even if class consciousness did not fully emerge until after 1832, people prior to this time were aware of social and economic distinctions, and spoke of such differences in terms of a tripartite division of society. Moreover, if class consciousness constitutes class, then such a consciousness was problematic from the start, for even as the culture acknowledged the existence of a middle class, they realized that it never constituted a seamlessly unified group. We need only turn to George and Weedon Grossmith's *Diary of a Nobody* (1892) to realize the complicated and fractured nature of middle-class identity even when class consciousness was a fact of life.[35] And if boundaries were unclear within the ranks of the middling sort, the divisions between themselves and all but the very highest echelons of the upper classes became increasingly hard to define throughout the period I consider, as the landed gentry depended to an ever greater extent on investments of their capital for income and the professions gained respectability and status. This confusion is registered in the culture's continued obsession with defining the true gentleman. In any case, class consciousness is often overrated as an analytical tool for theorizing both class and identity. As Michael McKeon notes, although full-fledged class consciousness does not emerge until the nineteenth century, 'it would be a mistake to insist too precisely on the fact of such consciousness as the *sine qua non* of the class orientation.'[36] Such class orientation is precisely what we see in reading the novel.

In mapping the history of an ideal as it was articulated in the novel, I necessarily emphasize the continuity of beliefs from one age to the next. While I hope that I have shown how married love and related concerns changed over time. I also stress that the ideal of consensual married love that became a dominant belief in the eighteenth century has had a long and influential reign – indeed, it has not yet lost its hold over our beliefs, expectations, and imaginations – and that the history of its ideological consequences also demonstrates continuity. In particular, the eighteenth and nineteenth centuries constitute an important block of time in terms of looking at the relationship between married love and women's subjectivity. Many of the cultural icons I discuss, such as domestic ideology and newer ideals of masculinity, emerged in the eighteenth century or earlier and continued to be dominant throughout the Victorian era, although scholars often identify them with one period or the other.[37] In short, the general thrust of the ideas I trace is a forward one, and I concentrate on this momentum.

Above all, I want to emphasize that I focus primarily on constructions of reality, both prescriptive and descriptive, rather than on reality itself. I am tracing the trajectory of a shift in attitude about marital motives – an 'ideo-logic,' the working through of whose implications and contradictions constituted a vital cultural project. I therefore concentrate on analysing representations of material and social conditions for what they have to say about 'the truth,' rather than on reporting history itself or assessing the accuracy of social commentary of the period or literary claims to realism, particularly on the part of the novel. This means that I do not attempt to determine whether or not people actually married for love, a project doomed to obfuscation and inaccuracy.[38] As Erica Harth observes, what is important is that they thought they should do so.[39] It was this belief, rather than an accumulation of individual histories, that most affected the discursive trajectories that I trace. But while I focus on ideology, and while I acknowledge that discursive practice often diverges from material reality, I also assume that the two are always related in complex, mutually generative, and dialectical modes. The middle classes might not have married into the upper classes as often as people thought, but the general assumption of an open elite was a crucial source of symbolic capital for this group, contributing to their acceptability as partners in business and policy, if not in marriage. And even if the rise of the companionate ideal did not improve women's lot in the eighteenth century, its revision of ideas about women's subjectivity provided ammunition for a feminist movement that had tremendous political and material results. The revision of assumptions about both class and gender generated enabling fictions that were inseparable from tangible realities as well as from the fictions that came to be known as the novel.

1
Married Love and Its Consequences

The Restoration and eighteenth century witnessed the emergence of a forceful ethical imperative to marry for love.[1] This ideal originated within the middle ranks of society, a group that increasingly identified themselves as the guardians of virtue. Their advocacy of married love challenged an older aristocratic paradigm, the marriage of interest, in which marriage was arranged by parents, kin, and family friends, in order to further the social, political, and economic ambitions of a family. This is not to claim that an ideal of married love sprang full-blown in the early modern period. Precedents in Western civilization can be found as far back as antiquity. More recently, marriage for love was advocated by humanists of the Renaissance, particularly Erasmus, and later by the Puritans, most famously Milton, who popularized this ideal and ultimately diffused it more widely within English culture.[2] But prior to this historical moment, the love match had been generally viewed as a desirable but inessential option. While, in the best of all possible worlds – such as the world of Shakespeare's comedies – lovers do marry one another, in the usual course of events, love need not precede the engagement, and so prudential matches were not thought to violate a child's chances for happiness or the moral sanctity of marriage. The promise to love of the Anglican wedding ceremony was viewed literally as a promise, a declaration made to another person with respect to the future. The wedding vow might be said to have had a performative, incantatory function. As married love became increasingly valued, this attitude was no longer tolerated. Although love was never thought to be the only factor in the marriage choice, it came to be seen as the necessary foundation – the *sine qua non* – for a successful and ethical Christian marriage. Such views about marital choice begin to appear consistently in texts of the seventeenth century, and were ratified repeatedly in those of the following two centuries.

Conduct literature provides an especially legible point of departure for tracing changes in attitude towards love and marriage; it also demonstrates the centrality of married love to the project of defining love correctly, as grounded in reason and companionship, and of addressing the progressive implications of married love for thinking about women's rights and duties. Intended as behavioural and ethical guides, these texts provide a useful means of reading a society's vision of its best self while also registering the anxieties that accompany this self-image.[3] Although, like other writings of the period that focus on gender and morality, conduct books are not free of contradictions, they nevertheless present a remarkably stable consensus on the topic of marital motives.[4] These guides are also useful in identifying the extent to which an emergent ideology about marriage was bound up with social origins. Conduct literature was usually written by middle-class writers; indeed, the genre was formative in constructing middle-class belief and identity.[5] Guides to conduct which evince attitudes different to those that are typical of the genre were almost always written by aristocratic rather than middle-class authors.[6] I will begin with a survey of the most popular advice books from the Renaissance through the nineteenth century, and I will return to the literature of conduct at several points in this study.

In the majority of treatises from the Renaissance and early seventeenth century love is invoked as a necessary aspect of marriage, but it is almost always dissociated from marital motives per se. In fact, marital motives receive little attention, and the fact that there is no urgency or anxiety about the subject suggests that it was not a significant issue. *A Godly Forme of Household Government* (1542) requires the husband to 'love, cherish, and nourish his wife as his own body,' but says nothing about the need for such love to precede the marriage.[7] *A Bride Bush* (1619) represents love as a matter primarily of will and religious devotion: 'A Christian man must love his wife not onley or principally because she is beautifull, witty, huswiflie, dutifull, loving and every way well conditioned: but chiefly, because ... [God] hath said, Husbands love your wives.'[8] And love can indeed follow marriage, since the 'naturall meanes' to create love is 'cohabitation: let them have one house, one table, one chamber, one bed, so shall they with most ease have also one heart and one soule.'[9] Robert Snawsel's *A Looking Glass for Married Folk* (1610) similarly depicts love as a matter of will, that it can be motivated by religion rather than by personal predilection: 'Before you can love one another, you must labour for the love of God.'[10] This suggests that loving one another is the consequence of loving God rather than a response to the charms or virtues of one's spouse. Another early seventeenth-century text, *Court of Good Counsell* (1607), foreshadows later treatises in some ways, particularly in its attention to the marriage choice, but has more in common with earlier ones in its conclusions and focus. Like *A Bride Bush*, it advises a man to 'to love [his wife] ... most hartely and unfaynedly, for so the Lawe of God commaundeth him for that is the strong foundation, which surely upholdeth marriage.'[11] But the *Counsell* also advises a suitor to assess his prospective wife's character – to 'know her good qualities and conditions' so he will be 'well framed to love her'[12] – and to choose carefully because '[t]he greatest joy, and sweetest comfort, that a man may have in this world, is a loving, kinde, and honest wife.'[13] Love is not only a matter of following God's commands but of personal predilection as well. The *Counsell* also dwells on the ethical consequences of failing to make one's marriage a loving one, a familiar theme of later guides: '[Love] being neglected by the husband, braedeth him great shame and Infamy,' presumably adultery.[14] But *Counsell* differs from its successors by assuming that choosing wisely will lead to a loving marriage, not that love, or even friendship, will lead to a wise choice. And mutuality is absent; *Counsell* discusses the husband's choice alone, never mentioning the necessity of a woman's choosing wisely.

Treatises of a later date, by contrast, reveal an increasing concern with defining proper marital motives, and warn against marrying for the wrong reasons, especially the pursuit of wealth or status. Most of these works address women and assume that a wife's feelings regarding the marriage choice are an integral part of the happy and virtuous marriage. Richard Allestree, in *The Ladies Calling* (1673), argues that successful marriages depend on appropriate motives, and exhorts young women to forbear venal temptations: 'In a word, Marriage is God's Ordinance, and should be considered as such; not made a stake to any unworthy design. And it may well be presum'd one cause why so few Matches are Happy, that they are not built upon a right Foundation. Some are grounded upon Wealth, some on Beauty, too sandy bottoms, God knows, to raise any lasting felicity on: whilst in the interim, Virtue and Piety, the only solid Basis for that Superstructure, are scarce ever consider'd.'[15]

The Ladies Calling also insists that a young woman should not marry someone for whom she feels an aversion, which signifies that her sentiments before marriage are crucial in determining a suitable spouse. Like the earlier *Court of Good Counsel*, *The Ladies Calling* advises choosing wisely, dwelling on the disastrous personal as well as ethical consequences of failing to do so, often in fairly graphic terms. But it does so from the point of view of the woman: 'I confess I cannot see how she can, without a sacrilegious Hypocrisy, vow solemnly to love where she at that instant abhors: and where the married state is begun with such a Perjury, 'tis no wonder to find it continu'd on at the same rate, that other parts of the Vow be also violated ... A loath'd Bed is at once an acute and lingring Torment.'[16] Successful marriage demands *mutual* affection, not simply a man's gratification, and such affection cannot be produced by will alone.

Daniel Defoe was equally censorious of improperly motivated marriages, and he advocates reciprocity between husband and wife. Like Allestree, he does not assume that love is likely to follow a marriage thought appropriate by parents for financial or social reasons. In *Conjugal Lewdness* (1728), he writes,

> Some are of the Opinion, prudential Matches, as they call them, are best. They tell us, 'tis the Parents business to choose Wives for their Sons, and Husbands for their Daughters; that let them be tied together first, they will toy together till they love afterwards; that Property begets Affection, and that if all other Things hit, they may run the risque of the Love with less inconvenience.
>
> But I must enter my Protest here: I think they that make a Toy of the Affection, will make a Toy of the Matrimony; they seem to know little of the Misery of those Matches who think they are to be toyed into Love after Consummation.[17]

Mrs Pennington, in *An Unfortunate Mother's Advice to Her Absent Daughters, In a Letter to Miss Pennington* (1761), warns daughters who make the same mistakes that parents do: 'The Advantages of great Superiority in Rank or Fortune has frequently proved so irresistible a Temptation, as, in Opinion, to out-weigh not only the Folly, but even the Vices of its Possessor; A grand Mistake! ever tacitly acknowledg'd by a subsequent Repentance, when the expected Pleasures of Affluence, Equipage, and all the glittering Pomp of useless Pageantry, are experimentally found insufficient to ballance [*sic*] the Deprivation of that constant Satisfaction, resulting from the social Joy of conversing with a reasonable Friend.'[18] A good match, 'founded on Reason and Religion, cemented by mutual Esteem and Tenderness, is a Kind of faint Emblem (if the Comparison may be allowed) of the promis'd Reward of Virtue in a future State.'[19] Dr Gregory, in *A Father's Legacy to his Daughters* (1774), is of the opinion that 'a married state, if entered into from proper motives of esteem and affection, will be the happiest ...'[20] In James Fordyce's view (*Sermons to Young Women*, 1765), marrying for the sake of ambition is not simply an error in judgment, but evidence of poor character. He asks ironically, 'What has a modish young fellow to do with those antiquated notions of gallantry, that were connected with veneration for female excellence, invincible honor and unspotted fame? Is it not enough for him, if he intends to strike the matrimonial bargain, that by himself, or an old cunning father, he can drive a good one, to get possession of some woman, whose fortune joined to his own ... shall enable him to glitter in public, and in private to gratify other favourite inclinations more freely?'[21] Fordyce clearly has a woman's welfare and happiness in mind. Whatever their differences, these writers are unanimous in condemning the marriage of interest, for wealth or status alone, and in advocating affection between prospective spouses.[22]

Among the propertied classes, conduct-book adjurations not to marry for money or status never precluded a general awareness that marriage was crucial in determining the social and economic structure of English society. Nor, in most cases, were readers advised to marry solely for love. As I hope to show, an emphasis on love above all, a belief we have inherited, was the product of Victorian times, and even then, a range of practical considerations still entered into finalizing real marriages.[23] By oversimplifying the marriage dilemma, much of the literature of this period belies the fact that love was a necessary component of the marriage choice rather than its only motive: the opposition between the marriage for love and the marriage of interest, or between desire and duty, became a standard trope. Paradoxically, this very stance of disinterestedness was implicated in the politics of socio-economic ambition and identity. This is not to say that individual writers were insincere in their advocacy of marriage for love, but simply that their position was ineluctably overdetermined by the politics of marriage, no matter how pure their personal motives.

Such overdetermination was unavoidable because married love represented the interests of the middle classes in precisely those worldly terms which their disparagement of wealth and ambition seemed to deny. This group stood to benefit substantially from an alliance with the landed gentry and aristocracy who were their social, and often, despite their own wealth, their economic superiors; marriage was an obvious way to form such alliances. The ethical imperative of married love provided the middle classes with a rationale for urging marriage between different social groups; Cupid's traditional blindness could be applied to social standing as well as personal attributes.

As Erica Harth has demonstrated in her astute analysis of the debates surrounding Lord Hardwicke's Marriage Act of 1753, the significance of married love as a strategy for middle-class upward mobility was obvious to members of Parliament.[24] Hardwicke's Act sought to annul what contemporaries called 'clandestine marriage,' ceremonies performed without either posting banns in Church or obtaining a licence, or, in the case of minors, without obtaining parental consent. Unions that had not been conducted according to form would no longer be considered legitimate. By curtailing easy access to marriage, the Act gave parents greater opportunity to influence their childrens' marriage choices and to prevent socially or economically undesirable love matches. Those who wished to elope would now have to ride to Gretna Green in Scotland. It is not surprising that members of Parliament divided with respect to the Act along the lines of social affiliation: opponents identified themselves with the interests of the middle classes, supporters with the nobility.

A desire to keep open a putatively important avenue to upward mobility underlay middle-class opposition to the Act, while the gentry and aristocracy hoped to obviate the threat of social contamination and downward mobility with its passage. As one member of Parliament pointed out, the Act would make a 'distinction' between the 'noblesse' and the 'burghers,' a goal to be desired or abhorred, depending on one's point of view.[25] Supporters thus openly contended that giving parents greater control over marriage was advantageous because it protected genteel families from debasing intermarriages. Attorney General Ryder argued, 'How often have we known the heir of a good family seduced, and engaged in a clandestine marriage, perhaps with a common strumpet? How often have we known a rich heiress carried off by a man of low birth, or perhaps by an infamous sharper? What distress some of our best families have been brought into, what ruin some of their sons or daughters have been involved in, by such means, every gentleman may from his own knowledge recollect; and every gentleman must allow, that such misfortunes ought to be prevented, if possible.'[26] Ryder does not question the rightness of pairing wealth with status, or of shoring up the power of both. John Bond even went so far as to observe that because the wealth of noble families is so vulnerable, 'we should contribute towards a poor lord's being always sure of matching himself with some rich heiress, and thereby restoring the lustre and the independency of his family.'[27] Opponents responded with arguments that addressed both the social and the moral health of England. The Act would allow parents from a small elite to monopolize most of England's wealth and power, and this would be detrimental to the country as a whole. Henry Fox observed that '[t]o accumulate the whole wealth of a society into a few families is inconsistent with the happiness of every society, and ... with the constitution, and to throw it all into the hands of our nobility is inconsistent with our constitution in particular.'[28] Robert Nugent argued, 'Riches is the blood of the body politic: it must be made to circulate: if you allow it to stagnate, or if too much of it be thrown into any one part, it will destroy the body politic as the same cause often does the body natural: if this Bill passes, our quality and rich families will daily accumulate riches by marrying only one another.'[29] Moreover, Nugent found Hardwicke's Act unethical because it discourages marriage for love: '[I]t seems to be flying in the face of Providence, by enacting that that passion which God Almighty has made the cause, and which ought to be the cause of every marriage, shall not be the cause of any marriage in this country.'[30] Similarly, Charles Townshend argued that the consideration of wealth or rank should have nothing to do with marriage: '[S]urely riches can never make that [kind of marriage] honourable which would otherwise be infamous, nor can poverty make that infamous, which would otherwise be no way dishonourable.'[31] These arguments show that the politics and morals of married love were inextricable.

The strengthening or weakening of class boundaries through marriage was not the sole consideration at stake in the Act; there were certainly other goals and consequences involved, such as the elimination of fraudulent marriage and the hardships women and children would face if previously legally sanctioned unions were suddenly annulled. But even writers who prioritized these different concerns acknowledged the prominence of class as a factor in evaluating the morality and efficacy of the Act.[32] For conservatives, its passage was a victory, a defence of society against insidious subversion. For liberal thinkers, it was a defeat for progressive views about status, liberty, and love.[33]

Despite the passage of Hardwicke's Act, and the resistance to the love match it demonstrates, an ideal of married love promulgated by the middle classes gained wide acceptance among the gentry and nobility in the course of the eighteenth century.[34] This happened because an alliance between these two groups, ratified by intermarriage, benefited both. For although intermarriage with the middling sort threatened the identity of the upper classes, it also provided a way to strengthen their power and position, enabling them to combine forces with an increasingly prosperous part of the population, and, thereby, to consolidate England's elites as a social bloc in contradistinction to the lower classes. Moreover, marriage with the middle classes was at least tolerated, if not embraced, because the threat to separate interests was a chimera; these groups were already interconnected and allied. With the exception of the most elite members of the upper classes, primarily the aristocracy, whose ranks for the most part remained closed to outsiders, the boundaries between the upper and the middle classes were blurred and permeable. The need to provide income for younger sons through the military and other professions, and to find viable matches for daughters, necessitated intermingling between various social strata, making the delineation of boundaries increasingly difficult.[35] As Peter Earle observes, by the eighteenth century, 'there would have been few members of the London business world who were not quite closely related to county families, and few county families who did not have a relative earning a living in London.'[36] In this social world both upward and downward mobility were common, so that the contours of these groups constantly shifted as well.

If the upper classes were to marry their social inferiors, however, they needed the justification of exceptional circumstances, and this is precisely what love provided. Their desire to maintain a social superiority and separate identity meant that, despite the advantages of allying wealth with position through marriage, they could not openly negotiate such pragmatic alliances. Certainly, wealth had always been an important consideration in upper-class marriages, and a belief in the propriety and benevolence of arranged marriage was part of an aristocratic ideology that survived among a minority despite the rise of married love.[37] Indeed, the wealth of the moneyed interest would have been especially attractive to the upper classes at this time, since the practice of strict settlement forced heads of families to keep their estates intact for the eldest son while providing portions for their younger children and maintaining the lavish standard of living that signified their power.[38] Rank and family, however, were traditionally considered even more significant than wealth in defining social status. Thus, although arranged marriage continued to be accepted in aristocratic circles throughout the eighteenth and nineteenth centuries, the upper classes never sanctioned what might look to us like its close cousin, the purely mercenary marriage. Because the status barriers limiting entry to powerful social circles ensured upper-class political sovereignty, it was not to this group's advantage to accept misalliance openly as a common practice; to do so would have been to endorse social mobility and consequently, the division of power between social groups. Furthermore, legitimating marriage for money meant overtly sanctioning the values of the marketplace, which the upper classes scorned, despite their participation in market practices. It was in opposition to such practices that they distinguished their own sort of wealth from that of the moneyed interest: a gentleman did not have to work for a living.

When the upper classes allowed economic considerations to override all else, they compromised their position, as Hogarth's famous series of prints 'Marriage à la Mode' acerbically illustrates. Sir William Temple, writing at the end of the seventeenth century, condemned noble families who marry purely for money: 'These contracts would never be made, but by men's avarice, and greediness of portions with the women they marry, which is grown among us to that degree, as to surmount and extinguish all other regards or desires: so that our marriages are made, just like other common bargains and sales, by the mere consideration of interest or gain, without any of love or esteem, of birth or of beauty itself, which ought to be the true ingredients of all happy compositions in this kind, and of all generous productions.'[39] Although Temple is ostensibly warning readers to avoid a practice which compromises the ethics and happiness of prospective spouses, his deployment of the language of the marketplace ('common bargains and sales') indicates that he is anxious about social contamination. That he considers birth an appropriate foundation for marriage (on the same footing as 'love,' 'esteem,' and 'beauty'), while condemning marriage for financial gain alone, shows that the mercenary marriage, not the marriage of interest, is his target, a distinction that middle-class theorists of love would not recognize.

Criticism of the mercenary marriage by the upper classes was commonplace in imaginative literature. In Aphra Behn's *The Rover* (1677), for example, the courtesan Angellica describes mercenary marriage as an alternative form of prostitution: 'Pray tell me, sir are not you guilty of the same mercenary crime? When a lady is proposed to you for a wife, you never ask how fair, discreet, or virtuous she is, but what's her fortune.' Willmore (the rover), whose identification with aristocratic ideology is established by his loyalty to the banished Charles II, agrees: 'It is a barbarous custom, which I will scorn to defend in our sex, and do despise in yours.'[40] But if marrying their social inferiors for money was out of the question, marriage for love offered the upper classes a way to negotiate economically advantageous marriages without compromising their status or integrity. These love matches could function as the exceptions that proved the rule of stable class boundaries.

The middle classes also needed love to justify such matches. It would have been particularly awkward for them to advertise a willingness to barter wealth for status; it was precisely such a desire, characterized as offensive social climbing and an undignified interest in getting the most for their money, for which they had been traditionally satirized, as in Philip Massinger's *A New Way To Pay Old Debts* (1633). Sir Giles Overreach hopes that his enormous wealth, which he has acquired by ruining gentlemen, will enable his daughter to marry a lord and thereby outrank nobly born ladies.[41] The middle ranks defended themselves from such pejorative characterizations by generating a body of literature, especially in the early eighteenth century, which countered negative representations of greedy traders with opposing, positive ones of gentleman merchants. Most famous are Lillo's *The London Merchant* (1731) and the writings of Addison and Steele, which portray the merchant as a respectable citizen whose commercial activities are central to England's prosperity.[42] But even more than the need to counter negative images, the moral high ground identified with married love was part of a new identity, vital to elevating the status and confirming the power of the middle classes. In the long run, this was even more significant than ensuring the possibility of intermarriage with their social superiors.

For the middle classes, married love was part of a larger cultural project that consisted of no less than the reform of English society on ethical, Christian principles. Their self-appointed but generally accepted role as England's moral guardians was fundamental to what we might call reciprocal hegemony between the upper and middle ranks – a division of authority along complementary axes, motivated by a symbiosis of interests among England's elites.[43] The upper classes continued to lead the country, both socially and politically.[44] But the middle classes determined its values and representational codes, which relied above all on an appeal to Christian virtue as the only legitimate foundation for belief and practice. Literature was essential to this process of cultural revision, which was formulated and disseminated in essays, conduct books, plays, and novels, all essentially middle-class venues.

Such an arrangement suited all. The middle ranks did not seek to organize as a group or to challenge the political sovereignty of the upper classes primarily because it was not necessary to their prosperity to do so. If the separate identities of the gentry and upper middle classes were confused by interfamilial and professional connections, a similarity of interests further blurred the lines of division. In the course of the seventeenth century, the aristocracy and gentry had themselves become capitalists, deriving a portion of their income from farming the land on their estates and investing in the commercial and financial ventures of the City, while capitalists were purchasing land and living like country gentlemen. By the time of the Hanoverian succession, with the French wars settled and the Whig oligarchy firmly established, landed peers and members of Parliament perceived that it was to their advantage to work to further England's commercial and imperial interests, since their own investments and financial ventures depended on policies favourable to business and trade. The upper classes therefore pursued political and economic policies that benefited all who possessed either property or wealth, regardless of social origin.[45] And the middle ranks remained content with indirect access to the highest reaches of status and power, adopting a political non-assertiveness that became a source of England's stability: the very lack of a collective political identity on the part of the middle classes obviated the one potentially serious threat to the status-oriented structure of English society.[46] Nor did they seek to alter the outward signs of elevated status, but imitated them instead; upward mobility was advertised by the appropriation of marks of gentility, such as the landed estate.[47] They preferred to join the club, or set up a similar club, rather than to dismantle the system that produced the club; the outer trappings of gentility, its manners and lifestyle, still defined the good life. But even if this newer elite did not participate in politics directly, and although they were content to support the very mechanisms and signs of elitism that worked to exclude them, they implicitly challenged the feudal triad of status, wealth, and power by revising cultural assumptions and thereby acquiring a form of cultural capital that buttressed their economic gains. If their power was ideological rather than political, it was ultimately no less forceful or influential. Like all forms of symbolic capital, these revisions of aristocratic ideology had a pragmatic, economic component, even when they appeared to be purely ethical or aesthetic.[48]

This is not to underestimate the recalcitrance of aristocratic ideology, particularly in its later incarnation as conservative ideology.[49] The middle classes acquired cultural capital through revising morals, but the aristocracy and gentry retained the reins of political power through much of the nineteenth century in part because of the longevity of certain older beliefs that remained impervious to this process of revision. Despite the fluidity of social groups, the diversity of sources of income, and the difficulty of drawing clear distinctions between different segments of the propertied population, English society remained obsessed with hierarchy, and people continued to believe in separate moneyed and landed interests. People of the middle ranks frequently aspired to rank, hoping to legitimate their economic rise in social terms. The very imitation of aristocratic institutions marked them as desirable. Moreover, aristocratic ideals were bolstered by the endurance of paternalism, the upper-class management and care of the lower classes, particularly in the country. And the analogous system of patronage remained strong within the civil service and the professions well into the nineteenth century, although it frequently came under attack.

While aristocratic ideals continued to be influential, they were continually being eroded and transformed by middle-class ethics and values. This process frequently took the form of redefining aristocratic social customs and literary genres, 'eating away, as it were from within, at a social structure whose external shell still seems roughly assimilable to the status model.'[50] The rehabilitation of the concept of honour illustrates this process. Aristocratic honour is based on a heroic, pugilistic, ethos of bravery, aggression, and belligerent jealousy about one's rank and reputation. In contrast, middle-class honour depends on virtue, and includes such qualities as humility, charity, and benevolence. 'Virtue ... is real Honour; whereas the other Distinctions among Mankind are merely titular,' observes Addison in *The Spectator* 286.[51] Hence the middle classes campaigned vigorously against duelling, recasting this time-honoured aristocratic practice for defending personal reputation and resolving disputes as cold-blooded murder. Addison and Steele were vociferous opponents of duelling, which they denounced in *The Tatler* and *The Spectator* papers. 'I must confess,' writes Steele in *Tatler* 25, 'when I consider what I am going about, and run over in my Imagination all the endless Crowd of Men of Honour who will be offended at such a Discourse [against duelling]; I am undertaking, methinks, a Work worthy of an invulnerable Hero in Romance, rather than a private Gentleman with a single Rapier.'[52] Steele's analogy cleverly enacts the recoding of honour which is the aim of his essay by figuring the traditional 'Hero in Romance,' a proponent of aristocratic honour, and often a duellist himself, as a hero who can eradicate this immoral practice.[53] Propounded in the same body of literature that reformed the code of honour, marriage for love is an integral part of this process of redefinition.

Such revision of cultural categories provides an unusually clear instance of the workings of symbolic capital, a phenomenon which is often so highly mediated that its operations are difficult to trace. Aristocratic ideology posits characteristics such as strength, bravery, and good character as innate, as we see from countless romances and stories of knights disguised as men of 'low degree,' whose essential nobility sooner or later emerges. Of course, typically aristocratic 'innate' abilities such as good swordsmanship would have been accessible only to the upper classes, for whom tuition in such skills was routine. But if possessing honour and being a 'gentleman' (another word whose definition shifted) depended on inner qualities alone, rather than on accomplishments, or birth, or wealth, then the upper reaches of society were indeed open to all who qualified.[54] Not everyone can be an excellent swordsman, but everyone can be, and ought to be, an excellent Christian. Similarly, if a lover's desirability depended on inner worth, then marriage within the very best circles was theoretically possible for all. Even if middle-class infiltration of the highest echelons of English society was more of a fiction than a reality, and even if countless mechanisms of snobbery and exclusion persisted, evaluating worth in terms of morals legitimated the upper middle class as an alternative elite whose sons and daughters were suitable spouses for the nobility.

The Companionate Ideal and Contractual Subjectivity

If changing notions about love and marriage were crucial in forming the identity and undergirding the power of the middle classes, such innovations were also part of a 'long revolution' for women that transformed their social and legal status in the course of the next two centuries.[55] Marriage for love insisted on a woman's autonomy in one crucial area, the choice of a husband. And if a woman was free to choose her spouse, she was by implication a trustworthy adult, capable of other significant choices and actions. John Stuart Mill argued in precisely these terms, connecting the marriage choice with women's suffrage: 'To have a voice in choosing those by whom one is to be governed, is a means of self-protection due to every one ... and that women are considered fit to have such a choice, may be presumed from the fact, that the law already gives it to women in the most important of all cases to themselves: for the choice of the man who is to govern a woman to the end of her life, is always supposed to be voluntarily made by herself.'[56] The expectation of companionship in marriage similarly suggested women's autonomy: if a man's wife was also his friend, she had to be more than a mere cipher.

Flying in the face of such logic, and prior to the great reforms in marriage law of the late nineteenth century, a woman's moment of choice condemned her thereafter to a total erasure of identity under common law. Her status was aptly characterized by the influential eighteenth-century jurist William Blackstone: 'The very being or legal existence of the woman is suspended during marriage, or at least is incorporated and consolidated into that of the husband.'[57] Because a wife had no independent legal identity, she was unable to participate in business or any other legal or financial arrangements independent of her husband. She could not own property, and her husband was entitled to any money or goods she brought to her marriage and any wages she might earn.[58] Wealthy women, however, were not always as poor in resources. If her family made a settlement of separate property held in trust for her under the legal system of equity, a woman might have access to her own money.[59] She might even have rights de facto – the rights that economic independence accords – although such rights were never given in her own name but rather in the name of her property.[60] However, it was increasingly the case that marriage settlements failed to make a significant practical difference; in the course of the eighteenth century judicial rulings defined the law in such a way as to prevent married women's access to 'their' separate property. And whether she were rich or poor, the law placed a wife almost completely in the power of her husband, no matter how abusive he might prove: he could beat her, lock her up, and live openly with his mistress, and she had almost no recourse at law. A hundred years after Blackstone's infamous definition, little had changed. In 1868, the Victorian activist

Frances Power Cobbe observed that women were classified in the same legal category as 'criminals, idiots, and minors.'[61]

Arguments linking the status of women as active partners in marriage with society's obligation to increase their rights and opportunities can be found throughout feminist arguments of the eighteenth and nineteenth centuries. Mary Wollstonecraft contended that 'passive, indolent women,' produced by a society that denies them freedom and limits their education and opportunities, do not make good wives because they cannot provide suitable companionship for their husbands: 'It is a melancholy thing for a father of a family, who is fond of home, to be obliged to be always wrapped up in himself, and to have nobody about him to whom he can impart his sentiments.'[62] Nor do women deprived of education and rights have the skills needed to be effectual mothers, for how should a woman void of reflection be capable of educating her children? (see, e.g., 83, 119). Such arguments became a staple of Victorian feminism. Like Wollstonecraft, Cobbe argues that laws oppressive to women are incompatible with wifely love and devotion. If men believe 'that a woman's whole life and being, her soul, body, time, property, thought, and care ought to be given to her husband' and that 'nothing short of such absorption in his and his interests makes her a true wife,' then denying women their rights undermines rather than furthers this goal: 'Is perfect love to be called out by perfect dependence? Does an empty purse necessarily imply a full heart? Is a generous-natured woman likely to be won or rather to be alienated and galled by being made to feel she has no choice but submission? Surely there is a great fallacy in this direction ... real unanimity is not produced between two parties by forbidding one of them to have any voice at all.'[63] Along similar lines, Marion Reid, another activist, contends that 'social equality ... [and] the possession and exercise of political privileges [by women] ... would be of benefit also to man, by ennobling the influence over him of that being who is the natural companion of his life.'[64] Conversely, a marriage that is neither consensual nor companionate negates a woman's independent subjectivity altogether. The Marquis of Halifax's *The Lady's New-year's Gift: or, Advice to a Daughter* approvingly links the arranged marriage, a practice he deems necessary to maintain the sovereignty of the aristocracy, with the complete effacement of women's rights, desires, and needs.[65]

The perception that ideals of marriage did not accord with its sociolegal reality was not just an intuitive insight or a matter of observation. It was an inference grounded in contract theory, which provided both a legal and a philosophical language for urging appropriate reforms. Even more important, it enabled a drastic revision in thinking about women's subjectivity. According to contractarian feminist arguments, the marriage contract, like the social contract, is a relationship entered into voluntarily for the benefit of both parties; love is indeed the marker of this voluntariness.[66] Marriage should therefore live up to its allegedly contractual nature. Political subjects retain rights and liberties; a wife ought to do so as well. To put this another way, endorsements of marriage for love, such as we have seen in conduct literature, discursively produce the contractual subjectivity of women. Married love interpellates women as autonomous agents who possess the intellectual capacity to enter into contracts, and who are therefore due the social and legal sanctions of civil society.[67]

Among the earliest and most well-known writers to articulate a feminist reading of contract was Mary Astell, a seventeenth-century Tory who criticized liberal thinkers for being contractarians where men were concerned and 'patriarchalists' towards women (a criticism that anticipates feminist critiques of our own day): 'If Absolute Sovereignty be not necessary in a State, how comes it to be so in a Family. The Domestic Sovereign is without Dispute Elected, and the Stipulations and Contract are mutual. Is it not then partial in Men to the last degree, to contend for, and practise that Arbitrary Dominion in their Families, which they abhor and exclaim against in the State? For if Arbitrary Power is evil in itself, and an improper Method of Governing Rational and Free Agents, it ought not to be Practis'd any where.'[68] This contractual logic was not confined to a few isolated thinkers. Susan Staves demonstrates that when ideals of contract were invoked in judicial decisions involving disputes over property, women were granted increased access to their separate property and increased autonomy. This result was 'intolerable,' and so by the end of the eighteenth century, 'the courts retreated from contract ideology in this field and reimposed ... deeper patriarchal structures.'[69]

Appeals to contract later became fundamental to Victorian feminism, especially in arguments urging the reform of marriage law. The most systematic and thorough expositor of the relationship between contract theory and women's rights was John Stuart Mill, whose work I discuss in chapter 4. But the invocation of contract was a familiar trope in the writings of other activists as well. In 1825, William Thompson angrily denounced the marriage contract for its failure to be a true contract: '[M]an condescends to enter into what he calls a *contract* with certain women for certain purposes [e.g., children] ... Each man yokes a woman to his establishment, and calls it a *contract*. Audacious false-hood! A contract! where are any of the attributes of contracts ... to be found in this transaction? A contract implies the voluntary assent of both contracting parties. Can even both the parties, man and woman, by agreement alter the terms as to the *indissolubility* and *inequality*, of this pretended contract? ... Such a contract, as the owners of *slaves* in the West Indies and every other slave-polluted soil, enter into with their slaves.'[70] Caroline Norton, urging the reform of the common law in 1855, framed a similar argument. 'As *her husband*, he has a right to all that is hers: as *his wife*, she has no right to anything that is his. As her husband, he may divorce her (if truth or false swearing can do it): as his wife, the utmost "divorce" she could obtain is permission to reside alone, – married to his name. The marriage ceremony is a civil bond for him – and an indissoluble sacrament for her; and the rights of mutual property which that ceremony is ignorantly supposed to confer, are made absolute for him, and null for her.'[71] A marriage contract is not a true contract if marriage laws fail to evince the contractual logic that the wedding ceremony purports.

Contract and Separate Spheres

Classic liberal theory has recently been criticized by feminists who point out that it is premised on masculinist assumptions that have ulti-mately done women more harm than good. Susan Moller Okin argues that contract theorists consign women to a separate domestic sphere in which they are isolated and powerless, 'naturally' subject to husbands whose interests supposedly encompass their own. Such segregation is premised on sexual difference – women are sentimental and irrational, and therefore unsuited to public life. As Okin and others have also pointed out, contract assumes a male political subject, ignoring or negating the recognition and accommodation of women's needs and differences. The concept of equal, genderless (but really male) political subjects has been used to deny women maternity leave and to gain control of children from the mothers who bore them.[72] Carole Pateman suggests that this gendered inequity is part of the very fabric of liberal theory. Creating her own allegory of contractual origins in response to the legal fiction of the social compact, Patemen posits a 'sexual con-tract': political right originates in male sex-right or conjugal right, which then guarantees the subordination of women. Classic liberal theorists incorporated this right, implicit in the theories of their patriarchalist opponents, thereby transforming 'the law of male sex-right into its modern contractual form.'[73] Like Pateman, Wendy Brown argues that the masculine identity of the liberal subject (as formulated by contract theorists) is not contingent but essential; he possesses characteristics that confer his specifically masculine status, including autonomy, self-interest, and acquisitiveness. Although the masculine liberal subject can be, physiologically, a man or a woman, liberal theory denies liberty to all because its 'formulation of liberty *requires* the existence of encumbered beings' and can therefore 'never be fully universalized.'[74]

This gendering of place and function, which identifies women with domestic life and men with public life, is of course known as the ideology of separate spheres. Given the assumption within contemporary political theory that a gendered and hierarchized separation of functions has been foundational to women's oppression in the past and continues to be so today, it is worth considering the controversy surrounding this concept. According to traditional historical accounts, by about 1780, industrialization had shifted significant sectors of industry from home to factory and other centralized locations, thereby depriving women who had manufactured goods at home of jobs and income.[75] At the same time, the commercialization of agriculture had taken away rural women's ability to contribute economically to their households. And as an emergent middle class predicated its identity on a glorified domesticity grounded in the gendered division of work and identity, women in the middling ranks were increasingly associated with the domestic sphere. Thus, in the course of the eighteenth century, women became progressively disempowered, confined to the home, and identified exclusively with domestic concerns and responsibilities, a process that was fully entrenched by the Victorian era.

While this paradigm is still widely accepted, the concept of separate spheres has been criticized in recent historiography and literary history on several grounds. One argument is that a dramatic separation of spheres did not take place. The idea that women and men have different 'spheres' of operation and that women are associated with the home and men with public life is a traditional concept, not at all unique to or even unusually predominant in the periods associated with its hegemony. After all, Aristotle refers to these distinctions. And when women did work in the early modern period, their work was usually significantly differentiated from that of men. Moreover, women's labour in earlier times might not have accorded them the prestige and autonomy that modern scholars attribute to it.[76] Second, modern definitions of 'public,' 'private,' and 'domestic' differ from historical ones. 'Private' and 'domestic' often encompassed duties and concerns that we think of as 'public'; conversely, 'public' referred to matters that we associate with the domestic. We are therefore liable to misinterpret the significance of past writings that refer to women's association with the domestic, or to the distinction between public and private life.[77] Third, assuming women's ostensible confinement to the domestic, as we use the term in contradistinction to public life, women were not disempowered, for they wielded tremendous if often covert authority. They defined the hegemonic terms of subjectivity itself;[78] they participated in their husbands' professional lives in central if tacit ways that advanced the standing of their families in social and economic terms;[79] and they engaged in public life in areas that were putatively an extension of their domestic function, particularly religious and philanthropic work, but which took them well beyond a narrowly domestic existence.[80]

While criticism of a simplistic deployment of 'separate spheres' is valid, it is nevertheless important to remember that whatever the extent of their power, autonomy, and self-activation, women nevertheless confronted non-negotiable limits to their rights and opportunities, a brick wall rather than a glass ceiling. Common law deprived married women of rights, property, and legal identity, and no woman, single or married, was accorded the status or entitlements of citizenship until well into the twentieth century. More important for my purposes than the accuracy of the separate sphere ideology is the fact that in this period 'the domestic' and 'separate spheres' were dominant categories within discussions of women's place and power. It is therefore more productive to view separate spheres not as a historical fact or a myth of modern scholarship but rather as what Laura Brown calls a 'cultural fable' of the eighteenth and nineteenth centuries. Brown explains that a cultural fable is 'a formal construct ... characterized by a set of related figures that have a distinctive structure or are in a dynamic relationship... [T]hey intersect with and elaborate one another so as to project a set of meanings, affects, or even ironies that constitute a common imaginative project.'[81] The many versions of the 'story' of separate spheres for men and women, with their varying investments and implications – how men and women in the state of nature, or the civilized world, or the fallen world came to have distinct arenas, concerns, and duties – testify to the flexible and often contradictory interplay of its elements. Here are some of these narratives: men forced women into the domestic sphere because they knew that women were superior and had to be kept down to establish their own power; God in His wisdom assigned men and women natural tasks, as is evident from their biological differences; men are stronger than women and so the law of nature sanctions a gendered division between domestic and public life.

It is in the eighteenth century that the traditionally accepted distinctions between men's and women's concerns attained the status of a cultural fable insofar as they generated 'a common imaginative project' rather than simply received wisdom. One way to trace the transformation from gendered functions to 'separate spheres' is through women's increasing association with the domestic in print culture.[82] Moreover, there is a consensus among women writers themselves that association of women with the home intersects with issues of power, status, and self-esteem. There is no doubt that Victorian feminists protested women's confinement within a domestic sphere, but such complaints appeared much earlier as well. For instance, the observation that men undervalue or constrain women by identifying them with and limiting them to the domestic is a trope of women's poetry throughout the eighteenth century, and it is worth noting that for all the evolution of the meaning of 'domestic' between that time and our own, these poets do use the word with all its negative connotations. Here is Elizabeth Thomas in 1722, articulating a familiar lament of later feminists, albeit in an eighteenth-century poetic style:

> Unhappy sex! how hard's our fate,
> By Custom's tyranny confined
> To foolish needlework and chat,
> Or such like exercise as that,
> But still denied th'improvement of our mind!
> 'Women!' men cry 'alas, poor fools!
> What are they but domestic tools?
> On purpose made our toils to share,
> And ease the husband's economic care.[83]

And Esther Lewis in 1748 (writing ironically from a man's point of view):

> We never choose a learned fair,
> Nor like to see a woman try
> With our superior parts to vie.
> She ought to mind domestic cares,
> The sex were made for such affairs.[84]

Even women who welcomed their identification with domesticity and derived both prestige and authority from it ostensibly accepted its exclusionary terms.[85] In short, while historians and literary critics might validly question the degree of separation between men and women's spheres, as well as traditional accounts of the origins of such separation, the importance of this concept to contract theory now and in the past is beyond doubt.

Contract and Feminism, Past and Present

In order to analyse the theoretical ground of women's contractual subjectivity and explain why contract was so important to feminisms of the past, I want to historicize the topic by turning to the writings of John Locke, the most influential theorist of contract in England. Locke's *Two Treatises of Government* informs earlier feminist arguments even though, as recent writers have shown, to view Locke in feminist terms requires a reading that is both partial and naive. But this was not always obvious: as the terrain of the feminist struggle has shifted, so has our point of view. That wives today have a legal identity has transformed the way we look at contract.

Even the feminists of the past who drew on Locke's theories would have been able to recognize that his statements regarding women are contradictory. Locke's inconsistencies stem from his specific agenda: to discredit Sir Robert Filmer and other Royalists. In his *Patriarcha*, Filmer had invoked a traditional analogy between marriage contract and social contract in order to argue that a king's authority in the realm is like the husband's authority in his family: both are total and indissoluble.[86] Locke responds to these claims with two contradictory strategies. First, he implicitly grants Filmer's analogy, which leads him to make several protofeminist statements in order to limit the king/husband's sovereignty. The husband's power within the family extends 'but to the things of their [his and his wife's] common Interest and Property, [and] leaves the Wife in the full and free possession of what by Contract is her peculiar Right.'[87] Subjection is negotiable. In fact, women are not necessarily subject to their husbands at all, because 'there is here no more Law to oblige a Woman to such a Subjection, if the Circumstances either of her Condition or Contract with her Husband should exempt her from it, then there is, that she should bring forth her Children in Sorrow and Pain, if there could be found a Remedy for it' (173). Mothers as well as fathers are entitled to their children's respect and obedience (303). A woman may have authority over the family as well as the man (321). Women may even divorce or separate from their husbands, and retain custody of their children, if the laws of the country in which they live permit this (321).[88]

Locke's other tactic, however, is to deny Filmer's analogy between family and state, maintaining that the husband's authority in the family is entirely distinct from the monarch's authority over his subjects. This allows him to assert a patriarchy almost as rigid as Filmer's own. Locke therefore defines conjugal power as 'the Power that every Husband hath to order the things of private Concernment in his Family, as Proprietor of the Goods and Land there, and to have his Will take place before that of his wife in all things of their common Concernment' (174).[89] Male domination is an ineluctable fact of life; women are already subject, even in the state of nature: 'God ... gives not, that I see, any Authority to *Adam* over *Eve*, or to Men over their wives, but only foretels what should be the Womans Lot, how by his Providence he would order it so, that she should be subject to her husband, as we see that generally the Laws of Mankind and customs of Nations have ordered it so; and there is, I grant, a Foundation in Nature for it' (174). In this passage, Locke relies implicitly on the characteristic Protestant distinction between Providence and free will to assert that if men are not entitled to authority over women (because God has given humans the free will to determine their social arrangements), they possess it nevertheless (this is the order of things we have brought about, which Providence foretells and ordains). These contentions separate the family from civil society, public from private. Here indeed is a locus classicus of the ideology of separate spheres which, as we have seen, critics of liberal theory point to as a primary source of women's oppression.

But Locke's usefulness to feminism consisted less in his specific claims about women or the family than in his general analysis of contractual relationships. According to Locke, all contracts have certain immutable limits that are guaranteed by human birthright. Both men and women are born into the state of nature, which exists prior to civil society. Although there is no formal government at this point, the state of nature is nevertheless orderly, for it obeys the 'law of nature,' a God-given coda of rights and responsibilities that people intuitively apprehend through their innate powers of reasoning.[90] This 'law' applies to everyone except 'lunaticks, Idiots, and children, until they reach the age of reason' (240). With these exceptions, all are equal, since the state of nature is a condition 'wherein all the Power and Jurisdiction is recipocal, no one having more than another' (269). And each person has 'a *Liberty* to dispose, and order, as he lists, his Person, Actions, Possessions, and his whole Property, within the Allowance of those Laws under which he is; and therein not to be subject to the arbitrary Will of another, but freely follow his own' (306). It is significant that by property Locke means more than mere belongings; property includes 'Life, Liberty and Estate' (323) and also designates 'property in one's own person' – one's body and one's labour power (what C.B. Macpherson calls possessive individualism).[91] Indeed, Locke's attitude towards property involves him in one of his major contradictions concerning women. For Locke, property is merged so completely with identity, liberty, and well-being that the husband's complete control of his family's common property is, in effect, on Locke's own terms, a negation of his wife's natural rights – a transformation of subjectivity into subjection.[92]

Neither the social contract nor any other contract may violate these inalienable liberties. The only purpose for which one person may legitimately exercise power over another is to punish a crime, and such power is not absolute or arbitrary (357). Locke therefore asserts that an individual cannot contract to give another absolute power over him/herself: 'This *Freedom* from Absolute, Arbitrary Power, is so necessary to, and closely joyned with a Man's Preservation, that he cannot part with it, but by what forfeits his Preservation and Life together. For a Man, not having the Power of his own Life, *cannot*, by Compact, or his own Consent, *enslave himself* to any one, nor put himself under the Absolute, Arbitrary Power of another, to take away his Life when he pleases' (284). It follows that a self-destructive contract is not valid, and if a contract is illegitimate, or if either of its parties violates its terms, that contract is dissoluble (367).[93]

These limits to the power of contract suggest the contracting subject's irrevocable autonomy. In Locke's terms, the marriage contract was not a true contract but a state of war, and every wife had the right to divorce her husband – indeed was not truly married. If we judge with attention to historical specificity the political status and function of the autonomous, 'contractual' self implied by Locke's guarantees, we see why his theory was so liberating for women. This becomes clear when we compare Pateman's discussion of possessive individualism, or property in one's own person, which is often judged to be a negative concept for feminism of our own period, with Mary Poovey's treatment of the same issue with respect to the nineteenth century. Pateman argues that the concept of property in one's own person 'enables the opposition between freedom and slavery to be dissolved.'[94] Because one can alienate aspects of oneself, such as one's labour, one can enter into contracts that entail virtual if not actual slavery (despite Locke's contention that one cannot contract to enter into slavery). While Poovey agrees that this alienable subjectivity enables forms of exploitation, she suggests that within the political and social structures of Victorian England, the oppression of patriarchy can be defined in contrast to the very capacity for oppression in the labour market: the 'slavery' of the worker is freedom from the point of view of a woman subject to common law prior to the passage of the married women's property bills. In nineteenth-century England, the 'proprietary [i.e., alienable] self' underwrote 'the fundamental criterion of subject status – the individual's capacity to recognize and act on his own interests.' Gender difference and female subordination were predicated to a large extent on the fact that 'the difference written into the proprietary subject' (i.e., the ability to alienate aspects of the self) did not apply to woman, 'who was not so divided ... This apparently fixed difference was then taken to anchor not only the kind of labor men and women performed, but also the opposition between the public sphere, where alienation was visible and inescapable, and the home.'[95] From this point of view, it is not contract that authorizes a hierarchically gendered division, but the absence of contract. It was precisely by denying married women the recognition of a proprietary, or as I call it, a 'contractual' self that the law rendered women fundamentally different from and subordinate to men – even if that form of subjectivity was itself a potential instrument of oppression.[96]

Despite the gender bias of Locke's theory, many aspects of which, as we realize today, imply the subordination of women, Victorian feminists were able to draw on contractual ideals to argue for women's inclusion within liberalism's umbrella of rights and liberties. Ironically, the institution of marriage, the very target of their criticism for its assignation of power to the husband, created the ideological ground for utilizing contract in their battle for reform. Married love was one articulation of a liberal 'structure of feeling' that emphasized the entitlements and protections of contract, including the idea that society is – and should be – based on voluntarism rather than force. The new ideal of married love had tremendous emotional and theoretical purchase within this new way of thinking. As J.R. Gillis observes, '[c]onjugal love was the model and the guarantee of a stable, consensual society that ... early capitalists hoped would replace the old order of privilege and birth.'[97] As parties to this most intimate of contracts, women were able to argue that they too belonged within this new order.

Women's Passion: An Open Secret

The suggestion of women's autonomy was threatening for myriad psychological and political reasons, the most urgent of which concerned their potentially wayward sexuality. If men relinquished control of women – particularly husbands' control of their wives – property might descend to illegitimate heirs. Samuel Johnson pithily captures the essence of such fears about women's virtue and the patrilinear descent of property: 'Consider of what importance to society the chastity of women is. Upon that all the property in the world depends. We hang a thief for stealing a sheep; but the unchastity of a woman transfers sheep, and farm and all, from the right owner.'[98] Rousseau expressed the connection between paternity and patriarchal control at length and with particular force: for him, paternity was an obsession, and the only important virtue in a woman was chastity. The danger that women might be unfaithful both necessitates and justifies their subjection.[99] Rousseau's fears, however exaggerated, reflected an anxiety at the heart of contemporary patriarchal thought. Nor had this changed much a century later. When bills to grant married women the right to own property, and hence to possess a modicum of independence from their husbands, were being debated in Parliament in the late nineteenth century, opponents feared that such autonomy would undermine the institution of marriage, and might even lead to women's straying from the marriage bed. Lord Penzance, who led the opposition to married women's property rights in the House of Lords, speculated that if a married woman could own property and was therefore able to participate in business, 'Being at full liberty to contract with the outer world, [she] might carry on any trade she pleased without her husband's consent, so that a man might be startled by the information that his wife had determined to set up a rival shop in his neighbourhood ... [He] might be still more startled at hearing that she had entered into a partnership with her cousin, who need not be a woman.'[100] Freedom for women signalled sexual licence.

One solution to the threat of a wayward feminine sexuality was simply to assert that it did not exist. Cultural critics have detailed the rise of 'passionlessness,' the denial of female sexuality.[101] By the middle of the eighteenth century, the 'proper lady' had come into her own; in the Victorian age, she became the 'angel in the house,' maternal, saintly, and pointedly non-sexual. It might not be accidental that as marriage for love became a cultural ideal, so did women's lack of sexual passion. It was much safer to believe that women married for companionship than to think they could be motivated by sexual desire. But female passion never entirely disappeared. The fallen woman was a continual reminder that female sexuality could reassert itself at any moment, in any woman.[102] Moreover, passionlessness co-existed with alternative cultural definitions that acknowledged women's capacity for both intense feeling and erotic responsiveness.[103]

Women could not be passionless, because feeling was believed to be the source of virtue, a point that was emphasized by philosophers of sentiment in the eighteenth century and that continued to be an influential ethical paradigm in the following century.[104] This is not to claim that popular attitudes about the passions were unambivalent, unchanging, or unilateral. Towards the end of the eighteenth century, for instance, strong feeling was suspect because it was associated with revolutionary excess.[105] Conservatives and progressives accused one another of possessing a dangerous sensibility.[106] Nevertheless, even within this climate of distrust, feeling continued to be associated with virtue. The writings of the renowned conservative Edmund Burke illustrate this ambivalence. While Burke's description of the Parisian mob's assault on the French Royal family illustrates the horror of unregulated feeling, he depends on evoking such horror precisely by manipulating the reader's pathos: this is one of the most sentimental of scenes in an age that abounded with the literature of tears.[107] However much Burke might have disparaged passion, he solicits the proper ethical response by sympathetic identification rather than argumentative persuasion.[108] Once the late eighteenth-century period of reaction ended, attitudes towards feeling became less conflicted, as the popularity of the Romantic movement in literature and the arts clearly shows. And rare is the Victorian novel whose good characters are not men or women of feeling.

Because of prevailing ideas about physiology, even the purest feelings were tinged with eroticism. Emotion, or 'sensibility,' was believed to be a physical as well as psychological phenomenon, and was described in contemporary medical treatises in terms of movements within the body. As R.S. Brissenden notes, '"sensibility," "sentiment" and "sympathy" were terms with precise meanings in the newly developing sciences of physiology and neurology.'[109] Science was reflected in popular belief, which often identified strong feeling, including benevolence, with sexual response. Diderot writes, 'There is a bit of testicle at the bottom of our most sublime sentiments and most refined tenderness.'[110] Likewise, the latitudinarian divines use erotically suggestive language to emphasize the pleasures of benevolence. Echoing Diderot Richard Kidder maintains, 'There is a Delight and Joy that Accompanies doing good, there is a kind of sensuality in it.'[111] Charles Brent is even more explicit: 'There is for certain, even now, a most Divine and Heavenly Pleasure in doing Good ... some good Men have indulged and epicuriz'd in it, till they have been tempted to call it downright *Sensuality*.'[112] In the eighteenth century, much of the concern about women's novel reading was that works of sensibility were sexually arousing, even when they dealt with benevolent feeling rather than love. Henry Mackenzie suggests in *The Man of Feeling* that prostitution is the logical conclusion to a course of reading comprising plays, novels, and 'those poetical descriptions of the beauty of virtue and honour, which the circulating libraries easily afforded.'[113] If the feelings that generated benevolence were to some extent erotic, then women must be capable of sexual passion, despite their iconic status as ladies and angels. To lack strong feeling, moreover, was also to lack the capacity for sympathy and compassion, the foundations of virtuous action. Passion might invoke the dangers of sexuality, but it nevertheless guaranteed a non-sexual kind of purity. The person who responded spontaneously responded selflessly.

The necessity of both suppressing and acknowledging women's capacity for passion explains a paradox central to many novels. It was axiomatic that a woman was never supposed to fall in love before a man had made serious overtures. To do so was to be guilty of indelicacy. Yet novel after novel portrays a morally superior heroine who falls in love with a worthy man before he has made his intentions clear, or even realized his own feelings. Even that most proper and passive of heroines, Fanny Price, falls in love with Edmund long before he recognizes her attractions. Yet despite their violation of etiquette, such heroines are always morally superior, in part because of their ability to love of their own volition, rather than simply to reflect male desire. That they can love without expectation of any return is the sign both of their ability to recognize worth in others and their own selflessness. In *Sir Charles Grandison* Harriet Byron's analysis of her feelings brilliantly captures the novel's duplicity about women's desire: 'It is, I hope, a secret *to* myself, that never will be unfolded, even to myself, that I love a man, who has not made professions of Love to me.'[114] She must keep this knowledge secret (even to herself), because it is wrong, but we all must know the truth of her feelings because they are so right.

Married Love and Sexual Difference

Yet another reason that women could not be construed as 'passionless' is that their supposedly excessive capacity for feeling justified their subjection. In this view, women need male supervision because they are too emotional and therefore likely to behave transgressively. On the one hand, women were increasingly construed as less passionate than men, an optative characterization that ensured the proper descent of property. But on the other hand, women's feelings, and female sexuality in particular, required the control, both social and legal, of paternalistic law. The contention that women are excessively responsive, always on the brink of losing self-control, is in fact part of a core of arguments that allege male supremacy on the ground of sexual difference. In the opposition Man/woman, 'woman' is the inferior term that delimits the superiority of 'Man,' who rules precisely because he is not woman. Male identity and power depend on female inferiority and powerlessness for self-definition; a man's difference entitles him to sovereignty while a woman's condemns her to subjugation. And such differences were believed to be biological and immutable facts of nature that expressed the will of God.[115]

This totalizing and determinate view of sexual difference emerged in the course of the eighteenth century. Although women's inferiority had traditionally been premised on their difference from men, such differences had not been considered immutable or irrevocably other: they were a matter of degree rather than kind. In this period, as Thomas Laqueur explains, popular and medical belief shifted from a 'one-sex' to a 'two-sex' model of conceptualizing sexual difference. Departing from traditional thought, new theories of medicine and psychology considered women not as lesser versions of men in terms of anatomy and character, as had formerly been the case, but as fundamentally and

essentially distinct. 'Woman' no longer signalled a social category associated with certain biological attributes, but a biological one that
defined women altogether: 'Distinct sexual anatomy was adduced to
support or deny all manner of claims in a variety of specific social, economic, political, cultural, or erotic contexts.'[116] Sexual difference therefore became a fulcrum in debates about women's proper role. Those
who argued for male supremacy averred that an essential sexual difference produced other differences in character and capability between
men and women (i.e., the two-sex model). Their opponents attributed
most of these allegedly innate sexual differences to education and custom. For these progressive thinkers, even the differences that were
unchanging facts of biology did not render women inferior to men, nor
did they justify subordination or the limitations on women's opportunities in education, employment, the law, and so forth.

The centrality of sexual difference to ideologies of gender can be seen
in a debate in mid-eighteenth century pamphlets between Sophia, 'a
lady of quality,' and an anonymous opponent.[117] In *Woman Not Inferior
to Man: or, A Short and Modest Vindication of the Natural Right of the Fair-
Sex to a Perfect Equality of Power, Dignity, and Esteem, With The Men*,
Sophia sets out to 'examine, whether there be any *essential difference
between* the *sexes* which can authorize the *superiority* the *Men* claim over
the *Women*.'[118] She concludes that ostensible differences are not innate,
but are rather the result of custom and men's self-interest: of 'the many
absurd notions that men are led into by custom ... there is none more
absurd, than that of the great difference they make between their own
sex and ours.' The belief that '*Men* are really superior to *Women*' has led
to 'the dependence we now are in' (6). The qualities that have enabled
men to dominate are brute strength and aggression – the 'law ... of the
stronger' (36) – which are irrelevant in moral or intellectual terms,
the true criteria for assessing value: 'If brutal strength, in which we
acknowledge their pre-eminence, is a sufficient plea, for their trampling
upon Us, the lion has a much better title over the whole creation' (18).
The crux of all Sophia's arguments is the assertion that women are the
equals of men because they have souls: 'And since there is not at most
any greater difference between the souls of *Women* and *Men*, there can
be no real diversity contracted from the body: All the diversity then
must come from *education, exercise*, and the *impressions* of those external
objects which surround us in different Circumstances' (23).

In *Beauty's Triumph (Part the Second), Being an Attempt to Refute
Sophia's Arguements; and to Prove the Natural Right of the Men to Sovereign*

Authority over the Other Sex, Sophia's male opponent argues that custom is proof not of the contingency of women's oppression, but rather of its necessity. The universality of women's subjection is in fact evidence that custom itself has its source in reason, and not that reason has been perverted by custom. And such reason points to nature rather than nurture as the determinant of difference and inferiority. Demonstrating a repugnance for women's bodies worthy of Swift, he asserts repeatedly that a woman's different and inferior body is the sign of her inferior character. '[T]heir souls are as different as their bodies, and ... there ought to be as great distinction between the two sexes in all the functions of life, as there is in that of instrumentally producing it. All which consider'd, no *Woman* in her senses can doubt of the subjection of that sex to ours, being founded on the laws of nature and reason' (88).[119] Above all, women are incapable of reason. Their follies, such as preoccupation with trivial concerns, which Sofia attributes to 'different circumstances,' are evidence of their unfitness for serious thought: 'If the business of the mind were nothing more than to contrive a dress, to invent a new fashion; to set off a bad face; to heighten the charms of a good one; to understand the oeconomy of a tea-table; to manage an intrigue; to conduct a game at *Quadrille*; and to lay out new plans of pleasure, pride, and luxury; the *Women* must be owned to have a capacity not only *equal*, but even superior to us. But, as the understanding of Man has infinitely higher objects to employ its speculations on, objects beyond the very aim of the ablest of *Women*; their intellectual faculties are so evidently inferior to his' (106).[120]

Married love was at odds with such beliefs about the unyielding boundaries of sexual difference: a companionate ideal of marriage undermined rigid and hierarchical conceptions of men's and women's roles by emphasizing the husband and wife's reciprocal contributions to the relationship. When men and women married for the right reasons, mutual regard was always assumed to be an important component of their feelings. Such regard was believed to depend on having interests and views in common.[121] If men and women shared common intellectual and moral ground, then how could there be absolute difference between them? This is not to say, however, that those who endorsed married love were necessarily progressive in their ideas about women. On the contrary, much eighteenth- and nineteenth-century writing attempted to undermine the progressive implications of companionship. While a belief in the deeply satisfying nature of friendship between husbands and wives was a mainstay of English culture from the seventeenth century on, at the same time, a woman was expected to accept her subordinate status and limited range of opportunity, as conduct literature shows.[122] As we shall see, pointing to the absurdity of this contradiction became a familiar feminist strategy.

While their writings are more subtle and articulate than the tedious rant that often characterizes *Beauty's Triumph*, Rousseau and Wollstonecraft nevertheless rely on similar arguments about sexual difference. In *Émile*, Rousseau claims that the most basic of biological differences, the fact that women bear children, determines their natural and irrevocable subjection. In order to address her childbearing and nurturing duties properly, a woman must be entirely dependent on her mate: 'She cannot fulfil her purpose in life without his aid, without his goodwill, without his respect; she is dependent on our feelings, on the price we put upon her virtue, and the opinion we have of her charms and her deserts. Nature herself has decreed that woman, both for herself and her children, should be at the mercy of man's judgment.'[123] Because of this necessary dependence, women's characters differ from those of men. Their biological destiny thus explains their personalities and preoccupations.[124] Women are naturally inclined to love finery, and to thrive on admiration because their lives are necessarily directed towards attracting men. Little girls love dolls because dressing them anticipates their own adornment: 'in due time she will be her own doll' (331). And so it follows that '[l]ittle girls always dislike learning to read and write, but they are always ready to learn to sew' (331). These behaviours are not simply adaptive strategies for survival formed in response to women's social positioning by men, as feminists would argue, but innate ways of responding to the world. Sexual difference also determines cognitive ability; women are more cunning than men ('[c]unning is a natural gift of women' [334]) because their inferior position prevents their demanding what they want directly.[125] However, although women are clever and manipulative, they lack the masculine capacity for abstract reasoning: 'The search for abstract and speculative truths, for principles and axioms in science, for all that tends to wide generalisation, is beyond a woman's grasp; their studies should be thoroughly practical' (349). This narrow view of women's functions and abilities of course precludes any enlargement of their opportunities for learning or employment. 'Vague assertions as to the equality of the sexes and the similarity of their duties are only empty words,' asserts Rousseau smugly. 'They are no answer to my argument' (325).[126]

Wollstonecraft's *A Vindication of the Rights of Woman* is an extended refutation of Rousseau's views on women, especially as he articulates them in *Émile*.[127] Wollstonecraft argues repeatedly that the characteristics which Rousseau cites as proof of sexual difference are really the product of a thorough and insidious process of enculturation, implemented both to assure men's power and to appeal to their sensuality. Because Rousseau and men like him believe that 'merely the person of a *young* woman, without any mind ... is very pleasing,' they construct a system of gender-training which produces such 'mindless' women who focus entirely on their appearance: 'To render it [a woman's body] weak, and what some may call beautiful, the understanding is neglected, and girls forced to sit still, play with dolls and listen to foolish conversations; – the effect of habit [i.e., mindlessness] is insisted upon as an undoubted indication of nature' (179). This training condemns women to an epistemology of the material and sensual. When men are similarly educated, they become equally foolish. Wollstonecraft gives the example of soldiers who, like women, are 'sent into the world before their minds have been stored with knowledge, or fortified by principles' (105) and who therefore lack 'depth of understanding,' which is 'as rarely to be found in the army as amongst women' (106). 'Where then is the sexual difference, when the education has been the same?' (105). Like Sophia, Wollstonecraft willingly concedes that men are physically stronger than women (80). But she argues that even in this area of evident superiority, training has done much to accentuate and exaggerate innate differences. Throughout the *Vindication*, she criticizes mistaken ideals of female delicacy which have rendered women much weaker than they need be.[128] Yet of all the false and destructive ways in which Rousseau characterizes women, Wollstonecraft believes that none is so pernicious as his dismissal of their capacity for reason. She counters that if women have immortal souls, as Christians believe, then they must have reason: 'the nature of reason must be the same in all, if it be an emanation of divinity, the tie that connects the creature with the Creator' (143).[129] Depriving women of substantive education is thus not only unfair but blasphemous, because it deprives them of the means to conduct life's most important work, the preparation of the soul for immortality; 'for, can that soul be stamped with the heavenly image, that is not perfected by the exercise of its own reason?' (143). Here, as in other areas, women's ostensible difference from men is the product of upbringing: 'Let their faculties have room to unfold ... and then determine where the whole sex must stand in the intellectual scale' (120).

Given his assertion of total distinction between the sexes, it is not surprising that in Rousseau's view men and women lack the common ground necessary for companionate marriage. Although Rousseau is a firm believer in marriage for love, love for him consists in romantic, sexual infatuation, not mutual regard. Women are objects of desire and passion, but they are never friends. So far from Rousseau's thinking was the possibility of companionship between men and women, so convinced was he of their essential and unalterable difference, that he thought men and women should live apart most of the time.[130] Rousseau's representations of men, women, and love suggest that a belief in the fixity of sexual difference is incompatible with definitions of married love that are based on friendship, and, conversely, that companionship is incompatible with such rigid categorization. Wollstonecraft, predictably, argues the very opposite, that relationships lacking in mutual respect and companionship cannot be the basis for a fulfilling marriage. By depriving women of education, men deprive themselves of the intelligent company that makes a marriage successful: '[A]n improved understanding [produced by freedom and education] only can render society [i.e., the relationship between husband and wife] agreeable ... the woman who strengthens her body and exercises her mind will, by managing her family and practising various virtues, become the friend, and not the humble dependent of her husband' (189, 113).

By the Victorian period, sexual difference was still the basis of belief in women's subordination and in the rightness of restricting their opportunities, but there was a crucial change. Such difference was not always figured pejoratively, and it did not always extend to women's intellectual capacity, or include denying women a sound education.[131] This was due largely to the centrality of Christianity within daily life, sparked by the rise of evangelicalism, which had an extraordinary impact on 'respectable' people, especially in the middle classes.[132] Christianity accorded women an elevated, idealized moral status. Women, because they were more susceptible to feeling than men were, and because feeling was the ground of true religion, were potentially closer to God. Their 'passionlessness' rendered them pure, and therefore worthy of respect. In evangelical Christianity in particular, the emphasis on each individual's responsibility for his or her soul implied the principle of religious equality; men and women might not be equal on earth, but they were equal before God.[133] In pragmatic terms, women had an important place within various religious movements; they formed voluntary associations, distributed tracts and Bibles, taught in Sunday schools, and raised money for religious and charitable causes. Their activism in social campaigns, such as abolitionism and attempts to improve conditions for the poor, drew them increasingly into the public sphere.

Most important with respect to cultural paradigms of womanhood, love, and marriage, Victorian Christianity tended to conflate domestic ideals with religious ones, assuming that the influences of home were crucial in shaping both the character and the morality of children. Paramount among the sources of spiritual education and regeneration to be found in the domestic sphere was the woman (wife and mother) herself, who was expected to provide companionship, solace, and the personal influence that would keep her children and husband true to their Christian beliefs. Thus while Christianities of various kinds asserted women's subordination and exclusion from the public sphere on the basis of sexual difference – the mainstay of earlier misogynistic characterizations of women – at the same time, the respect they accorded women's morals, spiritual qualities, and practical capability undercut this assumption. Dorothy Mermin sums up the contradiction at the heart of both religious precept and domestic ideology: 'The virtues that were thought to preclude women's participation in public affairs – the piety, selflessness, and unlimited capacity for love that defined true femininity – could instead be used to justify it.[134]

In particular, this restrictive yet laudatory view of women brought to the fore the conflict between a companionate ideal of marriage and the sexual difference which authorized women's subordination and exclusion from the public sphere. We can see this clearly in the work of Sara Lewis, one of the most influential voices of domestic ideology.[135] In her manifesto *Woman's Mission*, Lewis invokes sexual difference as the fundamental reason for women's remaining in the domestic sphere, under the authority of their husbands. Biology accounts for women's most important mission, to form the moral characters of their children, a responsibility that belongs to mothers because they care for children in their earliest years, when people are most receptive to instruction.[136] Because 'sentiment precedes intelligence' in the child's development, a mother, whose emotional connection to the child is stronger than anyone else's, is her child's most capable teacher. Indeed, '[i]t appears as though Nature had expressly co-ordained the relation of mother and child with a view to this influence' (21). Moreover, such teaching occurs not only because children want to please their mothers by following precepts, but also because children imitate their mothers:

'What she wishes us to be, she begins by making us love, and love begets unconscious imitation' (22). Women perform an equally important task by exerting a benevolent moral influence on their husbands and other male relatives: they 'instil into *their* relatives of the other sex the uncompromising sense of duty and self-devotion, which ought to be their ruling principles!' (52).[137]

In order for women to fulfil these duties – and here we see a familiar argument cast in more attractive terms – their characters are formed differently from those of men. Women possess selflessness, what Lewis calls 'self-devotion,' to a far greater degree than men, which enables them both to be devoted mothers undistracted by other concerns and to set an example of Christian virtue for their families. A woman's total devotion to her family to the exclusion of other pursuits is therefore not only a practical necessity, but also a powerful exemplar of the unselfishness she inculcates. Lewis explains, 'There must be a deeper principle [self-devotion] than usually lies at the root of female education, to induce women to acquiesce in the plan which, assigning to them the responsibility, has denied them the *eclat* of being reformers of society ... the manifestation of such a spirit is the one thing needful for the regeneration of society' (53). And it is this Christ-like quality in particular that will constitute the moral salvation of humankind: '[w]e claim for them [women] no less an office than that of instruments (under God) for the regeneration of the world, – restorers of God's image in the human soul' (11). But the fulfilment of such an exalted mission depends on women's 'moving in the sphere which God and nature have appointed, and not by quitting that sphere for another' (11–12). In short '[t]he greatest benefit which they can confer upon society is to be what they ought to be in all their domestic relations, i.e. to be what they ought to be' (51).

While Lewis agrees with Sophia's opponent and Rousseau that sexual difference should determine a woman's place, she does not share their fundamental misogyny. Instead, she assumes women's 'moral and intellectual equality' with men, asserting this as the basis for a happy marriage (49 and *passim*). For reciprocity in marriage entails not only friendship, although this is essential, but also the moral influence that a husband needs and a wife can provide, influence that cannot come from an inferior; a wife can exert influence effectively only because she is capable of understanding the issues confronting her husband in public life. Setting aside the question of caring for children (which does not enter into Lewis's discussion of wifely influence), if a wife is as intellectually capable as her husband, why does she not simply participate in business along with him, bringing her superior moral influence to bear in the public world, rather than operating behind the scenes? Lewis herself acknowledges that this question has been raised: '[B]ecause their talents and virtues place them on a footing of equality with men, it is maintained that their present sphere of action is too contracted a one, and that they ought to share in the public functions of the other sex' (44–5).

One answer lies in Lewis's concept of the wife as an exemplar who demonstrates her selflessness by renouncing personal ambition. This selflessness is called into question, however, when Lewis hypothesizes women's entry into the public sphere: 'It is by no means affirmed, that women's political feelings are always guided by the abstract principles of right and wrong; but they are surely more likely to be so, if they themselves are restrained from the public expression of them ... Now conscience and charity (or love) are the very essence of woman's beneficial influence, therefore everything tending to blunt the one and sour the other is sedulously to be avoided by her. It is of the utmost importance to men to feel, in consulting a wife, a mother, or a sister, that they are appealing *from* their passions and prejudices, and not *to* them as embodied in a second self' (52). Women's superior moral purity is shown to be dependent on circumstances rather than innate: women do not stay at home because they are pure, as Lewis usually maintains, rather, women are pure because they stay at home. If women were subject to the same pressures and temptations as men, they would think and behave in similar ways. A man's 'second self' turns out to be a double rather than a complement. The unravelling of Lewis's text thus allegorizes the challenge of an ideal of married love to patriarchal conceptions of sexual difference.[138]

The progressive and conservative positions I have surveyed were certainly not the only ways in which sexual difference was construed. Contemporaneous with the version of liberal feminism endorsed by Wollstonecraft and others, an alternative tradition of feminist thought emphasized sexual difference as a strategy for increasing women's power, especially within the home. Sexual difference is not an essentialist category but rather what Chantal Mouffe and Ernesto Laclau term an 'element,' capable of articulation in various ways and of appropriation by various political and ideological stances.[139] Sara Lewis's work in particular shows how flexible and unstable this concept actually was. But the conservative and progressive stances discussed nevertheless represent the most influential articulations of sexual difference within discourses of women's place and rights, because of the ways in which liberty and freedom were defined in a culture that identified strongly with liberal principles. What Carole Pateman argues regarding the 'equality versus difference' debate in our own day applies as well to the past: '[W]ithin the existing patriarchal conception of citizenship, the choice always has to be made between equality and difference, or between equality and womanhood. On the one hand to demand "equality" is to strive for equality with men (to call for the "rights of men and citizens" to be extended to women), which means that women must become (like) men. On the other hand, to insist, like some contemporary feminists, that women's distinctive attributes, capacities and activities be revalued and treated as a contribution to citizenship is to demand the impossible; such "difference" is precisely what patriarchal citizenship excludes.'[140] Since difference was so intertwined with subordination, the liberal attitude that downplays sexual difference came to predominate within Anglo-American feminism. It is this intellectual legacy that feminists today are still struggling to abandon or recuperate.

Married Love and the Threat to Masculinity

Married love further undermines sexual difference through its inclusion within a larger cultural trend discussed above: the middle-class reformation of English morals. Because traditional attributes of aristocratic manhood were also popular ideals of masculinity in general, the assault on corrupt aristocratic morals necessarily involved redefining manliness.[141] The ideal husband, the kind of man who would marry for the right reasons, is very much a part of this phenomenon: the qualities that make a good Christian, such as sexual restraint and compassion, are also the attributes of a good husband. New versions of masculinity therefore undermined sexual difference, by repudiating traditional markers of manliness and by embracing 'feminine' traits. For instance, by failing to exhibit masculine aggression, both sexual ('womanizing') and pugilistic ('duelling'), the man of virtue risked effeminacy. His capacity for feeling also threatened to compromise his manhood, because impassivity had traditionally been an important attribute of masculinity and feeling was increasingly identified as a feminine trait from the late eighteenth century on, despite its status as a source of virtue within different systems of belief.[142]

The imperative to maintain the boundaries of sexual difference while at the same time redefining masculine identity generated a tolerance for paradox. This often took the form of splitting the male subject to incorporate both old and new versions of masculinity. The division between home and workplace, for instance, became a division within individual identity. At work a man might have to be hard, competitive, heartless – the aggression of the duelling, whoring gentleman transformed into that of the ruthless capitalist – while at home he could revert to his true self, a Christian gentleman. Dickens captured the absurdity of this fragmentation in his character Wemmick, a parodic version of man's dual nature. The increasing separation of work from home throughout this period, which undergirded the ideology of separate roles for men and women, thus affirmed both the masculinity of the public world and the essentially 'feminine' nature of the good husband. The sexual double standard split the male personality in a similar way. Men's sexual transgressions were dismissed as unimportant surrenders to nature, dissociated from their relationships with good women. The problem with these conflicted notions of masculinity is that Christian morality precluded such temporizing, demanding benevolence and chastity of men as well as women. Scrupulous moralists therefore had a double imperative: to oppose overdetermined and unethical definitions of masculinity while also defending the manliness of the good Christian man.

One solution to this problem was an ingenious redefinition of the terms of masculinity itself, a redefinition that upheld the boundaries of sexual difference in the very process of transforming them. In this process of revision, self-control became a crucial category.[143] In the works of moralists, manly impassivity is frequently shown to depend not on the absence of feeling but on the ability to contain it. The result is that the good Christian man still appears to be impassive (and therefore masculine), but is really sensitive (and therefore compassionate, charitable, and so forth). In a particularly ingenious deployment of this strategy, Adam Smith tortuously reformulates manly impassivity as the product of emotion rather than its absence: '[o]ur sensibility to the feelings of others, so far from being inconsistent with the manhood of self-command, is the very principle upon which that manhood is founded.'[144] As he explains, we regulate our own behaviour by internalizing the way in which others see us, incorporating the spectator as 'the man within.' Self-command is therefore based not on imperviousness to feeling, but on a form of sympathy, the introjection of others' responses to us. And such self-command is the true index of manliness.

In a similar fashion, throughout *The Christian Hero*, Steele criticizes traditional classical stoicism because it depends on the lack rather than the control of feeling, and therefore provides no true test of manhood. All virtuous people feel, but only true men are capable of restraining and directing their emotions. Steele's writings also attack other traditional venues for manliness by redefining their terms. He writes, '[A] Coward has often Fought, a Coward has often Conquer'd, but *a Coward never Forgave*.'[145] Bravery is best exemplified by Christian charity, rather than martial prowess, which is merely 'an Imposture, made up of *Cowardice*, Falsehood, and Want of Understanding' [emphasis added].[146] Seduction, another traditional manly pastime, is also recast in an unflattering light as 'the Practice of deluding Women'; the seducer is merely a 'Rascal,' a word that impugns both character and social position.[147]

This defensive revision of the terms of masculinity continues well into the nineteenth century, finding pointed expression in the cultural phenomenon known as 'muscular Christianity,' for which Thomas Hughes's *The Manliness of Christ* is a central text. Like Steele, Hughes takes pains to establish that the virtuous male, modelled after Christ, is entirely masculine. In writing this treatise he was prompted by a fear that the working classes were not receptive to joining Young Men's Christian Associations because they believed that to do so might impugn their masculinity: 'there was a wide-spread feeling ... that these associations ... did not cultivate individual manliness in their members, and that this defect was closely connected with their open profession of Christianity.'[148] He argues that this belief is based on the misguided assumption that Christianity feminizes men because it demands meekness and self-effacement. Hughes asserts repeatedly that on the contrary, Christianity requires courage, the true foundation of manliness. The struggle for moral perfection, which is the goal of Christianity, can be attained only through constant battle against evil. Christ's character was perfect 'not only in charity, meekness, purity, and long-suffering' but in 'courage' as well. Real courage, however, consists of more than physical bravery and disregard for personal safety and determination; these are instances of 'animal courage,' which can be directed towards evil as well as good purposes (18). True courage, and hence, true manliness, lies in the sublimity of self-sacrifice: 'Courage can only rise into true manliness when the will is surrendered; and the more absolute the surrender of the will the more perfect will be the temper of our courage and the strength of our manliness' (33). In these terms, Christ's crucifixion is the epitome of manly action.

Despite their ingenuity, these revisions of masculinity were often disingenuous. By reincorporating the traditional definitions of masculinity that they opposed, they necessarily compromised their own values. Although Hughes recasts the 'feminine' characteristic of self-sacrifice (after all, this was Lewis's crucial characterological distinction between men and women) as an expression of masculinity, physical bravery and endurance are nevertheless important components of his definition, distinguishing it from women's selflessness. The male form of self-sacrifice also involves bodily risks that women would not be expected to take. Most important, men would not be expected to efface themselves in the quiet feminine manner Lewis advocates, an equivocation that *Manliness* accomplishes by reference to theology. Christ's self-sacrifice takes place in the context of God the Father's power. The Trinity enables a gendered splitting of male subjectivity in cosmic terms: Christ can demonstrate womanly qualities such as selflessness and mercy because God the Father safeguards masculine ones, such as sternness and aggression. What the Son renounces through his sacrifice will be exercised by the Father on Judgment Day.

I return to Steele for one further illustration of the problem. Steele's 'private gentleman' who campaigns against duelling characterizes himself as 'an invulnerable Hero in Romance,' opposing the 'the Crowd of Men of Honour' who perpetuate this immoral and barbaric custom.[149] But this metaphor implicates him in the very social practices he excoriates. If the 'spectator' is a hero for standing up for his beliefs through self-restraint, he nevertheless invokes his own heroism through an appeal to the categories of masculinity that he opposes. Even if Steele's battle is only in print, and even if it is really fought within the confines of his own domestic space, he must define himself as a manly man, always ready for a fight. There was no satisfactory way to resolve this problem because sexual difference was a necessarily recalcitrant feature of collective belief and psychology: it could not be challenged without disturbing the (im)balance in legal and social relations between men and women.

Why the Novel?

An ethical imperative to marry for love rather than interest articulated a liberal definition of marriage that conflicted with strongly entrenched patriarchal ideals. A variety of sources can be used to map the nature of this conflict, as well as to show the ways in which married love was implicated in the politics of class as well as gender. Yet the novel's appropriation of courtship as its primary subject, its central place within the collective consciousness of the eighteenth and nineteenth centuries, and its multiplot form render it a privileged site for untangling the ideological complexities of love, marriage, and gender. Having identified the 'function' of love both in its idealistic form as an ethical ideal and in its practical application, as a tool of class identity and consolidation, I would like to suggest one further crucial reason for looking to the novel. The novel utilized narrative to express beliefs about love that could not be voiced openly in non-fiction.

For reasons that will become clear in the following chapters, passion rather than companionship constituted a superior form of love from the standpoint of both ethics and utility. The careful consideration that went into choosing a companion was too like the self-interested prudence that motivated the marriage of interest; without some element of involuntariness, love could neither motivate unions between families of different social or economic standing, nor, more importantly, could it inspire ostensibly disinterested marriages. But love had to be of the proper kind or else it was no better than lust or senseless infatuation. Love had to comprise an emotional response to the worth of another person. This was a distinction that could not be made in non-fiction, for there was no rhetorical way of distinguishing a good form of passion from its inferior look-alike.

Conduct books reveal the problem with passion. From the seventeenth century on, these works generally advocate married love. So important is the obligation to marry for the right reasons that, despite conduct literature's insistence that a daughter obey her father without question, it grants daughters the right to veto unwanted suitors. Indeed, this is the one instance in which the genre sanctions a woman's right to disagree with and assert herself against male authority. But while conduct literature endorses marriage for love, it also defines love in such restricted and affectless terms that it is cleansed of all strong feeling. Conduct literature, after all, cannot endorse passion without also defying a fundamental principle of the ideology of conduct: that a woman must be cautious and prudent in all her interactions. Passion borders dangerously on lust, which is not only the potential source of a woman's undoing, but also immoral on its own terms.

These books take pains, therefore, to discuss love in ways that accord with their generally cautious outlook. They repeatedly warn against trusting impetuous feeling. And when writers attempt to define love, they almost always describe friendship, or what writers today call 'companionate love.'[150] For instance, the author of *The English Gentlewoman* warns, 'Discuss with your selves the purity of love, the quality of your lover, ever reflecting on those best deserving endowments of his, which either make him worthy or unworthy of your love ... It will be more usefull and beneficial to you, to checke your wilde fancy, if any such seaze upon you, than to give way unto it, and consequently undoe you. Repentance comes too late at marriage-night.'[151] Allestree, in *The Ladies Calling*, complains that '[too] great a Devotion is paid to Lust instead of Virtuous Love ... The thoughts of their [i.e., the lovers] future temporal conditions (like those of the eternal) can find no room amidst their foolish Raptures; but as if Love were indeed that Deity which the Poets feign'd, they depend on it for all, and take no farther care. And the event do's commonly too soon instruct them in the deceitfulness of that truth; Love being so unable to support them, that it cannot maintain itself; but quickly expires when it has brought those Lovers into those straits, from whence it cannot rescue them.'[152] Other writers attempt to define such 'vertuous love' more specifically. Mrs Pennington emphasizes that friendship ought to be the basis of married love: 'Few People are capable of Friendship, and still fewer have all the Qualifications one would choose in a Friend; the fundamental Point is a virtuous Disposition; but to that should be added, a good Understanding, solid Judgment, Sweetness of Temper, Steadiness of Mind, Freedom of Behaviour, and Sincerity of Heart ... Happy is her Lot, who, in an Husband, finds this invaluable friend!' She defines a successful marriage as 'founded on Reason and Religion,' 'cemented by mutual Esteem and Tenderness.'[153] Dr Gregory admonishes his daughters, 'Do not give way to a sudden sally of passion, and dignify it with the name of love – Genuine love is ... founded in nature, on honourable views, on virtue, on similarity of tastes and sympathy of souls.'[154] James Fordyce warns that 'the witchcraft of a fair outside is always dispelled by familiarity. Nothing can detain affection or fix esteem, but that kind of beauty which depends not on flesh and blood ... Sense, spirit, sweetness, are immortal.'[155]

Sara Lewis, writing early in the next century, was certainly no enemy to strong feeling, as her evangelical cast and championing of feminine sensibility reveals. Yet she is as cautious as her predecessors when she attempts to define the kind of love that is an appropriate foundation for marriage. Like earlier writers, Lewis advocates marriage for love as 'the one principle on which their [young women's] future happiness may be founded or wrecked' (73) and condemns marriage for social or economic ambition. She is also careful to explain the kinds of feelings that must be shunned. Girls should be taught to guard themselves against romantic notions in order to be able to 'distinguish true love from the false spirit which usurps its name and garb ... to abstract from it the worldliness, vanity, and folly, with which it has been mixed up' (76). Boys should be protected from encountering representations of lust, which can be found in 'heathen writers,' whose works are 'effeminate and corrupt' (73). Lewis defines genuine love as a union based on 'moral and intellectual grounds' (77). Her formulation is almost devoid of feeling.

What could not be said could, however, be demonstrated. In the eighteenth-century novel, overt discourse about love, as voiced by both characters and narrators, almost always advocates companionate love, but the narratives themselves override this endorsement. Novels repeatedly celebrate passion – all the worthiest heroes and heroines marry for something stronger than friendship – at the same time as they show that legitimate kinds of strong and involuntary feeling must be inspired by the inner worth of a prospective spouse. In Jane Austen's *Sense and Sensibility*, although Marianne finds happiness with Colonel Brandon, marrying him for the kinds of motives repeatedly urged by conduct literature, Elinor is rewarded for her superior character and behaviour with the fulfilment of her passion. In novel after novel, the heroine's instincts – instincts that often defy the advice of conduct literature as well as the advice of the heroine's guardians – are vindicated in the end.

In the Victorian novel, companionate love either disappears as a category or is shown to be a decidedly inferior option. Jane Eyre knows that marriage with St John Rivers ought to be an attractive prospect but finds herself reluctant to make this commitment. When Rochester's voice summons her to return, her instinctual loyalty to her passion is vindicated. A sensible, dutiful marriage with St John is obviously wrong, while her union with Rochester is right, despite all its difficulties and inappropriateness. In *Middlemarch*, Dorothea's motive in marrying Casaubon is obviously companionate love – a wish for mutual companionship – which is intensified by her desire to promote some great work in the world. To her sorrow, she finds that Casaubon can provide neither friendship nor purpose. Her later love-match with

Ladislaw shows that feeling is a better guide than prudence, a moral supported by the union of Fred and Mary; Mary prefers Fred to Fare-brother although marriage to the latter would be a more prudent choice. Although Lydgate's love for Rosamund illustrates that passion can err, these other stories show that this is a risk worth taking.

If novels illustrated modes of feeling that could not be expressed directly, they also suggested progressive points of view that authors would not openly admit to, or with which they disagreed, but which were nevertheless implied by a generalized cultural logic. The novels of Richardson, Austen, Trollope, and Oliphant considered in this study clearly demonstrate that married love challenged female subordination and self-effacement. Although the novel as a genre is only one kind of text among a plethora of others that bear witness to the rise of married love and its ideological consequences, in many ways its narratives present the fullest and most complex testimony to this development.

2
Virtuous Libertines and Liberated Virgins: *Sir Charles Grandison*

Samuel Richardson's *Sir Charles Grandison* is structured around an event that seems to defy both the novel's insistent and pervasive moralistic tone and its characterization of Sir Charles as a moral paragon: Sir Charles is in love with two women at the same time. Love for more than one woman is precisely the behaviour that distinguishes the rake, the kind of man Sir Charles himself excoriates. How can the exemplar of English integrity, who is not merely another worthy hero but a 'vision of Christ as a realistic eighteenth-century gentleman,'[1] be involved in what he himself rightly defines as a 'divided or double Love'?[2] Why is this paradox necessary for Richardson?

Sir Charles suffers a divided love because Richardson wants to endorse competing and contradictory cultural ideals of love, 'companionate' and 'sentimental.'[3] Companionate love is not what we today would call love, but rather a form of friendship, based on a reasonable assessment of the nature and compatibility of a prospective spouse. Comprising prudence and judgment, companionate love provides an alternative to romantic attraction and pure physical desire, both unstable forms of passion that could not guarantee proper marriages, and both associated with an aristocratic ideology hostile to middle-class interests. As *Grandison* and other novels show, this category was itself subsumed by sentimental love, a dialectical resolution of reason and passion. Indeed, it is almost exclusively in novels and other forms of imaginative literature that we find sentimental love, for other types of writing, such as conduct literature, lacked a way to distinguish proper forms of passion from improper ones. Strong feeling was always too much of a wild card – volatile, unpredictable, and uncontrollable – to be sanctioned overtly.

Distinguishing between appropriate and inappropriate kinds of love became a regular feature of English fiction; from the eighteenth century on, novel after novel represented a spectrum of possible modes of feeling and kinds of relationships in order to differentiate and choose among them.[4] For Richardson in particular, typologizing love was very likely a deliberate process. In a letter to Hester Mulso, he insists on the need to make distinctions between different kinds of feeling. He claims that he is 'not willing that love, *indiscriminately taken*, should be called noble'; he 'will not, *without discussion, without examination*, allow it an equal claim [with friendship]' [emphasis added].[5] It is just such discussion, examination, and discrimination that gives his last sprawling novel direction. Love was of course Richardson's great subject, and he had been attentive to its various guises in his earlier works. In their simplest sense, both *Pamela* and *Clarissa* are about the differences between pure and base desire, wise and foolish love. But *Grandison* is Richardson's most crystalline and categorical expression of such differences, a novel in which making distinctions itself becomes a primary focus. By representing alternative modes of feeling as a dialectic, *Grandison* maps the nebulous terrain of love in a schematic fashion, thereby providing a guide for the generations of novelists who followed.[6]

Epistolarity is rarely as significant in this novel as in *Pamela* and *Clarissa*; instead, multiplot form is the dominant structural principle, allowing the comparisons and evaluations that *Grandison* establishes as its project. In the most important of its many stories, *Grandison*'s double plot bisects the novel along the lines of Sir Charles's divided love; this legitimates and hierarchizes what Harriet Byron, the novel's heroine, calls 'different sorts of Love' (3:302), at the same time as the resolution of the plot masks the paradoxes inherent in conflicts between competing cultural definitions.[7] But while *Grandison* shows that some forms of love are better than others, it nevertheless clearly asserts the value of love as a motive for marriage. This stance conflicts with the novel's fundamental endorsement of patriarchal marriage, which is grounded in assertions of the ontological superiority of men and the rightness of women's subordination.[8] An ideal of consensual married love, with its basis in individual will and its promise of mutual fulfilment, articulates liberal principles for women as well as men. Consensual marriage evokes a contractual notion of selfhood, one that suggests that women have a degree of autonomy incompatible with total subjugation. Such autonomy also raises the threat of women's potentially errant and transgressive sexuality (kept in check by their subordination), and hence to the legitimate descent of property. Just as important, the kind of 'excellent man' who marries for love and remains faithful, of which Sir Charles provides the paradigm, undermines sexual difference, a traditional mainstay of patriarchy. By rejecting some traditional markers of masculinity, such as combativeness and promiscuity, and embracing other characteristics that were identified as feminine, including the capacity for conscience and feeling, the 'new man' was in danger of being too much like a woman.[9]

Grandison attempts to resolve these problems. If we are uneasy about its hero's roving heart, then his autogenerative excellence exonerates him in the end: according to this novel's circular and tautological assertions, Sir Charles cannot be wrong, because he is by definition right. He provides an exceptional case, a man whose excellence will never be equalled, and whose circumstances will never be repeated. In another of its important subplots, *Grandison* undermines the progressive, contractual ethos of marriage by scapegoating Sir Charles's sister Charlotte, the novel's one 'feminist,' an advocate of women's rights and liberties.[10] Charlotte's abjection provides a fantasy of assuagement for men's anxieties about women's power, while her 'passionlessness' disassociates women's autonomy from married love. The novel defends Sir Charles's masculinity by revising the terms of manliness itself, so that self-control becomes its most significant distinguishing feature. While none of these strategies is entirely successful, as the objections of Richardson's readers through the years have shown, the intricacy and intellectual pleasure of this novel inheres to a great extent in its ability to posit these often contradictory premises and to provide ingenious solutions.

'Different Sorts of Love'

As we have seen, an ethic of married love originated within the middle classes and helped to consolidate their alliance with the upper classes. Love provided a rationale for marrying across class lines by providing the exceptional circumstance that proved the rule of stable class boundaries. Whether or not the middling sort actually married into families of a higher class, the fact that such marriages were believed to take place ratified their presence as an alternative elite, with similar goals vis-à-vis England's economic and political policies. But if an ideal of married love were to facilitate shared hegemony between England's elites, love itself had to be defined in ways that precluded misalliance with social inferiors.[11] The project of defining love was taken up by middle classes, and like the ethic of married love itself, was evidence that this group increasingly generated – in their own image and in their own interests – the morals and representational codes that governed polite society.

Before the seventeenth century, love had usually been portrayed in English letters as physical desire or romantic passion.[12] In light of the new ethic of married love, neither was a suitable motive for matrimony. Following a well-established tradition in Christian thought, physical desire, often linked to aristocratic male libertinism, was deemed immoral. Not only does lust lead to a plethora of sins, including the corruption of pure women, but it is wrong in and of itself. Even within marriage, desire is sinful if unredeemed by more tender feelings. In Defoe's view, married lust turns holy matrimony into 'conjugal lewdness,' and 'the divine Institution is made a Stalking-horse to the brutal Appetite.'[13] Moreover, it was believed that unions motivated by lust (always the man's) were seldom happy, for such desire was soon sated and bound to seek a new object. It was common knowledge that if the rake married, he would eventually seek the renewal of his pleasures in a mistress.[14] Mrs Pennington therefore warns her daughter: 'Numerous have been the unhappy victims to the ridiculous opinion – *A reform'd libertine makes the best husband* ... Be it your care to find that virtue in a lover which you must never hope to form in a husband.[15] Licentiousness was as bad as avarice: indeed, throughout the period, they constitute the twin perils of marital motive, and are often equated with one another. Mary Astell observes, '[t]here's no great odds between his [a man's] Marrying for the Love of Money, or for the Love of Beauty, the Man does not act according to Reason in either Case, but is govern'd by irregular Appetites.'[16]

Romantic love was somewhat more respectable, but still unsuitable as a basis for marriage. Although it had a history dating back to antiquity, for the novelists of the eighteenth century, it was associated primarily with recent popular literature: the enormously popular French romances of the seventeenth century, many of which had been translated into English; the numerous English imitations they inspired; and the scandalous novels of Behn, Manley, and Haywood.[17] Hence Mrs Shirley, Grandison's female sage, blames romances for her former, mistaken notions of love and is glad that literary tastes have changed for the better. She tells her young listeners, 'The reading in fashion when I was young, was Romances. You, my children, have, in that respect, fallen into happier days' (3:398). She regrets that in her youth, when she was the girlish Henrietta rather than the venerable Mrs Shirley, she was 'over-run with the absurdities of that unnatural kind of writing,' from which she derived 'very high ideas of first impressions; of eternal constancy; of Love raised to a pitch of idolatry' (3:398). Because of these 'romantic notions,' she almost rejected her husband Mr Shirley's offer of marriage, despite the fact that he was 'a good sort of man; a sensible man' whose 'character was faultless' (3:398). 'But what was a good sort of man to an Oroondates?' she asks, referring to the hero of La Calprenède's *Cassandra* (3:398). Moreover, she feared that if she married Mr Shirley, she might later fall in love with someone else, 'the kindred soul, who must irresistibly claim my whole heart' (3:399), as does the main character in Mme de Lafayette's *Princess of Cleves*, a book she owns and admires (3:400).[18]

From Mrs Shirley's youthful misconceptions, we can extrapolate the conventions of romantic love: it is involuntary and always strikes the lover at first sight; it is passionate and fixated on one object, since a second love is impossible; it inspires the male lover with courage and daring. It is important to keep these conventions in mind when looking at the ways in which *Grandison* and other novels revise romantic love. Despite its emphasis on the worthiness of the lovers, for middle-class moralists, romantic love was fraught with pitfalls if taken seriously as a motive for marriage. Because romance as a genre represents lovers as accountable and responsible to their own feelings above all else, it suggests the beauty of sacrificing all for love, a questionable moral stance. The novel in particular (for example, Richardson's own *Clarissa*) shows how such emotions might inspire a young girl to elope, thereby defying her parents and risking her own ruin. Moreover, the very suddenness of love at first sight precludes the sound judgment considered necessary for any important step in life, for such love might or might not have a basis in reality. Sir Charles observes that love at first sight (i.e., romantic love) is not a suitable foundation for marriage, since it 'must indicate a mind *prepared* for impression, and a sudden gust of passion, and that of the least noble kind; since there could be no opportunity of knowing the *merit* of the object' (2:357). In the romance, we almost never encounter representation of the development of relationships between lovers. For these reasons, despite all its passion, romantic love could ironically inspire an unhappy, loveless marriage.

The middle classes had another reason to be hostile to lust and romance as modes of feeling, because they were identified with aristo-

cratic ideology and its exclusionary elitism. Libertinism was an aristocratic invention that invoked the innate superiority of the nobly born:
the libertine believes he can ignore conventional rules and morals
because he is superior to everyone else.[19] Romantic love has its origins
in courtly, aristocratic romances that equate worth with birth. This is
why in romances, love is never subversive of the social order; com-
moners are shown to be undesirable to those of exalted rank, the implication being that attractiveness itself is constituted by the innate
superiority of aristocratic blood. (In Charlotte Lennox's *The Female
Quixote*, Arabella, whose head has been turned by her reading of
romances, assumes anyone worth speaking to must be a noble in disguise.) Middle-class moralists could not acknowledge status as a
ground of desire any more than they could acknowledge it as a basis
for worth. Thus in Mrs Shirley's account, romantic love is already partially revised: she tells of all its affective characteristics – how love feels
– but they are cleansed of their association with aristocratic ideology;
social status is insignificant in her list of ideal qualities. Once shorn of
its association of birth with worth, romantic love threatened to open
the floodgates of social mobility if sanctioned as a motive for marriage.
As Sir Charles's sister Charlotte says, '[i]f Love be not a voluntary passion, why not [fix her affections] upon a hostler, a groom, a coachman,
a footman – A grenadier, a trooper, a foot-soldier?' (3:405), all unsuit-
ably lower-class persons. If love rather than interest were to become
the basis for marriage, as moralists insisted, it had to be defined in
such a way as to encode internal social controls. Companionate love
provides this safeguard.

As Mrs Shirley continues to elaborate on her youthful folly, she
advocates companionate love to her young listeners, which protects
married love from the dangers of unregulated passion, and which the
novel overtly endorses. She recounts how her good friend Mrs Eggleton cured her of romantic notions by urging her to accept her suitor Mr
Shirley's proposal, even though she was not passionately in love:
'Esteem, heightened by Gratitude, and enforced by Duty ... will soon
ripen into Love: The only sort of Love that suits this imperfect state;
a *tender*, a *faithful* affection' (3:398). Mrs Eggleton denies the legitimacy
of her young friend's ideas of love, arguing that '[t]he passions are
intended for our servants, not our masters' (3:399). In her view, practical motives are not to be ignored when choosing a husband – Henrietta
is 'one of many Sisters' (3:398) – although the primary consideration
should not be economic. That Henrietta does not dislike Mr Shirley,

together with the fact that he is a 'worthy man,' is enough to constitute a preference. Mrs Eggleton concludes, 'I would not by any means ... have you marry a man for whom you have not a preferable inclination; but why may you not find, on admitting Mr Shirley's addresses, young, agreeable, worthy, and every way suitable to you, as *he* is, that he is that man whom your inclination can approve?' (3:399).

Although a preference is necessary for marriage, this preference can be generated at will, as Mrs Eggleton's locution 'whom your inclination can approve' suggests. The unusual use of the word 'inclination' as the active agent of the clause enacts Mrs Eggleton's revision of romantic love: inclination should be an act of will rather than a passive predilection. Furthermore, the foundation of companionate love is not passion but esteem, which is inspired by 'merit,' a combination of intellectual and moral qualities, the most important of which is virtue. Although 'understanding' (intelligence) is a desirable characteristic, a good man who is not particularly intelligent (such as Charlotte's husband, Lord G.) is still a suitable lover.[20] Assessing the character of a prospective spouse is thus the most important part of determining his or her eligibility; this precludes love at first sight. And contrary to the romantic belief that true lovers are made for each other, companionate love implies that any two worthy people are capable of being happy together. As Charlotte says, 'The man who loves virtue for virtue's sake, loves it where-ever he finds it: ... there will be tenderness in his distinction to every one, varying only according to the difference of her circumstances' (2:352). Companionate love is indeed a 'voluntary passion.'

Like the redefinition of honour that I discussed in the previous chapter, companionate love serves middle-class interests. Equating attraction with virtue, it exemplifies the middle-class revision of aristocratic codes. Once the criterion for the marriage choice becomes individual moral worth, the significance of social identity is greatly diminished. Just as one does not have to be a nobleman to possess honour, one does not have to be from the upper classes to be worthy of love. Moreover, companionate love precludes undesirable alliances. The fact that it is voluntary means that the lover can avoid directing his or her affections inappropriately. A suitor can make the decision to cross class boundaries in quest of superior merit – such is the basis on which the Count of D. seeks Harriet's hand in marriage – but he does not do so indiscriminately. And since a person who loves virtue must be a good person, he would not wish for a marriage likely to injure his family or the object of his affections. As Sir Charles says, a man whose love is a 'pure flame' would never 'seek to gratify his own passion, at the expence of the happiness or duty of the object pretended to be beloved' (1:332–3).[21] Because titles and estates were inherited through the male line and a woman adopted her husband's rank, a man who esteemed a woman of superior social rank would restrain his feelings, as their marriage would be detrimental to her economic and social standing.[22]

Sir Charles experiences companionate love for his Italian pupil Clementina. He chooses to love her only after she falls in love with him first. Before this, he appreciates her attractions, without personally desiring her. He confides to his mentor Dr Bartlett: 'I had never seen the woman ... that I *could* have loved so well, had I not restrained myself, at first, from the high notion I knew they [her family] had of their quality and rank; from considerations of the difference in religion; of the trust and confidence the family placed in me; and by the resolution I had made, as a guard to myself from the time of my entering upon my travels, of never aiming to marry a foreigner' (2:176). Sir Charles's statement shows that he does not restrain strong and unbidden emotions, as he does in the case of his English friend Harriet, as we shall see. On the contrary, he rationally acknowledges that Clementina possesses qualities that are capable of inspiring love. The emphatic 'could' of his statement, which signals an act of will, reveals that his love for Clementina will require deliberation.

Sir Charles's responses to Clementina always involve thought rather than feeling. For instance, when he imagines marriage to Clementina before it has been suggested by her family, his daydreams are motivated by rational considerations of the advantages of such a match: 'For my own part, it was impossible (distinguished as I was by every individual of this noble family, and lovely as is this daughter of it, mistress of a thousand good qualities, and myself absolutely disengaged in my affections) that my vanity should not sometimes be awakened, and a wish arise, that there might be a possibility of obtaining such a prize: But I checked the vanity, the moment I could find it begin to play about and warm my heart' (2:123–4). Sir Charles is thus momentarily tempted by Clementina's family's position and her own merits, both of which he coolly assesses. His metaphor, which figures vanity as a flame (it plays about and warms his heart) emphasizes that passion is not the basis of Clementina's attraction. Sir Charles's alteration of a conventional metaphor (flame as love) reveals his true motive for desiring Clementina: vanity inhabits the place of love in the metaphor, as it does in Sir Charles's emotions.

The Erotics of Virtue

Although companionate love precludes the threat of unregulated social mobility by its incorporation of sound judgment, it nevertheless creates problems within the very terms of the ideological riddles it ostensibly solves. Marriage for love ideally deflects random social mobility by providing seemingly exceptional cases of marriage between different social groups. But it does not completely obviate the threat to the hierarchical structure of English elite society, since the 'exception' can in theory become rather than prove the rule. Companionate love solves this problem by encoding the social control of desire so that it focuses only on appropriate objects. But this solution paradoxically recreates the original problem: companionate love has the potential to re-establish class lines on nearly as rigid a basis as those of the marriage of interest. Love must be involuntary if it is to enable marriages that transgress established norms; other words, companionate love might authorize marriages that, from a self-interested point of view, a family might not have sought, but which it can nevertheless accept without too much difficulty. Companionate love justifies the Count of D.'s suit to Harriet, who is a member of the gentry. But it does not authorize the marriage between Mr B. and Pamela.[23] A completely 'voluntary passion' would not be capable of altering the social order, not even to justify the limited number of interclass marriages that were deemed suitable and necessary to the economic health of the nation.

Companionate love, moreover, continually threatens to collapse into the very motives of interest that it presumably opposes. Although interest is supposedly subordinated to inclination in the companionate marriage, since one should not marry unless a preference exists, this preference, based as it is on a balanced and deliberate judgment, is in danger of overvaluing the material or social advantages of marriage. This situation is illustrated by the marriage between Sir Charles's ailing uncle, Lord W., and the impoverished Miss Mansfield. Lord W. is aging, suffering from gout, and in need of a nurse; Miss Mansfield's family has fallen on hard times. Although Harriet claims that the marriage is appropriate, since 'discretion and gratitude are the cornerstones of the matrimonial fabric' (3:281), the sort of gratitude that Miss Mansfield owes to Lord W. is very different from that which Harriet herself feels for Sir Charles. Harriet is initially grateful to Sir Charles for rescuing her from a kidnapper, and later for his love, while Miss Mansfield is grateful for the material advantages Lord W.'s interest brings to her and her family. Although Harriet praises the match between Lord W. and Miss Mansfield by citing the conventional arguments for marriage based on companionship – 'Lady W. had no prepossessions in any other man's favour. My Lord loves her' (3:281) – the plot reveals that the marriage is one of convenience, since the 'lovers' agree to marry before either can have gained sufficient knowledge of the other's worth or character. Lord W.'s marriage shows that *Grandison* wants to advocate a certain kind of marriage of convenience because it is serviceable, while revising its true motives (marriages of interest are morally unacceptable). That the discourse of companionate love can be applied in this process of revision reveals the permeability of the boundary between prudence and interest.

These dilemmas are solved by the last and best of the novel's 'different sorts of love' – sentimental love – as exemplified by Harriet's and Sir Charles's feelings for one another.[24] On the surface, Harriet's love resembles romantic love. She adores Sir Charles at first sight and persistently denies her ability to care for another man. Even when it appears that he is certain to marry Clementina, Harriet refuses to consider the Count of D.'s proposals, claiming that her heart is '*already* a wedded heart: It is wedded to his [Sir Charles's] merits ... I can never think of any *other*, as I *ought* to think of the man to whom I give my hand' (2:289). As Harriet falls more and more deeply and (ostensibly) hopelessly in love, she suffers all the conventional symptoms of the romantic lover. She grows pale, sickly, and thin; she blushes and sighs; and she prefers solitude to company. Sentimental love, like romantic love, includes sexual desire: Sir Charles is dashing and handsome, and as Harriet herself confesses, her love is 'perhaps a little too personal' (2:13). In fact, unlike companionate love, the effects of sentimental love are always registered on the body.

Harriet's love is not romantic, however, because it is inspired by Sir Charles's merit. If Harriet adores Sir Charles at first sight, it is because her very first sight of him provides proof of his moral worth: in an action befitting the most impassioned romantic hero, Sir Charles risks his life in a disinterested act of goodness and mercy to save Harriet's honour. It is because Sir Charles is so much more virtuous than the merely good men Harriet esteems that her response to him is so much more intense. Indeed, when she reflects on the events of the kidnapping, she consistently imagines Sir Charles as a hero of romance, a 'mighty prince (dreams then make me a perfect romancer) and I am a damsel in distress' (1:285). Her fantasy of the romance plot is a correlative of her passionate feelings: if she pictures Sir Charles as a hero of romance, it is because she experiences the exalted passion of the romantic heroine.[25] The reasonable criteria of companionate love thus inspire the passionate affect of romantic love; the flamboyant plot and exalted passion of the romantic ethos remain intact yet their driving force is virtue. Merit has been eroticized in a dialectical resolution of reason and passion.

Sir Charles experiences similar feelings. He reveals his 'sentimental love' for Harriet in an intimate conversation, in which he confesses his involvement with Clementina, yet lets her know that she is the true object of his passion: 'And now, madam, said he [and he was going to take my hand, but with an air, as if he thought the freedom would be too great – A tenderness *so* speaking in his eyes; a respectfulness *so* solemn in his countenance; he just touched it, and withdrew his hand] What shall I say? ... Honour forbids me! – Yet honour bids me – Yet I cannot be unjust, ungenerous – selfish! ... And, bowing low, he withdrew with precipitation, as if he would not let me see his emotion. He left me looking here, looking there, as if for my heart' (2:132). In marked contrast to his encounters with Clementina, Sir Charles struggles to control himself. He cannot resist touching Harriet. Moreover, his feelings are betrayed by his body language, the infallible sign of sentimental love. He obviously has tears in his eyes ('he would not let me see his emotion'), as the muted pun on 'precipitation' (hurry and moisture) emphasizes. The dashes in his speech indicate his overwrought condition. He is so overcome with emotion that he departs from the usual procedures of etiquette, quite a statement from this 'complete gentleman'; he fails to conduct Harriet out of the room and abruptly leaves her in great agitation, casting '[l]ooks that seemed to carry more meaning than his words' (2:134). Although Sir Charles does not (cannot) completely voice his thoughts about the conflict he is suffering ('Honour bids me – Yet Honour forbids me'), the context of the conversation makes it clear that honour bids him to be faithful to Clementina and forbids him to make his addresses to Harriet. Even Harriet herself, who misconstrues this conversation in Clementina's favor on several occasions, finally understands that Sir Charles's confusion and distress indicate his love. She writes to Lucy, 'Does it not look, my dear, as if his *Honour* checked him, when his *Love* would have prompted him to wish me to preserve my heart disengaged till his return from abroad?' (2:386–7).

Sir Charles's love for Harriet, unlike his feeling for Clementina, is involuntary. Although he claims that he had restrained himself from loving Clementina because circumstances were not conducive to their union, how much truer ought this to have been where Harriet is concerned, when he had already pledged himself to another woman. And yet Sir Charles cannot subdue his love for Harriet any more than she can suppress her love for him. Although both are capable of restraining their passion in the interest of virtue and justice, the initial impulse to love is unsought and immediate. Thus Sir Charles, like Harriet, loves at first sight; as he later confesses: 'the moment I saw you first ... I loved you' (3:284). And Sir Charles's passion registers the courtly, bodily language of love throughout the novel. He blushes several times at the mention of Harriet's name in connection with his own (2:81, 339, 658). When he speaks of Harriet, '[h]is voice then is the voice of Love' (2:352). The most devoted reader of romance could wish for no more.

Sentimental love takes its name from the mid-century conception of sentiment itself, for sentimental responsiveness provides the implicit model for this kind of love, which corrects the ethical and disciplinary deficiencies of other modes of feeling. Richardson and his contemporaries thought of sentiment as a combination of reason and spontaneous feeling, a double valence that safeguards the sentimental subject from the opposing dangers of irrationality and calculation, as does sentimental love.[26] Moreover, sentimental love transforms the very physicality which is so often a source of danger (lust) into a virtue. As John Mullan notes, sentiment takes the body as an absolute ground and guarantor of sincerity: 'the vocabulary [of sentiment] is that of gestures and palpitations, sighs and tears ... powerful because it is not spoken,' whereas speech 'can ... be a terrain of possible conflict and imposition, blandishment and deceit.'[27] The sentimental ethics of 'embodiment' thus enables the ingenious co-optation of romantic feeling on the part of sentimental love: its imprint on the body becomes the sign not only of its involuntariness and eroticism, but also of its ethical character.

Sentimental love retains the encoded social controls of companionate love, but they operate subconsciously. This is made clear early in the novel when Harriet reassures her friend Lucy that falling in love is nothing to be ashamed of: 'What better assurance can I give to my Uncle, and to all my friends, that if I were caught, I would own it, than by advising *you* not to be ashamed to confess a sensibility which is no disgrace, when duty and prudence are our guides, and the object worthy?' (1:66). In Harriet's locution – an unwitting description of sentimental love – the lover must be 'caught,' surprised by love, yet at the same time guided by motives that would seem to preclude such a passive and unconsidered entanglement. This is possible only if duty and prudence are internalized. While the companionate lover deliberately obeys the dictates of his or her social world, the sentimental lover is a thoroughly disciplined subject.

Sentimental love thus allows for the limited social mobility that companionate love, with its emphasis on consideration and evaluation, paradoxically threatens to inhibit. Since it is passionate and involuntary, it can inspire the interclass marriages that companionate love precludes. At the same time, however, because the foundation of sentimental love is virtue, it cannot lead to a truly subversive passion. Sentimental love is therefore superior to companionate love, since it synthesizes the best aspects of all other 'sorts of love': it retains the proper motives of companionate love, yet it is purified of the taint of interest through its spontaneity.[28] Its superiority is obvious in *Grandison*, since it is the sort of love experienced by its morally superior hero and heroine; as ideal characters, they achieve an ideal love.[29]

'A very apparent difference'

Grandison's need to endorse two different forms of love involves a fundamental contradiction within the novel's code of virtue, as I have suggested already. However excusable Sir Charles's involvement with two women might be, and however rarefied his love for each, a double love conjures the Lovelacian demons of libertinism and polygamy.[30] This creates the paradox of a less-than-perfect paragon, a problem which generates a certain amount of defensiveness within the text. Characters repeatedly comment on the extraordinary nature of the characters and circumstances involved. For instance, Charlotte observes, 'There might be a law made, that the case should not be brought into precedent till two such women should be found, and such a man; and all three in the like situation' (3:195). The unavoidable nature of Sir Charles's entanglement in this triangle is also stressed by both himself and others. Although he and Harriet are in love, he has not 'sought to engage her affections' (2:383). Far from encouraging the love of two women, Sir Charles cannot help inspiring unsought passion in the female breast: 'A woman of virtue and honour cannot *but* love him' (2:381). The type of love triangle that would ordinarily be the consequence of morally questionable behaviour on the part of a gentleman is here generated by

Sir Charles's very excellence – by his sense of honour and his love of virtue; he cannot help but respond to both the vulnerable Clementina and the morally excellent Harriet.[31]

The most ingenious of Richardson's solutions to the paradox of a virtuous double love is also the novel's notable formal quirk: the curious absence of Sir Charles in his eponymous novel.[32] *Grandison* must reveal Sir Charles's thoughts and emotions in order to establish both his virtue and the nature of his feelings for Clementina and Harriet. But it does so in indirect ways. Sir Charles's interiority is always mediated, but his feelings are nevertheless always legible. He writes relatively few letters, and they are rarely of the self-probing kind typical of Harriet's correspondence. His most revealing moments are almost always reported by other characters, thereby blunting their confessional quality – and yet such moments of revelation occur with regularity. Even his direct statements are often elliptical. When he confesses his love to Harriet, he fails to complete his sentences ('Honour bids me – yet honour forbids me').

It is not surprising, therefore, that when Sir Charles experiences his conflict most intensely, after he meets Harriet and before he reveals his love, we have almost no direct access to his feelings. Once he returns to Italy, Richardson is compelled to have him correspond so that his readers (both characters and readers of the novel) can have a record of events. His failure to do so would be a violation of verisimilitude. In these letters, he writes not simply with his confidant, Dr Bartlett, in mind, but with a view to his larger audience. His request that Dr Bartlett censor his letters if 'any-thing should fall from my pen, that would possibly in your opinion affect or give uneasiness to any one I love and honour' (2:458) tells us that he does not plan to be completely self-revealing. His other set of extended correspondence, written before his return to England, is also assembled for Harriet's perusal at Dr Bartlett's discretion. Although these letters, which narrate his previous Italian adventures (when he becomes betrothed to Clementina), consist almost entirely of his own text, they are entitled 'Dr. Bartlett's letters,' thereby indicating once more that a protective editorial presence guards Sir Charles's most intimate subjects. This strategy of indirection ensures that we know the truth about Sir Charles's double love, yet we do not experience it fully through his eyes. We are therefore distanced from his internal struggle and spared the moral queasiness of a divided affection. Through Richardson's persistent sleight of hand, different sorts of love and different sorts of lovers – the very material of aristocratic excess – accord with middle-class Christian virtue.[33]

Sir Charles's impeccability thus exonerates him in what appears to be a morally dubious situation. But the very moral qualities that guarantee his innocence and establish his identity as a Christian gentleman and a proper husband threaten to undermine his masculinity by blurring the boundaries of sexual difference. Since virtue is inextricable from feeling, the virtuous Christian gentleman possesses a 'feminine' capacity for emotion. He also eschews traditional, primarily aristocratic, expressions of masculinity such as duelling and promiscuity. As Janet Todd observes, Richardson had to justify at length his [Sir Charles's] possession of the female virtues of modesty and chastity.'[34]

In Richardson's endorsement of a 'feminized' virtue for his hero, more than Sir Charles's manliness is at stake. Richardson's characterization of his hero is framed by contemporary debates about the nature and meaning of sexual difference, so that the soundness of Sir Charles's masculinity is inextricable from the justification of patriarchal social and legal institutions. As we saw in chapter 1, antifeminist writing of the eighteenth and nineteenth centuries insists that there are clear, innate, and unalterable distinctions between men and women that testify to men's superiority and justify women's subjection. Feminist writers of the period (most famously Wollstonecraft) maintain that, on the contrary, sexual differences are due primarily to custom, and that, were women to have the same freedoms and opportunities as men, they would prove themselves just as capable. In a debate with Sir Charles about the proper role and nature of women, Mrs Shirley argues this feminist position, averring that nurture not nature is responsible for the gendered characteristics that dictate '[m]an's usurpation' of 'women's natural independency' (6:242). Mrs Shirley admits that women are less capable than men, but she also contends that this deficiency is the result of custom and circumstance: 'For the advantages of education which men must necessarily have over women, if they have made the proper use of them, will have set them so forward on the race, that we can never overtake them. But then don't let them despise us for this, as if their superiority were entirely founded on a natural difference of capacity! ... For it is not the hat or cap which covers the head, that decides of the merit of it' (3:243). Because of these differences in upbringing, 'women are generally too much considered as a species apart' (3:243). Sir Charles disagrees, expressing the antifeminist doctrine that male superiority is an essential and ineluctable part of human nature: 'There is a difference ... in the *constitution*, in the *temperament*, of the two Sexes, that gives to the one advantages which it denies to the other ... Weaker powers are given generally for weaker purposes, in the oeconomy of Providence ... [I]t is my opinion, that both God and Nature have designed a very apparent difference in the minds of both, as well as in the peculiar beauties of their persons. Were it not so, their offices would be confounded, and the women would not perhaps so readily submit to those domestic ones in which it is their province to shine, and the men would be allotted the distaff, or the needle' (3:247–8). Where Mrs Shirley uses the metaphor of clothing to argue for contingent and external gender difference between men and women (difference in abilities is like a cap), Sir Charles locates an essential and hierarchized sexual difference in immutable bodily distinctions, which determine both a woman's subordination and her confinement within the domestic 'province.'

Richardson's dilemma, then, is to maintain distinctions between the sexes by asserting the essential masculinity of his virtuous Christian gentleman while simultaneously emphasizing his hero's sensitivity and chastity. Following other writers of his day, particularly Steele, he does this by designating self-control, rather than aggression or insensitivity, as the defining category of manliness. This serves to encode sexual difference within the very construction of virtuous masculinity that ostensibly undermines it. Richardson's respective characterizations of Sir Charles and Harriet show how restraint functions as an index of sexual difference. With respect to self-control, the best of women cannot measure up to the best of men. Both Sir Charles and Harriet love passionately and involuntarily; this is in the nature of sentimental love. But by an effort of will, Sir Charles controls the effects of this passion to a far greater degree than Harriet, revealing only what he wants others to see. Cognizant of the moral demands of a man in his position, Sir Charles returns to Italy willing to marry Clementina despite his strong feeling for Harriet. He might suffer brief moments of emotional vertigo (such as when he confesses his love to Harriet), and these moments are necessary to signal that strength of feeling that gives rise to his superlative virtue and his superlative love. But he quickly recovers his self-possession. Sir Charles's feelings never interfere with the performance of his duties or his proper behaviour.

Harriet's conduct under a similar trial, although certainly good, falls short of this standard. Had Sir Charles married Clementina, duty to her family and society would have dictated that she conquer her love and marry another eligible man. Her resistance to this idea shows that she is willing to allow personal feelings to interfere with what she knows is right. Unlike Clementina, Harriet remains in control of her faculties and is able to perform her household duties. But her depression affects both her health and demeanour; her lovesickness is obvious to all. When compared to Sir Charles, she clearly lacks self-command.[35] While women were increasingly identified with excellent powers of self-discipline, this characterization arose from the belief that they potentially lacked self-control to a far greater degree than men. The greatest fear was that women might lose control over their sexual impulses, precisely the area in which the rakes allow their desires to rule, and the strict forms of feminine decorum advocated by women themselves (what Harriet's Uncle Selby derisively calls 'femalities') were necessary forms of self-policing that kept a potential female chaos at bay. Harriet's 'weaker powers' therefore testify to the 'very apparent difference' that justifies her subordination.

By suggesting that true manhood consists in the ability to contain one's impulses, Richardson shows male aggression to be the product of frailty rather than strength. The rake's sexual rapaciousness and the duellist's sensitive honour originate not in superior masculine drives, as in the older, aristocratic ideology, but rather in a simple failure of self-command. By failing to control his desires and his anger, the libertine/duellist displays a 'feminine' chaos of the passions. To signal the effeminacy of traditional masculine behaviours, Richardson conflates the figure of the rake cum man of honour with that of the fop, that familiar dandy of Restoration drama who is notoriously unsuccessful with women. Linking predatoriness with dandyism, Sir Charles observes to Charlotte, 'There are, indeed, *men*, whose minds ... seem to be cast in a Female mould; whence the fops, foplings, and pretty fellows, who buz about your Sex at public places' (3:247). Sir Hargrave, Harriet's kidnapper, is just this sort of 'fopling,' predatory but ineffectual, aggressive but weak. The effeminacy of Sir Hargrave and other rakes is further emphasized through the reiterated threat of castration. In a skirmish prompted by sexual jealousy, Jeronymo receives a wound to his groin that renders him sexually inactive; Mr Merceda is nearly castrated as punishment for a seduction; and Sir Hargrave is metaphorically deprived of his instruments of prey when Sir Charles knocks out two of his front teeth in the course of rescuing Harriet (the metaphor becomes clear when we recall that during his frustrating courtship of Harriet, he had bitten her hand).[36] The metonymic logic of the narrative, which designates castration as an appropriate punishment for sexual transgression, doubles as a metaphor of the effeminacy of the rake; would-be conquerors, both sexual and combative, are incapable of fulfilling their desires. As Sir Charles says, figuring aggression as impotence, 'I have generally found, that those who are the readiest to give offence, are the unfittest, when brought to the test, to support their own insolence' (2:67).

Despite Richardson's rejection of 'masculine' attributes and his valorization of 'feminine' virtues, his revision of masculinity is only partially successful, for he defends his hero's perfect masculinity by appealing, at least in part, to the very qualities he condemns. Thus Sir Charles is revealed to be manly in aristocratic terms, an excellent fighter and lover, while the rakes are singularly unsuccessful at both love and war. We see this appeal to conflicting ideals of masculinity in an episode in which Sir Charles wounds two of his enemies in his house. He writes of this encounter to Dr Bartlett: 'You cannot imagine ... how much this idle affair has disturbed me: I cannot forgive myself – To suffer myself to be provoked by two such men, to violate the sanction of my own house! ... My only excuse to myself is, That there were two of them; and that, tho' I drew, yet I had the command of myself so far as only to defend myself, when I might have done any-thing with them' (2:67). Sir Charles demonstrates his superior powers of restraint by inflicting less damage than he might have done. Yet, however much he controls himself, he still fights, and within the terms of a Christian pacifist ethic, he is right to blame himself. Moreover, this incident demonstrates Sir Charles's skill in the manly arts, as well as his aggressive temper; he inflicts more damage in self-defence than his opponents do through outright attack. Mrs Barbauld criticized Richardson for this capitulation to the rules of honour: 'Sir Charles, as a Christian, was not to fight ... yet he was to be recognised as the finished gentleman, and could not be allowed to want that most essential part of the character, the deportment of a man of honour, courage, and spirit.' Ultimately, 'the code of the gospel and the code of worldly honour are irreconcilable.'[37]

Grandison hedges less in its insistence on male chastity. But Richardson's refusal to compromise on the issue of Sir Charles's virginity had its price; it left his hero open to ridicule, a fate he has certainly suffered. Colly Cibber's reaction to the idea of male virginity typifies generations of readers' responses: 'A male-virgin, said he – ha, ha, ha, hah!'[38] Richardson was well aware of the chance he was taking: Charlotte asks Harriet not to tell that 'this grace [is] supposed to be my brother's ... I would not have my brother made the jest of one Sex, and the aversion of the other; and be thought so singular a young man' (2:497). Yet, once again, Richardson acknowledges the cultural purchase of the ethos he rejects. Sir Charles's sexual restraint is shown to be a matter of choice; Sir Charles possesses all the skills and even the ardour of the libertine. His charms are irresistible to women: Clementina goes mad with love for him and Olivia offers to be his mistress. Lord W. reports that 'within this month past ... no fewer than Five Ladies, out of one circle, declared, that they would stand out by consent, and let you pick and choose a wife from among them' (2:43). Sir Charles can even play the rake when he wants to; he 'seduces' Lady Beauchamp into good behaviour through his bold and teasing manner. And when he becomes Harriet's accepted lover, he shows an appropriately manly eagerness, pushing for an early wedding date, and shocking Harriet by kissing her on the lips. As his sister Charlotte says, 'Had he been a wicked man, he would have been a very wicked one' (3:297). By being 'a Rake in his address, and a Saint in his heart' (3:93) Sir Charles establishes his claim to a virtuous libertinism. But this is a paradox that inevitably hovers between conflicting versions of manliness.

Charlotte, Marriage, and Patriarchy

If the qualities of the good Christian husband threaten to upset the patriarchal (im)balance of power by undermining sexual difference, the widely accepted mandate to marry for love invokes yet another, equally serious, challenge to men's supremacy. I have argued above that by entering voluntarily into a marriage, a woman becomes a contractual subject, and that as such, she theoretically possesses certain inalienable liberties. Locke claims that a party to a contract cannot bargain away either life or liberty.[39] While eighteenth-century marriage law and social custom denied a woman's theoretical claim to autonomy by rendering a wife economically dependent on her husband and subject to coverture (that is, having no separate legal identity), an ideal of consensual married love authorized a challenge to existing laws and institutions by its invocation of contemporary political theory.

Harriet's conflict with her libertine suitor Sir Hargrave shows that Richardson is aware that an ideal of consensual married love suggests women's autonomy and rights.[40] As a libertine, Sir Hargrave is necessarily a misogynist, hostile to women's independence and indifferent to their desires; by objectifying women, the libertine necessarily denies their personhood. Hence, *Grandison*'s rakes often discuss women in dehumanizing terms, most frequently figuring them as prey, a metaphor that Harriet's half-mad suitor Greville attempts to take literally when, in a paroxysm of frustration and desire, he bites Harriet's hand (1:101). As far as Sir Hargrave is concerned, then, Harriet's consent to their marriage is unimportant. He believes he has made a great concession to her honour by his willingness to postpone his rape until after the marriage ceremony. Harriet, however, would rather die than go through a forced marriage with a man she abhors. Although Harriet's objections stem ultimately from ethical, Christian ideas about marriage, these ideas affirm her well-developed sense of her own entitlement. Harriet's belief in her right to choose her husband both engenders and supports her sense of freedom and self-worth. Thus, in her arguments with Sir Hargrave during his courtship, Harriet resorts to the language of rights and equity in order to justify her rejection of him. She claims the freedom to refuse his proposal of marriage because she has 'the liberty so to act, so to govern myself, in essential points ... Sir, let me be intitled to the same freedom in my refusal that governs you in your choice' (1:113–14).

It is because Sir Hargrave has such different ideas about women that he disagrees with Harriet about the nature of marriage. At one point during her ordeal, Harriet asks, 'Would you, *can* you, be so little nice, as to wish to marry a woman who does not prefer you to all men?' (1:113). This question becomes important – indeed, intelligible – only if one accepts that a woman's feelings have anything at all to do with the marriage choice. If a woman's thoughts and desires are insignificant, as they are in Sir Hargrave's view, then money and position, precisely the allurements that would appeal to a woman's family, are all that are necessary to a proper marriage. The well-intentioned women who help Sir Hargrave in his escapade share his outmoded point of view: 'they seemed to believe, that marriage would make amends for every outrage' (1:153). But for the woman who expected to marry for love, this was no longer enough. 'I am proposing to exalt you, madam,' says Sir Hargrave, pleading with Harriet to surrender quietly. 'Vile, vile, debasement!' is her answer (1:157). Person, fortune, status – all of which Sir Hargrave pleads in his cause – are nothing without love.

Richardson, a firm believer in male sovereignty, was therefore faced with the problem of upholding an ethic of married love while at the same time negating the progressive implications of a wife's contractual subjectivity. Or, to put this another way, by endorsing an ethic of married love, Richardson was caught between two versions of marriage: a liberal ideal of consensual marriage that implied women's freedoms and rights, and a traditional patriarchal definition of marriage that denied such liberties. His solution was Charlotte Grandison, a scapegoat who dispels masculinist fear of the relationship between married love and woman's autonomy.

Harriet asserts her 'rights' only in her confrontation with Sir Hargrave; at other times, she is appropriately subservient to male authority, especially that of Sir Charles. But this is not true of Charlotte, the novel's one (proto) feminist, whose wish to free herself from the domination of men is a ruling passion. Charlotte's attempt to escape her father's tyranny prompts her abortive attempt to elope with her unworthy suitor, Captain Anderson (1:406). The same desire also explains her resistance to marriage, once she has realized that liberty and marriage are at odds ('MATRIMONY and LIBERTY – Girlish connection!' [1:406]). She later tells her brother that she would like to remain single for a while because 'One wants now-and-then a *dangling* fellow or two after one in public' (2:86). In other words, Charlotte would like to be able to continue her coquetry, one of the few ways in which a woman could exercise power, but one which was unavailable to a virtuous matron. After Charlotte marries Lord G., she bitterly resents his authority, complaining to Harriet, 'What a poor powerless creature is your Charlotte!' (2:359). Her reluctance to use her married name signals her longing for the relative autonomy of the single woman; after a lengthy and plaintive letter recounting a marital squabble, she signs herself 'Charlotte Grandison' (2:360). When Lord G. addresses her as 'my dear Lady G.,' she interprets this as a snub: 'The wretch called me by his own name, perhaps farther to insult me!' (2:393). In Charlotte's view, the institution of marriage is an insult to women.

Indeed, Charlotte's resentment of her subjection is at the heart of her many quarrels with her husband. She repeatedly takes offence at behaviour she construes as authoritarian and proprietary. When Lord G. asks her to accompany him to a breakfast, she suspects his motive is to 'make a shew of his bride, as his property' and to 'preserve to himself the consequence of being obliged by his obedient wife, at the word of authority (2:393). For similar reasons, she disregards her husband's request to dress for a court appearance, complaining to Harriet, '[w]ere I to choose again, I do assure you, my dear, it should not be a man, who by his taste for Moths and Butterflies, Shells, China, and such-like trifles [referring to Lord G.'s passion for collecting], would give me warning, that he would presume to dress his baby' (2:436–7).[41] She avenges herself appropriately for what she interprets as her husband's denial of her personhood: her favourite nickname for him is 'the monkey.' It is clear, however, that Charlotte is hostile to Lord G. not from personal dislike but because she resents the powerlessness and subordination she believes to be the inevitable lot of married women.

Charlotte's attitude towards money expresses the seriousness of her resentment. As noted above, although under common law a wife was not allowed to own money or property, her family could settle separate property on her, held in trust, under the legal system of equity. One especially controversial form of such separate property emerged during the late Restoration: pin money. This consisted of payments by a husband to his wife of a set yearly sum, designated to provide some necessities, such as clothing and tips to servants, but never food or rent.[42] In the case of a generous settlement, pin money could grant a wife a fair degree of financial independence, even allowing her, in extreme cases, to separate from her husband. Richardson and others thought this was a dangerous practice. Sir Charles therefore insists that Charlotte's allowance of pin money be small, even though Lord G.'s family are willing to be generous. Unknown to her brother, however, Charlotte has received a thousand pounds as a gift from her uncle. Keeping this money for private use, she turns it into an equivalent of pin money, thereby granting herself the autonomy that Sir Charles was so careful to forestall. Charlotte is not greedy; it is clear that the value of the gift lies not in goods but in power: 'I value not money but as it enables me to lay an obligation, instead of being under the necessity of receiving one' (2:351). Charlotte is horrified that her sister Caroline, who has received a similar gift, has given it to her husband. But Caroline, echoing Richardson's views in *Rambler* 97, explains that she and Lord L. 'have but one purse' (2:349). The equality that Charlotte transgressively appropriates is therefore Caroline's by virtue of having married a good man and trusted him fully. Of course, such parity is really an illusion, since Caroline's access to this money is a favour rather than a right, and Lord L. ultimately controls their finances. Nevertheless, Caroline shows that in a happy marriage, there is no need to struggle for independence or authority. When Charlotte eventually comes to see the error of her ways, she gladly gives her money to Lord G.

Charlotte's 'feminist' complaints – her desire for civic identity, economic power, and social authority – are especially threatening because the basic liberties that she covets are implicit in the notion of contract. Richardson's strategies to make marriage for love, which is a contractual agreement, safe from its liberal, progressive implications therefore depend on discrediting Charlotte in various ways. First of all, her resentment against her husband is shown to have no basis in reality. Lord G. is eminently reasonable and tolerates a great deal of perverseness and cruel teasing. For instance, when Charlotte refuses to accompany him to breakfast, she is obviously wrong, lacking not merely feminine deference, but common courtesy. Lord G. (who is not quite so stupid as he appears) recognizes her behaviour for what it is: 'a declaration of rebellion' (2:393), as she confesses to Harriet. Although Lord G. 'insists' upon her compliance, the manner of his insistence is anything but authoritative; he almost begs: 'Upon my soul, madam – Let me perish, if – and then hesitating – You use me ill, madam. I have not deserved – And give me leave to say – I *insist* upon being obliged, madam' (3:393). Lord G. is uncertain, plaintive, and timorous. In the end, he asks her permission to give her a command. Moreover, Charlotte wins the argument and does not go to breakfast. In general, Lord G. suffers from their quarrels, while Charlotte simply enjoys herself. So much for oppressive male authority, in Richardson's view. Given Lord G.'s obliging temper and manifest love, it is clear that Charlotte could have a happy marriage if she would only behave herself. The novel represents her feminism as a catalyst of her marital troubles, rather than a response to women's subjection. Charlotte's resentment is a chimera.

Yet, as in many of his 'solutions,' Richardson does not play fairly with his ideological deck of cards. He can undermine Charlotte so thoroughly because he locates her battle exclusively within the personal sphere of family relationships. Charlotte's resentment is legitimate with regard to social and legal definitions of marriage because marriage as an institution enables the exploitation and abuse of women, as feminists would point out repeatedly in the next century, but the novel represents Charlotte's resentment as a strictly personal issue, an individual quirk on Charlotte's part. *Grandison* suggests elsewhere that the quality of a marriage is solely a matter of individual responsibility, including, above all, the responsibility to choose a husband wisely. In this way, Richardson represents marital choice not as an argument for extending women's liberties, as liberal theory suggests, but rather as a justification for women to endure their married lot, whatever it might be, since they bring it on themselves. Lady Grandison, Charlotte's own mother, exemplifies the proper method for dealing with a bad husband: she submits entirely to his will, no matter how unreasonable or outrageous his behaviour. Yet this is not for lack of spirit: 'Lady Grandison's goodness was founded in principle; not in tameness or servility' (1:313). She clearly exemplifies Mary Astell's advice to women to use their husbands' tyranny to practisce their own virtue.[43] Lady L. does not need to exercise such stoicism, or take refuge in the protection of pin money or other separate property (wrong, in any case) because she has chosen her husband wisely. And as Charlotte herself ultimately realizes, she too has chosen wisely and has no ground for complaint.

Charlotte's bid for power is thus thoroughly discredited. First, she has no need for power because she has a good husband; second, women's insubordination is wrong, even in trying circumstances. But for this 'solution' to the threat of women's autonomy to work, one has to have already accepted Richardson's standards of public and private, right and wrong, as Charlotte herself does in the end. Richardson's undermining of Charlotte's feminism is ultimately a sermon for the converted. In the terms Richardson constructs, it is impossible for a truly good woman to invoke, let alone abuse, the implicit power of the contractual subject. Within these terms, so negligible and powerless is Charlotte's threat, that she herself ultimately characterizes her own insubordination as illusory. Once Charlotte decides to behave herself, she denies the seriousness of her previous rebelliousness, rewriting her challenge to male authority as 'playfulness,' and blaming 'mediators and mediatrices' for exacerbating their quarrels by intruding, and thereby taking her 'playfulness further than it would otherwise have gone' (3:408). She even transforms her derisive nickname for Lord G., the monkey, into a term of affection, dubbing her infant 'the marmouset.'

Charlotte and 'Passionlessness'

Charlotte's character addresses yet another implicit danger of married love and the contractual subjectivity it implies. As we have seen, one reason that the collective patriarchal imaginary so feared women's autonomy was that it threatened to unleash a chaotic female sexuality that would divert the legitimate descent of property. The only way women could be kept chaste or faithful, and hence, property could be kept in the right hands, was to keep women under the firm control of men. Married love was therefore doubly perilous, for it invoked not only women's independence but the erotic desire that made this independence so dangerous. Through a strategy of displacement that again scapegoats Charlotte, Richardson ironically links sexual transgression not with passion, but with its absence.

Charlotte repeatedly evokes the threat of sexual transgression. The first sign of Charlotte's potentially erring nature is seen in her plan to elope with Captain Anderson, a scheme that ostensibly enacts the worst fears of the middle and upper classes about the capacity for female passion to destabilize the social order. Anderson is the ancestor of Wickham in *Pride and Prejudice*, the dashing but low soldier of popular imagination, dangerously apt to attract a giddy woman of superior social station. With Anderson, Charlotte faces either a degrading marriage or her own 'ruin.' Later, the threat of adultery also haunts Charlotte. Her Aunt Nell suspects that her provoking behaviour with Lord G. might be motivated by unrequited love for Sir Charles's friend Beauchamp, whom Charlotte had once playfully suggested as a suitor. This inference is not surprising, since both romances and conduct books warned that a woman who does not marry for love might be susceptible to an illicit passion after her marriage. This is in fact the plot of *The Princess of Cleves*, one of the two French romances to which *Grandison* specifically refers.

Charlotte's 'raillery,' an unbridled propensity to wit and teasing that flouts the rules of decorum, evokes a less specific but equally potent threat about her sexual conduct. Because propriety was identified with feminine virtue, the least sign of indelicacy or erratic social behaviour augured more serious and irrevocable errors, as we see in the case of the hot-tempered Olivia. Olivia's willingness to become Sir Charles's mistress indicates that a volatile temper and impulsive nature easily metamorphose into inappropriate and uncontrollable sexual passion. Charlotte possesses a similar 'liveliness,' for which other characters, especially Sir Charles, frequently reprimand her. Although Sir Charles claims to admire his sister's 'charming vivacity' (2:114), he laments the fact that she does not 'regard times, tempers, and occasions' (2:338). He is therefore eager to see Charlotte safely married before he leaves for Italy, under the protection of a man who like himself would be capable of suppressing her inappropriate behaviour and verbal excesses.

Yet none of Charlotte's erratic behaviour is motivated by passion. As we have seen, Charlotte plans to elope not for love, but in order to escape her tyrannical father's household. She calls her relationship with Anderson 'an *entanglement* ... for I could not, with justice, say *Love*' (1:409), and once she is rescued by her father's timely death, her interest in her suitor vanishes. Likewise, Charlotte's allusion to Beauchamp is a ploy to forestall commitment to any man. She invokes the name of Sir Charles's friend to distract her brother because he is pressuring her to choose between Lord G. and another suitor. Charlotte is therefore able to honestly repudiate Aunt Nell's charge: I should hate myself, were I capable of treating Lord G. meanly, or contemptibly, with a thought of preference to any man breathing, now I am his' (2:505). In Charlotte's view, her cavalier treatment of her husband demonstrates not her vulnerable feelings, but on the contrary how little she is in danger of loving elsewhere. She tells her aunt, 'I know my own heart, madam. If I thought I could not trust it (and I wish Lord G. had a good opinion of it) I would not dance thus, as you suppose, on the edge of danger' (2:505). This answers Sir Charles as well: Charlotte's vivaciousness is the sign not of her teetering 'on the edge of danger' – a precursor to her fall – but rather, an indication of how little susceptible she is to temptation. Charlotte's liveliness falsely signals a philandering nature.

Indeed, Charlotte appears to be passionless. Although she comes to an affectionate rapprochement with Lord G., she never expresses ardour for a lover, either before or after marriage. She tells Harriet that 'Love-matches' are 'foolish things ... Mild, sedate convenience [the motive for her own match] is better than a stark staring-mad passion. The wall-climbers, the hedge and ditch-leapers, the river-forders, the window droppers, always find reason to think so. What nonsense, in matrimony? – Passion is transitory; but discretion, which never boils over, gives durable happiness' (3:30). Through Charlotte's immunity to passion, Richardson displaces the problem of women's desire, associating it paradoxically not with married love, but with its absence.

Charlotte and Sexual Difference

Charlotte's passionlessness, while dissociating both feminism and the wayward sexuality it ostensibly threatens from an ideal of married love, introduces yet another problem: just as Sir Charles's capacity for virtue and feeling threatens to undermine sexual difference, so does Charlotte's invulnerability to love, since women's greater susceptibility to emotion was considered an important marker of such difference. Even more alarming, Charlotte appears to possess a masculine capacity for self-control. Grandison therefore asserts the 'two-sex' model with regard to Charlotte, putting her securely in her place; sexual difference, which accounts for women's inferiority, is ultimately shown to be the basis for her capitulation to her husband.

Although the connection between lack of feeling and sexual transgression that I have noted in Charlotte's characterization is paradoxical, it is nevertheless familiar. The rake is another figure who combines
licentiousness with an absence of true passion. I have suggested above
that Richardson defends Sir Charles's masculinity by showing that his
hero possesses the most important attribute of manliness, self-control,
and that this quality is also a marker of sexual difference. The rake's
compulsive sexual conquest reveals his lack of this defining trait, and
hence, his effeminacy. Yet, just as Sir Charles possesses greater self-
command than Harriet, the rakes have greater self-command than
their female counterparts. That is to say, the rakes might be 'cast in the
female mould' when compared to Sir Charles, but they possess an
abundance of masculine restraint when compared to the novel's
female characters who are similarly guilty of indulging forbidden or
inappropriate passions, such as Olivia, whose outbursts express her
wayward and uncontrollable desire. The novel's rakes indulge their
passions because they choose to do so (just as Sir Charles chooses to
abstain). The rake is effeminate, not feminine.

The seduction/rape is emblematic of this difference. As James
Turner points out, '[l]ibertine sexuality cannot be understood simply
as a surrender to spontaneous physicality: it is inseparable from the
cerebral triumph over the opposite sex.'[44] The rake plots and schemes
in order to entrap his victim; he sees the better way but deliberately
ignores it. (Similarly, the duel is not a spontaneous expression of anger
but rather a choreographed confrontation.) Sir Hargrave's kidnapping
of Harriet depends on an elaborate, premeditated scheme that includes
planting a servant in Harriet's household, drugging and substituting
her chairmen, establishing a hide-out in the country complete with
female help to aid and calm Harriet, and hiring a disreputable priest so
they can be married clandestinely – hardly the impulse of a moment's
passion. Moreover, since the rake is driven by the love of conquest, his
desires are ignited most by the women who pose a challenge. Sir Hargrave urgently wants to marry Harriet because she fails to find him
attractive, just as Clarissa is Lovelace's ultimate challenge. And the
rake's lust for triumph includes men as well as women; this is why
rakes are also duellists. What appears as a lack of control from the perspective of the virtuous man's self-discipline is really a means to a different sort of control for the rake: power over others.

Charlotte has much in common with these libertines; Lady L. even
notes, '[h]ad you been a man, you would have been a sad rake' (2:350).

We have seen that like the rakes, Charlotte uses seduction as a form of power (she likes to 'keep a fellow or two dangling'). Unlike the women, good and bad, whose lack of control is genuine, Charlotte's 'failure' to restrain her 'raillery' is actually a well-planned and sustained protest of her subordinate status. In her highly plotted marital squabbles with Lord G., Charlotte demonstrates the 'manly' qualities of reason, intelligence, and self-control. Indeed, her verbal wit and exuberance invite comparison with male characters such as Uncle Selby. And she directs these powers towards triumphing over the other sex, thereby denying her proper role and place. Charlotte appears to lack the capacity for passion, although strong feeling was increasingly identified as a feminine trait in this period. And for much of the novel, she appears to be stronger and more tenacious than all the men she encounters, except Sir Charles, whom we know will win in every battle of wills with both men and women. While this characterization functions to dissociate marriage for love from the dangers of women's autonomy and sexuality, it reiterates the problem of sexual difference. By using Charlotte as a scapegoat to assuage anxieties about the companionate ideal, Richardson reiterates the same problem of sexual difference that he confronts by characterizing Sir Charles as a man of virtue and feeling.

Charlotte's womanliness is therefore asserted with a vengeance. If many episodes suggest that she is unlike – and hence superior to – other women, the cumulative effect of others reinscribes her as feminine and vulnerable. For instance, in the narrative of her ongoing battle with her husband, Lord G.'s superior strength of will ultimately triumphs, causing her to capitulate to his authority. As she explains her sudden change of heart to her sister (continuing to use the martial metaphors with which she always characterizes her relationship with her husband), 'I began to find the man could be stout. "Charlotte, thought I, what are you about? ... Make your retreat while you can with honour; before you harden the man's heart, and find your reformation a matter of indifference to him"' (2:518). Charlotte has been able to 'take the reins out of her husband's hands' only because he has failed to exert the strength of which he is capable. When Lord G. decides to act like a man, she is forced to take him seriously.

Of course the novel's reasoning is once again circular, because Lord G.'s strength derives to a great extent from the laws and social conventions that ensure women's subordination, and which are justified by 'innate' male superiority. These include definitions of feminine virtue that necessarily restrict Charlotte's own 'strength': she is supposed to obey her husband. Thus Charlotte realizes that if she destroys her chances for domestic happiness by alienating her husband, her life will have little variety or purpose because she is fundamentally a virtuous woman who values her home and husband. As she admits to herself, 'You have a few good qualities; you are not a modern woman; have neither wings to your shoulders, nor gad-fly in your cap: You love home' (2:518). Although this insight might come as a shock to those of us who have followed her exploits through the last four published volumes, it certainly confirms that she knows her place. Lord G.'s victory is especially significant in that it proves that even a woman who appears to be superior to most men (and Charlotte certainly appears superior to Lord G., who lacks serious occupations or interests) is not justified or capable of appropriating male privilege, and will inevitably succumb to men's power. Even the buffoonish, simple-minded Lord G. is shown to be stronger and therefore more suited to rule than his clever, accomplished wife.

Grandison also discredits Charlotte's claim to the essentially male characteristic of self-control. Although Charlotte manipulates events in her relationship with Lord G., even plotting her own reform, she is ultimately unable to manipulate herself or her destiny. Sexual difference, in the form of biological difference, robs Charlotte of her powers of control, trapping this arch-plotter in a narrative over which she has no authority: the story of her own pregnancy. It is biological destiny that causes Charlotte to fully acknowledge her powerlessness and defeat in her struggle against women's subjection. Writing to Harriet while she is pregnant, she describes her condition as a form of male triumph and female abjection, which she curiously figures as a male pregnancy: 'These vile men! I believe I shall hate them all. Did *they* partake [of pregnancy] – But not half so grateful as the blackbirds: They rather look big with insolence, than perch near, and sing a song to comfort the poor souls they have so dreadfully mortified' (3:117).

Charlotte's strange metaphor underscores her point that the differences between the sexes accord both power and advantage to men. Real pregnancy is bodily, painful, and dangerous while men's 'pregnancy' is no more than a figure of speech that expresses their pleasure and triumph in women's misfortune. Men 'look big' (are pregnant) with insolence because they have impregnated and therefore humbled women by subjecting them to the ordeal of childbirth.[45] Later, anticipating childbirth, Charlotte pictures herself as a 'milk-white heifer dressed in ribbands, and just ready to be led to the sacrifice' (3:358).

Using the metaphor of prey usually found in the rake's vocabulary, she implicitly renounces her claim to equality, accepting her status (already designated by marriage law) as a non-person, a 'heifer'; she is now no more than chattel. She also describes childbirth itself as a time of 'crying out,' an ordeal that reduces her usual verbal pyrotechnics to an involuntary and inarticulate scream. Despite Charlotte's superior intellect, in the end her female body is the most important thing about her. Only men can escape the tyranny of the flesh. Only men can claim the virtue of self-control.

Since the body is a source of humiliation for Charlotte, it is not surprising that biological difference also provides Lord G. with definitive proof that she accepts her womanly place. Her decision to breastfeed – 'an act that confessed the mother, the *whole* mother' (3:402) – reveals her conscious acceptance of womanhood and all that it involves, including subordination. Indeed, both Charlotte and Lord G. understand that breastfeeding signals her final capitulation in their long-standing struggle for power.[46] She is therefore determined to hide it from him: 'I intended that he should know nothing of the matter, nor that I would ever be so condescending' (3:402). But Lord G. discovers her secret by accident, entering the nursery unexpectedly. As Charlotte explains, 'The nurse, the nursery-maids, knowing that I would not for the world have been so caught by my nimble Lord (for he is in twenty places in a minute) were more affrighted than Diana's nymphs, when the goddess was surprised by Acteon' (3:402). But this Diana loses for having been seen. Even after her 'reformation,' Charlotte had shown enough of her old impertinence to give her husband some moments of anxiety (see, e.g., 3:261). But when Lord G. surprises her nursing their child, he knows he has nothing more to worry about:

My Lord then again threw himself at my feet – Pardon, pardon me, dearest creature, said he, that I took amiss any thing you ever said or did – *You* that could make me such rich amends – O let not those charming, charming spirits ever subside ... I loved you too well, proceeded he, to take any usage that was not quite what I wished it, lightly. But for some time past I have seen that it was all owing to a vivacity, that now, in every instance of it, delights my soul. You never, never, had malice or ill-nature in what I called *your* petulance. You bore with *mine*. You smiled at me: Henceforth, every thing you say, everything you do, will I take for a favour. O my Charlotte! Never, never more shall it be in your *power* to make me so far forget myself, as to be angry! (3:403)

Charlotte now loses the only power she had left as a married woman, the power to torment her husband, as Lord G. astutely observes (although he couches this observation in complimentary language). When Lord G. tells Charlotte that it is no longer necessary for her to part with her 'roguery,' she realizes that his ability to shrug off her teasing will rob it of its edge: 'Impossible, my Lord, to retain it [her Roguery], if it lose its wonted power over you' (3:403–4). Charlotte's chagrin is facetious, for she perceives Lord G.'s discovery as a fortunate event. She writes to Harriet, '[y]ou my dear left us *tolerably* happy. But now we are almost *intolerably* so' (3:402). But even within the positive terms of Charlotte's narration, the fact that this encounter is about power (a word used by both Charlotte and Lord G.) remains clear. Subdued by male strength and biological destiny, Charlotte fully acknowledges the claims of sexual difference.

'My reverence for *him*'

One problem remains. Despite the happy conclusion to Charlotte's marital troubles, Richardson was faithful enough to the terms of his own characterization to show that Charlotte's feelings for Lord G. still consist in friendship rather than passion. Harriet's assessment of Charlotte's relationship to Lord G. characterizes it as companionate love rather than passion: 'She hates not Lord G. There is no man whom she prefers to him. And in this respect, may perhaps, be upon a par with eight women out of twelve, who marry, and yet make not bad wives' (2:347). For according to beliefs of the day, Charlotte could not have controlled her behavior to Lord G. so successfully had she really been in love with him. Moreover, passion was not believed to develop from friendship, rather, the reverse was thought to be true; 'love' was more likely to mellow into friendship.[47] Yet, if Richardson allowed Charlotte's passionlessness to be genuine, he would have challenged a central belief about sexual difference. Charlotte must therefore be shown to be susceptible to feeling, particularly to love. She must be both passionate and passionless at the same time. Richardson accomplishes this by locating her feminine susceptibility to love in a relationship in which it can never be expressed. Charlotte's self-containment is therefore due not to the fact that she has escaped her essential female nature, rather, following conventional beliefs about love, Charlotte is incapable of passionate love for Lord G. because she loves another man. Charlotte cannot love Lord G. or any other suitor because she is in love with her own brother.

Although Charlotte never openly expresses such unthinkable feelings, her suppressed attraction reveals itself indirectly. That her feelings for her brother inhibit her attachment to other men is itself a sign of their erotic dimension; were these feelings purely fraternal, her brother would occupy a category separate from that of her suitors. But Charlotte confesses that 'this brother of mine makes me think contemptibly of all other men. I would compound for a man but half so good; tender, kind, humane, polite, and even chearful in affliction' (2:320). Moreover, Charlotte expresses her unusually strong cathexis to her brother in terms that imply sexual attraction: 'Sir Charles, whatever faults he might have had when he was from us, came over to us finished. He grew not up with us, from year to year: His blaze dazled me; and I have tried over and over, but cannot yet get the better of my reverence for *him*' (1:237). Charlotte speaks the language of romance here, sounding more like a heroine who knows she must conquer an impermissible passion than an affectionate sister. Charlotte's comment on Sir Charles's long and timely absence from the family also explains how it was possible for her to have developed such an attachment; eighteenth-century literature abounds in instances of long-lost relatives' (often unwitting) passion for one another. Moreover, in a novel that repeatedly figures virtue as a powerful catalyst of erotic response, Charlotte's 'reverence' dissolves easily into love.

Charlotte's body language further suggests her erotic fixation on her brother. When Sir Charles publicly humiliates Charlotte in order to reveal her liaison with Anderson, her nervousness prompts her to fidget in a sexually suggestive manner: 'And every-thing being removed, but the table, she play'd with her diamond ring; sometimes pulling it off, and putting it on; sometimes putting the tip of her finger in it, as it lay upon the table, and turning it round and round, swifter or slower, and stopping thro' downcast vexation, or earnest attention, as she found herself more or less affected – What a sweet confusion!' (1:397). Through this masturbatory fidgeting (the ring was a traditional figure for female genitalia) under Sir Charles's irresistible gaze, Charlotte symbolically enacts the consummation she cannot openly desire.

Charlotte's illicit passion is the source of Sir Charles's repeated misreadings of his sister's conduct. When Charlotte tries to postpone choosing from among her suitors, Sir Charles accuses her of waiting for 'a man in the clouds' (2:97). Evoking the language of pastoral romance to mock what he believes to be her unrealistic expectations, he asks what might inspire her with love for one of her devoted followers: Shall I retire with you to solitude? Make a Lover's *Camera Obscura* for you? Or, could I place you upon the mossy bank of a purling stream, gliding thro' and enamelled mead ... No witness but the grazing herd, lowing love around you; the feathered songsters from an adjacent grove, contributing to harmonize and fan the lambent flame' (2:98) What is strange about this passage is that Sir Charles occupies the lover's place in this scenario as if he realized that he were indeed the source of Charlotte's romantic longings. While neither sister nor brother can allow this knowledge to be conscious, repression will out.

Charlotte's marriage is motivated by passionate love after all, but for Sir Charles rather than her husband, who is at best the object of sedate, companionate feelings. Charlotte's desire to gratify her brother's wishes keeps her from avoiding a relationship for which she feels little enthusiasm. When Harriet begs her to call off her marriage if she does not truly love Lord G., Charlotte can only respond, 'What will my brother say?' (2:340). He is always first in her thoughts and feelings. Despite her raillery, her bid for power, and her independence, Charlotte has more in common with the retiring and unquestionably feminine Clementina than she does with the libertines whose bravado she mimics. Clementina must also choose another despite her love for Sir Charles, and she is also cruelly pressured by Sir Charles into so doing. Charlotte is like other women after all. The claims of patriarchy have been successfully defended from the dangers of liberal selfhood.

3

'No small part of a woman's portion': Love, Duty, and Society in *Persuasion*

Emma Thompson's brilliant adaptation of *Sense and Sensibility* is one of the most authentic of the many film versions of Austen's novels made in the 1990s. Thompson consistently follows Austen's ordering of events and reproduces her wording. Costumes and settings are historically accurate. Camera work conveys Austen's sense of etiquette for contemporary viewers: long shots, which introduce the characters' social calls, function as a metaphor of the formality and distance that govern social relationships in the eighteenth century. Yet despite Thompson's dedication to conveying the look and spirit of her original, her treatment of the novel's primary subject, the representation of love and marriage, differs from as well as follows Austen in telling ways. The most important of Thompson and Austen's shared assumptions is that love between prospective spouses is the proper foundation for marriage, and that other motives, such as status or money, are morally suspect. Willoughby is detestable in both versions, not only for his faithlessness and cruelty to Marianne, but also because he marries for wealth rather than love.

Fissures between film and book reveal that Austen and Thompson define acceptable kinds of love in different ways. Thompson's *Sense and Sensibility* departs most markedly from the original in depicting the story of Marianne Dashwood's marriage to Colonel Brandon. The novel shows that although Marianne enjoys a successful and satisfying second love, the emotional quality of this relationship is distinct from that of Marianne's love for Willoughby: 'Instead of falling a sacrifice to an irresistible passion, as once she had fondly flattered herself with expecting, – instead of remaining even for ever with her mother, and finding her only pleasures in retirement and study, as afterwards in her more calm and sober judgment she had determined on, – she found herself at nineteen, submitting to new attachments, entering on new duties, placed in a new home, a wife, the mistress of a family, and the patroness of a village.'[1] Instead of 'falling,' as she had for Willoughby (and the word connotes the potential for danger of such unreflecting passions), Marianne *submits* to her attachment to Colonel Brandon. Such submission involves conscious choice, and takes into account not merely personal desire, but the good of the community as well.

In marked contrast, Thompson's film represents both of Marianne's romances as grand passions. To emphasize that her second love is equivalent to the first, the film characterizes Colonel Brandon as a replacement for Willoughby – an ardent lover who inspires as intense a response as his predecessor.[2] This point is conveyed both by the narrative and by visual imagery. For instance, the scene in which Colonel Brandon carries a feverish Marianne back to Rosings after she has been wandering in the rain, distracted by her grief over Willoughby's treachery, closely resembles the scene in which Willoughby carries Marianne home after she has twisted her ankle, the incident that begins their relationship. The camera follows a similar trajectory with respect to both distance and movement, and the actors look alike: they are brown-haired and clean-shaven, of medium build and height, and both are dressed in dark clothing of a similar style.[3] This replication indicates to the viewers that they are about to witness another version of the same story. With regard to character, Thompson's handsome, energetic Colonel Brandon also resembles the Willoughby of both versions to a far greater degree than he does Austen's suitor of the infamous flannel waistcoat. In the novel, Willoughby's enthusiasm for literature attracts Marianne, while one of Colonel Brandon's faults is his lack of imagination and literariness. Colonel Brandon of the film turns out to be a man of letters as well, and he, like Willoughby, successfully uses literature to make love. Moreover, the lines we hear him read to Marianne, from *The Faerie Queen*, self-reflexively indicate the phenomenon of replacement: 'Nor is the earth the lesse, or loseth aught./ For whatsoever from one place doth fall,/ Is with the tide unto another brought.'[4]

Readers familiar with eighteenth-century novels, particularly those of Richardson, will realize that Austen is advocating companionate love in Marianne's story. Indeed, to a great extent, the didactic point of Austen's novel is to show that the loving partnership Marianne enters into with Colonel Brandon is as acceptable as Elinor's more passionate union. The novel also makes it clear that Elinor's attraction to Edward is based on an intuitive apprehension of his virtues and character ('sentimental love'), a perception enabled by her own sound ethics and judgment. Writing for audiences today, Thompson faced strong pressures to alter her original. We no longer credit the kind of love that Austen's Marianne feels for Colonel Brandon; in our stories, the only truly happy ending is the fulfilment of passionate feeling. Nor do we make distinctions between kinds of passion, distinctions that were crucial to eighteenth-century novelists and readers.

Film and book also differ in their attitude towards Marianne's independence. While Austen endorses Marianne's right to marry for love, she nevertheless shows that total autonomy for a young girl can be risky, and that Marianne would have been better off with parental strictures and guidance. Marianne's traumatic experience with Willoughby is due largely to the lack of intervention from her mother, who fails to exert her authority when appropriate. When her daughter appears to be secretly engaged to Willoughby, it is Mrs Dashwood's prerogative to inquire into the status of their relationship and to demand that they either declare their engagement or conduct their friendship in a less intimate manner. Yet even though Mrs Dashwood lacks judgment, and is as foolishly romantic as Marianne, her failure to intervene is to a great extent justified by her daughter's entitlement to marry for love. It is only because love is assumed to be the proper foundation for marriage that Mrs Dashwood can misinterpret Willoughby's behaviour, mistaking 'an intimacy so decided' for a proper engagement.[5] Austen emphasizes this point through Elinor's similarly mistaken judgment. For despite her uneasiness about the couple's secrecy, even the wise and temperate Elinor assumes they are engaged because they appear to be in love. She might question Marianne's conduct, but she does not question Marianne's right to engage herself, a privilege that enables her sister's mistaken disregard of decorum. While the film also shows that Marianne is headstrong and behaves improperly, and that she has a somewhat foolish and overly tolerant mother, it makes much less of the connection between Marianne's errant and self-destructive behaviour and her right to choose her husband for herself. Like many heroines in other films, Marianne simply falls in love with the wrong man. In short, the novel problematizes Marianne's autonomy, linking it with her freedom to make her own match, a connection virtually invisible in the film.

Thompson's departures from Austen are consistent with one

another. In the novel, Marianne's autonomy is problematic precisely because her passion for Willoughby is of the wrong kind – romantic and unreflecting – and a parent's sound advice is therefore crucial. If, as in the film, the error lies entirely with the object of her affection rather than in the quality of her feeling, it follows that Marianne's freedom is not an issue; anyone can be deceived. In the film, Marianne's disaster is nobody's fault; in the novel, both she and her mother are to blame. Hence, in the original, Marianne is both punished and rewarded with a marriage to Brandon: punished for her foolish romanticism by a less than passionate relationship, yet rewarded with a happy marriage because her foolishness, now corrected, was not entirely her responsibility.

Austen's depiction of an 'absent' parent allows her to justify Marianne; more importantly, it allows her to sidestep a fundamental contradiction within eighteenth-century ideals of love and marriage: conflict over the marriage choice. Children, especially daughters, were supposed to obey their parents, yet they were also obliged to marry for love. Parents were supposed to respect their children's wishes, yet they were also expected to guide their children's choices. When does advice become command? When does following one's heart become defiance? If parents refuse to or are unable to offer their judgment, then daughters do not have to confront the problem of disobedience, and they are even to a great extent exonerated from 'disobeying' – that is, from defying general parental/paternal social expectations, so long as their error stays within reasonable bounds. (By contrast, the transgressions of the two Elizas are unpardonable – no failure of parental guidance would justify their elopements.)

Through Mrs Dashwood's abdication of her rightful authority, Austen both evokes and dismisses the contradiction at the centre of beliefs about love and marriage. She would return to confront it in her last complete novel, *Persuasion*.

Conflicts in Conduct

Conduct books of the eighteenth century, which fervently preached the virtues of married love, attempted to resolve conflicts over the marriage choice between parents and children, especially daughters, by granting parents the right to strongly advise – to 'persuade' (the contemporary term for influencing the marriage choice) – their daughters to reject unsuitable lovers, while also allowing them to refuse men whom they find objectionable.[6] For instance, *The Ladies Calling* (1673), a guide that remained popular throughout the eighteenth century, states that it is proper for a daughter to be 'prescrib'd to' in 'choosing the fix'd Companion of her Life ... For where once the Authority of a Parent comes to be despis'd, tho' in the lightest instance, it lays the Foundation of the utmost Disobedience.' One of the 'highest injuries' a daughter can do her parents is to marry without their permission. However, a daughter has the right to refuse her parents' choice of a suitor: '[A]s a Daughter is neither to anticipate, nor contradict the Will of her Parent, so (to have the balance even) I must say she is not oblig'd to force her own, by Marrying where she cannot love; for a negative voice in the case is as much the Child's right, as the Parent's.'[7]

Despite its assumption of choice and agency for daughters, the conduct-book formula for resolving differences was so widely accepted that it influenced even the most conservative of commentators, such as Dr Fordyce, a firm advocate of subservience and restriction for women. Fordyce believes that parents are better able than daughters to judge the merits of a prospective husband because they will be guided by reason rather than feeling: '[A] parent, generally speaking, is much more likely to judge with soundness for a daughter, than she is for herself ... the deliberate advice, which is dictated alike by length of days, knowledge of the world, and earnest solicitude for a child's welfare, ought to be relied upon, rather than the hasty conclusions of juvenile desire.'[8] But when the issue is one of forced marriage, Fordyce turns around; he is now firmly on the side of children and feeling: 'But they would force you to sacrifice your happiness to a man whom you cannot love. There your submission is to stop. No rules of duty can oblige you to involve yourselves in misery and temptation, by entering into engagements to love and to honour, where your hearts with-hold their consent.'[9] In this case, children know best, and hearts, not parents, are the wisest guides. The ethics of marriage force even this staunch patriarchalist into a position at odds with most of his treatise. What is noticeable here is that Fordyce replicates the alignment of passion with independence that we see in *Sense and Sensibility*, an association that is crucial in *Persuasion*.

Fordyce, like Richardson and other writers, is caught between his allegiance to two conflicting versions of marriage: an ideal of consensual married love grounded in a Christian ethic and a patriarchalist conception of marriage consistent with traditional views of relationships between men and women. This problem leads him to a solution embraced by the larger culture: the typologizing of love in order to obviate the potentially disruptive effects of passion. As discussed above, strong feeling threatened the social order by raising the possibility of class miscegenation, which might upset the existing social hierarchy. Women's passion in particular was considered especially dangerous, for female chastity ensured the legitimate transmission of property. Furthermore, Fordyce's distrust of strong feeling was influenced by the conservative politics of his time. In the post-revolutionary era of reaction, the fear of female desire was overdetermined by the popular figuration of radical views and revolutionary violence as affective or sexual excess.[10] Fordyce therefore condemns passion, especially sexual attraction, a judgment that emerges despite his euphemistic language: 'juvenile desire' is an unreliable guide to making a good marriage because 'Fancy alone is too sanguine a counsellor to be a prudent one ... protestations of eternal fidelity, of uninterrupted affection, made in the heat of blood have no solid basis.' He distinguishes between '[l]ove grafted on esteem, or fed by it' and its 'worthless pretenders,' a phrase which connotes the subversive force of unregulated passion. If daughters are prevented from following 'worthless pretenders' — pretenders that take the form of their own feelings as well as their 'worthless' suitors – then parental guidance that serves to unmask such false claimants does not violate the ethical imperative to allow a daughter to follow her conscience and her heart.[11]

Yet Fordyce's attempt to accommodate a daughter's feelings only highlights the inadequacy of the conduct-book solution to conflicts in judgment. His distinction between true suitors and worthless pretenders is moot (and mute) in both perception and practice. A daughter might believe she is in love while her parents think she is infatuated. And in any case, judging correctly is difficult; neither Marianne nor her judicious sister, who represents a proper parental point of view, recognizes that both Marianne's feelings and Willoughby himself are 'worthless pretenders.' In much the same way, the power of mutual veto, which attempts to protect the interests and honour of both parents and children, leads potentially to a zero sum game: in the most pessimistic scenario, there is no coercion and no defiance, but there is also no husband and no marriage. Conduct advice is capable of producing just such a stalemate precisely because it refuses to prioritize the rights of parents or children with respect the marriage choice. And the possibility that these rights will conflict is as likely as the possibility that tastes and judgments will differ.

The Double Plot of *Persuasion*

Persuasion represents this deadlock between married love and filial obligation through the multiplot form: its primary plot and subplot align with opposing points of view that remain at odds with one another in the end. Yet, as with other oppositions in Austen's work, pride and prejudice and sense and sensibility being the most famous, the predominant binary pairing in *Persuasion* between feeling and prudence is exposed as illusory. Feeling can never escape thought, and more important, prudence always implicates feeling. If we are entrapped by Austen's binaries to begin with, lulled into the security of having made important distinctions (between pride and prejudice) or of having chosen correctly (sense over sensibility), we are always shown that we have been foolish for thinking that such neatly bounded categories might govern something as morally and psychologically complex as human judgment and behaviour.

Despite its brevity, *Persuasion* comprises multiple narratives, including those of the Elliots, the Musgroves, the Crofts, the Harvilles, and Captain Benwick. Following the conventions of the multiplot novel, *Persuasion*'s several stories often revolve around common themes, as when Captain Benwick's engagement to Louisa evokes the issue of constancy that has haunted the Anne/Wentworth narrative. What is atypical, however, is that the primary plot and subplot involve the same story and characters, the romance of Anne and Wentworth, so that the novel becomes a retelling of the same tale.[12] Such repetition with a difference invokes an analogy with writing, for Anne does nothing so much as revise her story, this time, with an alternate ending: she marries Wentworth instead of rejecting him.[13] Indeed, Anne is very much the author of her tale as well as her fate: control of the narrative is shared between Anne and the narrator, a collaboration that is formally expressed through the liberal use of free indirect discourse and focalization.[14]

Persuasion's 'subplot,' or first narrative, the story of Anne's failed engagement, endorses the conservative cluster of values we see in Fordyce: filial obedience, prudence, and a strong distrust of feeling. It assumes the superiority of judgment over feeling and parents over children as reliable guides to behaviour. Such values are inherently antifeminist, like Fordyce himself, in that they deny the autonomy and subjectivity of women, negating their desires and placing them firmly within the control of patriarchal, familial interests. Lady Russell's 'per-

suasion' of Anne to repudiate her engagement illustrates precisely
what Fordyce means by 'deliberate advice' – advice that is both prudent and efficacious. In this sense, it is significant that Lady Russell
achieves her goals through persuasion, and not force, a point established from the title onward. Although Lady Russell 'had almost a
mother's love, and mother's rights,' [15] she is not a true parent; she can
only advise, not command, nor does she try to do otherwise. She never
attempts to arrange a marriage for Anne, and when Anne later rejects
the eligible Charles Musgrove, Lady Russell accepts her refusal gra-
ciously, exhibiting perfect conduct-book behaviour.

Lady Russell's disapproval of Wentworth is grounded in prudent
considerations concerning the status of Anne's family and the security
of Anne herself. If Lady Russell is a surrogate mother, she is also a surrogate father (she stands 'in the place of a *parent*' (246) [emphasis
added]), whose patriarchal point of view is based on dynastic aspira-
tions for the Elliot family: marriage to Wentworth represents downward mobility. Yet despite her 'prejudices on the side of ancestry ...
[and] value for rank and consequence' (11), she disapproves of more
than Wentworth's lack of blood, the basis of Sir Walter's condemnation, and in fact, the irrelevance and fatuousness of his opinion contrast with the soundness and integrity of hers. Wentworth's lack of
status is only one aspect of his overall unsuitability. Lady Russell's
poor opinion of him originates as much in pragmatism as in snobbery,
for, being poorly connected, Wentworth has 'nothing but himself to
recommend him, and no hopes of attaining affluence, but in the
chances of a most uncertain profession, and no connexions to secure
even his farther rise in that profession' (26–7). These grim prospects
promise a life of hardship and uncertainty for Anne.

Following Fordyce's logic, Lady Russell shows a strong distrust of
feeling, which accords with her general social conservatism. It is not
surprising, then, that she finds Wentworth's passionate nature as odious as his uncertain prospects. Her aversion is described in language
that encodes his strong sexuality: '[F]ull of life and ardour, he knew
that he should soon have a ship, and soon be on a station that would
lead to every thing he wanted ... Such confidence, powerful in its own
warmth, and bewitching in the wit which often expressed it, must have
been enough for Anne; but Lady Russell saw it very differently. – His
sanguine temper, and fearlessness of mind, operated very differently
on her. She saw in it but an aggravation of the evil. It only added a dangerous character to himself. He was brilliant, he was headstrong. –

Lady Russell had little taste for wit; and of any thing approaching to imprudence a horror. She deprecated the connexion in every light' (27). Wentworth's 'wit' associates him with the risqué behaviour of the rake; its power of 'bewitching' evokes a familiar trope of infatuation. 'Ardour' and 'warmth' are also familiar in the vocabulary of love, especially to readers of novels. Wentworth's temper is 'sanguine,' which indicates an amorous disposition according to the physiology of the humours (outdated by Austen's time, but part of general lore). The 'imprudence' that horrifies Lady Russell connotes lapses in sexual conduct as well as in worldly calculation. Even in areas unrelated to romance, Wentworth evinces characteristics associated with sexual passion: strength of feeling, spontaneity, ebullience. Wentworth's general deportment is that of a lover. In following Lady Russell's advice, then, Anne, like her mentor, must distrust feeling, suppressing her own 'exquisite felicity' (26). She must also abjure the claim to know what is best for herself. By relegating her desire Anne relinquishes her autonomy, in accord with the antifeminist ethos of the subplot.

While parental authority, prudence, and women's subservience bespeak the values and determine the outcome of the first narrative, independence, passion, and a contemporary version of feminism do so in the primary plot, the story of events in the present that constitutes most of the novel.[16] Early on in this part of the novel, Anne rejects the conservative ethos that governed her behaviour eight years earlier, showing that she has come to realize that feeling is the most important guarantor of successful marriage: 'How eloquent could Anne Elliot have been, – how eloquent, at least, were her wishes on the side of early warm attachment, and a cheerful confidence in futurity, against that over-anxious caution which seems to insult exertion and distrust Providence! – She had been forced into prudence in her youth, she learned romance as she grew older – the natural sequel of an unnatural beginning' (30). Prudence, which seemed appropriate eight years earlier, is here cast in a negative light, as an almost unchristian sentiment, while feeling is viewed as a proper ethical response to events. Words such as 'warm' and 'confidence,' which have previously signalled the moral ambiguity of Wentworth's demeanour, are now part of the vocabulary associated with Anne, whose superior character is never in question. The narrator's play on the word 'natural' encapsulates this reversal of values. 'Natural' can mean '[t]aking place or operating in accordance with the ordinary course of nature.'[17] In this sense, the claim here is that the 'natural' triumphs over the unnatural, that which is '[n]ot in accordance with the usual course of nature,'[18] an apt description of Lady Russell's prudence, which has suppressed Anne's sexual desire for Wentworth. But 'natural' also means '[b]ased upon the innate moral feeling of mankind; instinctively felt to be right and fair.'[19] In this sense, the 'natural' is not that which is primary and unmediated, but that which is right in and of itself. The context of the passage points to this second definition; Anne's 'natural' desire is also what is 'natural' – what is moral and proper.

In the last sentence of this passage a shift from the free indirect discourse of the preceding sentences to the narrator's own voice signals to us that this change in values will apply to the narrative as a whole, as well as to Anne's feelings. 'Sequel' is a literary term that aptly describes the relationship of the primary plot to the subplot.[20] By describing Anne's enlightenment as a sequel, the narrator in effect suggests that the story we are about to read, which follows the 'unnatural' story of Anne's suppression of her feelings, will endorse the 'natural' lesson she has learned. Moreover, this lesson consists of 'romance,' another literary term.[21] Most critics assume that romance here means love, but the passage plays on its popular and technical definitions. Of course the two are related, since romances, in all their literary incarnations, from medieval tales of chivalry to contemporary trade paperbacks, recount tales of love. But romance had a specific and charged valence at this time: novelists often took pains to distinguish their genre by claiming that the novel inculcated prudence and morality in contrast to the glorification of impulsive passion depicted in romance. The term 'romance' thus suggests that Anne's hard-earned education (in romance) will reverse the novel's usual didactic trajectory from romance to prudence (the course followed by Austen's own Marianne Dashwood), as it reverses conventional moral codes: passion, not prudence, governs here.

Indeed, *Persuasion*'s primary narrative is all about feeling – its subtle nuances, its emotional benefits, and, as I will later show, its ethical value. Focalized primarily through Anne, it is above all the story of her varying responses – suffering, suspense, elation – as she and Wentworth move towards reunion. Wentworth returns to her because she is able to convince him that her feelings for him have always been strong and have remained constant; Anne's ability to acknowledge and communicate her emotional interiority thus ensures her happiness. Conversely, Wentworth's love for Anne comes to predominate over all other considerations. Moreover, in this part of the novel, marriage for love is shown to be generally for the best, whatever the consequences. The poor naval household we see here is not that of the chaotic Prices of *Mansfield Park*, whose large, unruly, and needy establishment illustrates the unattractive consequences of an imprudent match, but the industrious and orderly Harvilles, true exemplars of 'love in a cottage,' who prove that it is not only possible but desirable to weather hardship when love and affection compensate. The Crofts' happy marriage was the result of 'a cheerful confidence in futurity,' and the trustworthy Mrs Croft herself recognizes the importance of an 'early, warm attachment.' It is significant that the one marriage for love that is not entirely happy, that of Anne's own mother, is described earlier, in the first version of Anne and Wentworth's story, where it supports Lady Russell's point of view; its placement in the novel – its positioning with respect to plot rather than story – emphasizes its association with the values of this earlier narrative.[22]

Linked with this valuation of feeling in the second narrative is a contemporary form of feminism, embodied in particular by Mrs Croft. Hardy and independent, she contradicts the popular assumption of female weakness, so detested by Wollstonecraft as a means for stunting and controlling women.[23] Mrs Croft has little need of the sheltering available to women of her class, and is at home nowhere so much as on a naval ship. She is as caught up in the affairs of the navy as her husband the Admiral, so that his career is in effect a family business. And if they are companions at work, they are also partners at home – participants in a marriage which tries its best to ignore conventional ideas about women's roles and separate spheres.[24] While Anne lacks Mrs Croft's hardiness and stamina – she will not go to sea with her husband – she comes into a feminism of her own. Her education in romance is the first step, for in regretting her prudence, she repudiates Lady Russell's authority, as well as the patriarchal values it represents. Her behaviour does not reflect this change in attitude for quite a while, and in the scenes before Lyme, she appears to be the same retiring, self-effacing 'Miss Elliot.' But she gradually becomes more active in shaping her destiny, abjuring feminine helplessness and passivity. When faced with the emergency of Louisa's fall, she quickly takes control. Family and friends look to her for guidance: '[N]o one so proper, so capable as Anne!' says Charles Musgrove (114). Most revealing is Anne's pursuit of Wentworth, which almost exceeds the bounds of decorum. Changing appointments, switching seats at a concert, imploring others to remind Wentworth that he is invited to her family's party, Anne aggressively manipulates events to regain her lover. She finally brings him back by encrypting reassurance of her own love in an intimate talk with Captain Harville; such talk teeters on the brink of impropriety, for Anne does not know Harville well.[25] Anne takes risks in order to take charge.

Anne's talk with Harville, then, epitomizes the 'feminist' Anne, a woman who is not afraid to assert herself in order to get what she wants, and, just as importantly, who believes that getting what she wants is worthwhile. But this conversation is more than a gesture signalling Anne's increasing autonomy, for its feminism also inheres in what is said. Anne argues for the contingent, socially constructed nature of men and women's behaviour, while Harville insists that the differences between the two are essential and innate. These positions allude to a long tradition of debate over whether nature (the antifeminist position), or nurture, especially custom and education (the feminist position), is responsible for sexual difference. Their respective modes of reasoning are therefore even more important than the fact that Anne praises women and Harville disparages them. In Anne's view, women are more constant lovers than men not because they are inherently more faithful or emotional, but because of circumstances: 'We live at home, quiet, confined, and our feelings prey upon us. You are forced on exertion ... and continual occupation and change soon weaken impressions' (232). When Harville invokes literature as proof of women's natural inconstancy, Anne rejects its authenticity as a faithful record of nature, exposing the world of letters as a series of cultural practices that both enable and display male hegemony: 'Men have had every advantage of us in telling their own story. Education has been theirs in so much higher a degree; the pen has been in their hands. I will not allow books to prove any thing' (234).

Persuasion promises to repair this injustice to women – at least in one very local instance – for Austen, in the writing of this scene, takes the pen in *her* hands to inscribe an alternative to Harville's great tradition of masculinist literature. Not only does she write a scene in which her trustworthy heroine voices opposition to a genealogy of misogynist texts, claiming that they further the widespread assumption of women's inferiority, but in creating a character who is 'almost too good,'[26] Austen cultivates an alternative tradition of representation that depicts women in positive terms. Not only Anne's arguments, therefore, but her very existence, challenges the 'books' to which she objects.[27] In a moment which similarly repudiates custom, Wentworth, listening attentively, drops his pen, figuring the gendered reversal of position, power, and moral authority that marks Anne and Wentworth's relationship throughout the primary plot.[28] For contrary to the usual fare in the didactic novel, it is a man (not a woman) who must be educated to see his errors in judgment and to acknowledge his flaws; it is a man who is rewarded with a happy marriage once he is able to do so. Moreover, in this scene of 'penlessness,' Anne makes her desires and viewpoints known while Wentworth remains in the woman's position, silent and waiting to learn his fate.

Passion, Prudence, and Society

By the time of Anne and Wentworth's joyous reunion, it appears that feelings and feminism have triumphed over prudence and patriarchy. But just as we think the novel will finish with this progressive moral, Anne herself repudiates the obvious lesson that a daughter's 'rebellion' is sometimes justifiable, and instead, reaffirms the rightness of her decision eight years earlier:

> I was perfectly right in being guided by the friend whom you will love better than you do now. To me, she was in the place of a parent. Do not mistake me, however. I am not saying that she did not err in her advice. It was, perhaps, one of those cases in which advice is good or bad only as the event decides; and for myself, I certainly never should, in any circumstance of tolerable similarity, give such advice. But I mean, that I was right in submitting to her, and that if I had done otherwise, I should have suffered more in continuing the engagement than I did even in giving it up, because I should have suffered in my conscience. I have now, as far as such a sentiment is allowable in human nature, nothing to reproach myself with; and if I mistake not, a strong sense of duty is no bad part of a woman's portion. (246)

While Anne had never previously said, or even thought, that she ought to have defied Lady Russell, the thrust of her speech retracts her state of mind at the start of the primary plot – a state of mind so subversive that it could only be voiced through the narrator. Then, she was at least certain that Lady Russell was wrong, and that 'she should yet have been a happier woman in maintaining the engagement, than she had been in the sacrifice of it' (29); now, while Anne still does not agree with Lady Russell's advice, she is willing to concede that it was just as likely to have been right as wrong, and that she herself would have suffered more in defying her mentor than she did in capitulating. Retreating from her endorsement of a 'cheerful confidence in futurity against that over-anxious caution which seems to insult exertion and distrust Providence' (30), Anne now asserts that 'it was, perhaps, one of those cases in which advice is good or bad only as the event decides.' In this revision of her former sentiments, preordained 'Providence' has become contingent fortune, and the ethics of the marriage choice depend on practical hindsight rather than divine foresight. Anne enters fully into Lady Russell's point of view, affirming the values repudiated throughout her own 'natural sequel to an unnatural beginning.'

If this is hard to take for many readers, it is also hard to dismiss. Anne has been the moral centre of the novel, and her judgment has been impeccable throughout. This is Anne's last interchange of dialogue – her last word, so to speak. But if Anne is unwilling to draw the moral so many readers expect, the narrator does it for her: 'Who can be in doubt of what followed? When any two young people take it into their heads to marry, they are pretty sure by perseverance to carry their point, be they ever so poor, or ever so imprudent, or ever so little likely to be necessary to each other's ultimate comfort. This may be bad morality to conclude with, but I believe it to be truth' (248). While the narrator stops short of advocating defiance, she nevertheless legitimizes it: the rejection of parental advice has become a matter of custom, and it is therefore no longer shocking or egregious. Moreover, the ambiguity of the word 'morality' enables her to endorse such autonomy on the part of children, while hedging such an endorsement. Morality can mean 'the moral (of a fable, etc.),' and in this sense, she simply concludes from observation that when children are determined to marry, they will do so. But 'morality' also means '[m]oral discourse or instruction; a moral exhortation,' which implies that the narrator approves this 'moral,' and that it is 'moral' for people to marry when and whom they want, whatever the consequences.[29]

The narrator's reversal of Anne's sentiments represents a significant rupture. Throughout *Persuasion*, Anne and the narrator have been identified with one another through both congruence of judgment and formal devices. At the conclusion, however – that most important moment when we as readers draw our own conclusions – they divide. We expect the ending to be a synthesis of opposing points of view, much as *Sense and Sensibility* resolves its opposition between reason and passion, but

Persuasion offers dissolution rather than dialectic. The effect is to leave us with a palimpsest of opposing values and divergent narratives: prudence and passion, submission, and autonomy, Anne's story in the past and Anne's story in the present. The effect is, in other words, to replicate narratologically the division within conduct literature itself, which also voices irreconcilable views about the rights and duties of both children and parents. Yet despite these shifts in position between its two authoritative voices, *Persuasion* ultimately takes sides, endorsing the narrator's 'bad morality.' This stance is necessarily subtle and indirect, for Austen would have risked her reputation and continued publication by openly sanctioning a young woman's autonomy and desire, especially when these contest the values of duty, submission, and family loyalty. As Claudia L. Johnson observes, women writers had to be circumspect when voicing even mildly progressive views, or they would risk being classified as dangerous progressives, advocates of female liberty, adultery, the dissolution of the family and of society. They accordingly 'smuggle in their social criticism, as well as the mildest of reformist projects, through various means of indirection.'[30]

Despite Anne's reliability, it is hard to take her final judgment seriously because it makes so little sense on the novel's own terms. Like the liar's paradox, 'I always lie' (and so I must be lying, but then that means I'm telling the truth, but that is impossible because I always lie), Anne's statement of filial duty conveys its own absurdity. It is because Anne is so dutiful that she is able to follow Lady Russell's advice to begin with, and later, to vindicate such advice, despite her recognition of its dubious worth. But the fact that she does so makes a mockery of the very viewpoint she endorses; her final judgment is misguided precisely because she is able to make such a judgment. And it may be disingenuous after all. The narrator assures us that had it been necessary this time, Anne and Wentworth would not have failed in 'bearing down every opposition' (248). By hypothesizing Anne's refusal to yield a second time, she undermines Anne's conclusions, suggesting that however heartily Anne now exonerates persuasion, her views would be different if her happiness were threatened.[31] Moreover, such judgment runs counter to the undertow of affect in the novel; not only does the second narrative dominate in terms of sheer bulk (the tale of Wentworth's rejection, after all, takes only a few pages), but all *Persuasion*'s energy and passion inheres in the tale of reunion and the values it represents. This has been felt by generations of readers who have perceived the novel as critical of Lady Russell's advice – as critical of 'persuasion' altogether. A contemporary and disapproving reviewer writes that 'its *moral* ... seems to be, that young people should always marry according to their own inclinations and upon their own judgment; for that if in consequence of listening to grave counsels, they defer their marriage, till they have wherewith to live upon, they will be laying the foundation for years of misery, such as only the heroes and heroines of novels can reasonably hope ever to see the end of.'[32]

But *Persuasion* strikes its most potent blow against the conservative ethos of prudence by undermining its very foundation. Conservative ideology assumes a classic, metaphysical paradigm in which prudence represents a superior term in the opposition 'prudence/passion.' *Persuasion* shows that such difference between the two is ultimately illusory. Passion is what Derrida calls a 'dangerous supplement,' which implicates the term it opposes.[33] A context for this strategy can be seen in David Hume's *Treatise of Human Nature*, which also provides a model for the status of feeling in general in *Persuasion*, as I will later show.[34] Hume rejects the traditional philosophical exhortation to be guided by reason, the basis of most conduct-book advice, claiming that only feeling can motivate behaviour: '[R]eason alone can never be a motive to any action of the will: and ... it can never oppose passion in the direction of will.'[35] The work of reason is to figure out how we can fulfil our desires, how best to 'avoid or embrace what will give us ... uneasiness or satisfaction' (414). Hume summarizes this position in what has become one of the *Treatise*'s most famous passages: ''[T]is evident ... that the impulse [to aversion or propensity] arises not from reason, but is only directed by it ... We speak not strictly and philosophically when we talk of the combat of passion and of reason. Reason is, and ought only to be the slave of the passions, and can never pretend to any other office than to serve and obey them' (414–15). Contests between reason and passion are in truth nothing more than struggles between competing passions: those that are 'calm and weak,' and which we mistake for reason, as opposed to those passions that are 'violent and strong' (419). Although rational thought is theoretically possible, it is both rare and ineffectual. In practical terms, there is no 'outside' of feeling. Or, as Austen's narrator says, 'How quick come the reasons for approving what we like!' (15).

In *Persuasion*, Mr Elliot is a pivotal figure in the unmasking of reason, prudence, and objectivity. He initially appears to be a man who lacks feeling, an impossibility, of course, in Hume's terms. Anne distrusts her cousin because he is too controlled and unemotional: 'There was never any burst of feeling, any warmth of indignation or delight, at the evil or good of others' (161). Yet when all his misdeeds are known, Mr Elliot is revealed to be driven by his feelings: he is greedy and proud (he initiates contact with his cousins to prevent the possibility of a male heir), cruel (in his shameful treatment of the Smiths), and lascivious (the narrator thinks it likely that Mrs Clay will seduce him into a marriage). Mr Elliott does not lack feeling, but has the wrong feelings, and his prudence is merely a stance adopted in order to accomplish his selfish schemes. As Anne speculates early on in their acquaintance, Mr Elliot's control is simply the façade of 'a clever, cautious man, grown old enough to appreciate a fair character' (161).

And so it is with other characters throughout the novel, whose 'reasonable' behaviour is always shown to have its source in feeling. Mary instantiates this lesson parodically. When she wants to go out to dinner, she concludes that her ailing child will be better off with Anne: 'My being the mother is the very reason why my feelings should not be tried. I am not at all equal to it ... [To Anne:] You, who have not a mother's feelings, are a great deal the properest person' (56–7). What makes this statement so ironically ludicrous is that it has the structure of an argument, but it is so obviously an expression of desire. Lady Russell's logic is similarly hollow, although in a serious rather than comical register. Her disapproval of Wentworth might have many practical determinants, but she is ultimately motivated by aversion – indeed, her opinions and hatred are inextricable. Even Anne's prudent decision to end her engagement stems from her very love for the man she rejects: '[I]t was not a merely selfish caution, under which she acted, in putting an end to it. Had she not imagined herself consulting his good, even more than her own, she could hardly have given him up' (27–8). This thematic of passion offers the final quietus to Lady Russell's caution, to Fordyce's view that parents are better judges, and by implication to the antifeminism undergirded by such assumptions. There is no true disinterestedness that would justify a parent's moral authority. The opposition between parents and children, then, is not an opposition between reason and passion, but between passions for different objects.

In this contest of desires, moreover, children's motives are likely to be purer than those of their parents. As Mr Elliot shows, the line between prudence and self-interest is often non-existent. Lady Russell sees Mr Elliot as the very exemplar of prudence: 'He was steady, observant, moderate, candid; never run away with by spirits or by selfishness, which fancied itself strong feeling; and yet, with a sensibility to what was amiable and lovely, and a value for all the felicities of domestic life, which characters of fancied enthusiasm and violent agitation seldom really possess' (146–7). But what she fails to understand is that prudence rather than 'spirits' is likely to be a function of selfishness. Whether the hypocrisy of prudence is conscious or unwitting, moderation of feeling is often the sign of self-serving calculation. With the exception of Lady Russell, the advocates of prudence in *Persuasion* tend to be entirely selfish. Mr Elliot himself preaches the value of caution when he advises Anne not to disregard the importance of rank (150–1). It is no coincidence that the only other character to voice Lady Russell's views on marriage is the totally self-centred Mary, who does not wish Henrietta to marry Charles Hayter, for 'considering the alliances which the Musgroves have made, she has no right to throw herself away' (76).[36] With allies like these in her ideological camp, Lady Russell's position is weak indeed. Anne ('almost too good!') consistently represents the opposition, both in action and discourse, despite her defence of her mentor: 'She felt that she could so much more depend upon the sincerity of those who sometimes looked or said a careless or a hasty thing, than of those whose presence of mind never varied, whose tongue never slipped' (161). The narrative vindicates such instincts.

It is tempting to see a 'new' Austen in these attitudes, and critics generally view *Persuasion* as a departure from her earlier work, even when they agree about little else. But *Persuasion* is not quite the exception it is sometimes thought to be. If Austen's prior novels espouse the value of prudence, they also reveal its seamy underside, as when Charlotte Lucas marries Mr Collins in *Pride and Prejudice*. *Persuasion* reverses this ratio of praise to blame, as we have seen, and prudence rather than passion comes in for the most censure. But this is almost reluctantly the case. Prudence is never entirely discarded, even in the primary narrative. Wentworth's own sentimental education consists in part of learning that Louisa's nearly fatal impulsiveness is inferior to Anne's caution. Mrs Musgrove's large fat sighings over a son she never cared for are ludicrous not because she is overweight, but because she is excessive; her deportment betrays her inability to contain herself physically or emotionally. Anne never loses her self-control, or her ability to think before she acts; indeed, these qualities are part of her overall moral excellence. Anne's own mother married for love only to regret her lapse in judgment. The author who punished Marianne

Dashwood so thoroughly can still be heard, even in the narrator's cele-
bratory reference to bad morality. Moreover, Austen sidesteps the difficulties and potential objections to her own 'bad morality' by depicting
love of the highest order. Anne and Wentworth's love is not an impulsive infatuation – Anne is not Marianne Dashwood, or Lydia Wickham, or even Henrietta Musgrove. Anne's love for Wentworth is
grounded in an intuitive apprehension of his virtues ('sentimental
love'), feelings that are shown to be accurate in the course of time.
There is even a degree of contingency in the relationship that affirms
its rational nature, distinguishing it from romantic notions of fated and
exclusive love; Anne and Wentworth fall in love largely because 'he
had nothing to do, and she had hardly any body to love' (26). Whatever is innovative about this novel, and whatever is startling about
its judgments, it is fundamentally consistent with Austen's project
throughout her work: the deployment of narrative in order to interro-
gate her society's ethics and to formulate an acceptable moral order. If
Persuasion takes the side of love over prudence, it is because 'prudence'
is capable of producing a Mr Elliot, and Mr Elliot is precisely what is
wrong with society. The opposition between prudence and passion
ultimately represents a contest between ways of being in the world –
between narcissistic self-enclosure on the one hand, and extension
beyond one's own desires and needs on the other – an opposition, in
other words, between solipsism and sympathy.

   The premise that sympathy is the source of both virtue and justice –
the *sine qua non* of civilization itself – is central to Hume's *Treatise* (575–
7). Personal feelings are able to develop into public benevolence
through the faculty of sympathy, which makes possible our identification and empathy with others. As John Mullan explains, 'sympathy is
not selflessness; its operation does not guarantee that our actions will
be adapted to the sentiments of others. What it provides for is the
accessibility of those sentiments, and therefore a sociability not explica-
ble in terms of political or material necessity.'[37] By converting an 'idea'
of someone else's thoughts or feelings into an 'impression,' which we
then apprehend with personal intensity, sympathy makes possible the
transformation of inherently antisocial feelings into social ones. Hume
thus maintains that by reference to sympathy, 'we may easily account
for that merit, which is commonly ascrib'd to *generosity, humanity, compassion, gratitude, friendship, fidelity, zeal, disinterestedness, liberality,* and
all those other qualities, which form the character of good and benevolent [people]' (603; emphasis in the original). And our passions must

be tempered by such benevolence if society is to function: 'A propensity to the tender passions makes a man agreeable and useful in all the parts of life; and gives a just direction to all his other qualities, which otherwise may become prejudicial to society. Courage and ambition, when not regulated by benevolence, are fit only to make a tyrant and public robber' (603–4). Hume's choice of the phrase 'tender passions,' a conventional term for love in the period, implies that amorous relationships belong within this complex of moral virtues, the very linkage made by *Persuasion*.

Indeed, a Humean formulation of sympathy and morality operates throughout *Persuasion*. Here too, sympathy is an epistemological tool by which one understands the feelings and concerns of others. Mr Elliot, a 'tyrant and a robber' in Hume's words, epitomizes the connection between a lack of sympathy and the insidious passions that threaten the fabric of society. But morality is nevertheless a matter of individual choice and individual responsibility. Mr Elliot knows the better way, as we see from his ability to act the part of a good man, but willingly embraces evil; he is able to acknowledge his acquaintance with Mrs Smith to Anne without a trace of shame or self-consciousness. Nor does benightedness excuse bad behaviour. The narcissism of Anne's family might not be as destructive, but it is nearly as odious. The great sin in this novel – perhaps the only sin – is the failure of negative capability, the refusal to imaginatively inhabit another point of view. This is indeed what Wentworth is guilty of when he condemns Anne for ending their engagement, and then stubbornly holds a grudge for the next eight years. As he later confesses, 'I shut my eyes, and would not understand you, or do you justice' (247).

It is above all this willingness to get beyond the self that makes Anne morally superior. While Anne understands that judgment is circumscribed by personal concerns, she always attempts to override such limits. When she moves from Kellynch to Uppercross, she determines to inhabit her new neighbourhood mentally and emotionally as well as physically: 'She acknowledged it to be very fitting, that every little social commonwealth should dictate its own matters of discourse; and hoped, ere long, to become a not unworthy member of the one she was now transplanted into. – With the prospect of spending at least two months at Uppercross, it was highly incumbent on her to clothe her imagination, her memory, and all her ideas in as much of Uppercross as possible' (43). In a culture acutely aware of the signifying properties of clothing, this metaphor of dress would have resonated: our very ability to create a civilized society depends on our willingness and ability to refashion our minds to other points of view. It is through this exercise of cognitive flexibility, the hallmark of sympathy, that the inherently decent characters correct their errors. Once Anne and Wentworth are engaged again, Lady Russell (like Wentworth) must change her mind: 'Anne knew that Lady Russell must be suffering some pain in understanding and relinquishing Mr. Elliot, and be making some struggles to become truly acquainted with, and do justice to Captain Wentworth. This however was what Lady Russell had now to do. She must learn to feel that she had been mistaken with regard to both ... There was nothing less for Lady Russell to do, than to admit that she had been pretty completely wrong, and to take up a new set of opinions and of hopes' (249). Like Anne's 'clothing herself in as much as Uppercross as possible,' Lady Russell must 'take up' new ways of seeing: the metaphor here refers to company (a new set) rather than attire, but its implications are the same: society (as opposed to Society) depends on such efforts. Characters like Wentworth and Lady Russell must be shocked into such recognition. But Anne's determination to transform her cognitive life in recognition of her environment is consistent and self-motivated, extending to all her dealings with others. Anne is sympathetic in all senses of the word.

Rights and Needs

I have so far suggested that *Persuasion* exposes the inadequacy of the conduct-book solution to conflicts over the marriage choice through a plot and subplot that fail to be reconciled at the conclusion of the novel. Yet despite this ostensible lack of resolution, *Persuasion* takes the side of children and of feeling in the clash of values it portrays, in accord with a Humean vision of society that posits sympathy as the necessary foundation of sociality. In fact, the opposition between feeling and judgment is a false one, for there is no such thing as a judgment that is not influenced by desire. I would like to suggest that this choice in values constitutes a further criticism of conduct literature, a criticism not only of the advice it has to offer, but also of its very method of positing fairness. The mutual power of veto in the marriage choice addresses the rights rather than the needs of children and parents. By exposing the shortcomings of conduct literature, Austen implicitly criticizes the concept of rights and the body of classical liberal theory from which it derives.

Political theorists writing in our own day have contended that liberalism, with its emphasis on rights, fails to acknowledge or compensate for both gendered inequities and personal needs. *Persuasion* uncannily anticipates these insights. However, this involves the text in a paradox. By associating consensual married love with women's independence, *Persuasion* implies a positive reading of liberalism as a progressive force for women. Yet by teasing out the shortcomings of a discourse of rights for women, it also encodes a critique of liberal theory. In this sense, *Persuasion* replicates the conflicts among feminist scholars today, who question whether liberalism's emphasis on autonomy and rights is a powerful tool against women's oppression, or if liberal theory is irremediably masculinist.[38]

Discussions of liberal theory in our own time cite rights and needs as two organizing categories. Rights grant an individual freedom from unfair restrictions and incursions on the part of the state and of other individuals, while needs address a person's emotional and physical requisites for the reproduction of daily life. Rights and needs are viewed in oppositional terms, for which the overarching antithesis is male/female; this opposition therefore aligns with other gendered oppositions such as public/private and state/family. These divisions are the foundation of women's exclusion by Locke and other liberal theorists from the legal and social entitlements that the social contract is supposed to guarantee.

Although critiques of liberal theory are diverse in scope and focus, they share a fundamental premise: rights derive from an abstract, formal conception of equality, which assumes a homogeneous (white, male, unimpoverished, physically and mentally unimpaired) subject.[39] Since we do not all start from the same place and with the same advantages, a truly humane system of justice must recognize and allow for difference – in other words, it must acknowledge that in order to guarantee rights, we also have to recognize needs.[40] Thus, critics of liberalism often point out the ways in which binary, often gendered, oppositions perpetuate the very injustices that our rights allegedly obviate. These inequities, however, were formerly obscured by an ostensibly neutral strain of liberalism that appeared to apply the notion of rights to all. This is why feminists in earlier times invoked liberalism in general, as well as an ideal of consensual, married love that implied a woman's autonomous, 'contractual' subjectivity, in support of arguments for women's rights. But, as discussed above, scholars of a later age have revealed that the ostensible neutrality of liberal theory is in reality the ground of its masculinist bias, because the neutral subject of liberalism is always conceptualized as male.

The gendered divisions within liberal theory account for the failure of conduct literature to provide a satisfactory formula for resolving conflicts over the marriage choice. Conduct literature draws on the tradition of rights by setting forth entitlements and restrictions ('advice ... ought to be relied upon'; 'there your submission must stop'; 'a negative voice in the case is as much the child's right as the Parents'). The ethics of marriage, and the contractual subjectivity this implies, authorizes such advice: if a woman marries for love, she has the right to choose her husband, or, at the very least, the right to refuse her parents' choice. As I have been contending, this perception informs the representation of love and marriage in the novel as a genre. But a discourse of rights cannot possibly provide a fair solution to conflicts over the marriage choice: the denial of a child's wishes and the suppression of love (the result of a parent's veto) and the refusal of an unwanted match (the result of a child's veto) are not equivalent in emotional terms, although they might appear to be so within the abstract logic of rights. *Persuasion* dwells lingeringly on the pain and damage inflicted by Lady Russell's persuasion, which is qualitatively different from the mild disappointment she herself feels when Anne refuses Charles Musgrove. This disparity is not recognized by the supposed equity of conduct literature.

In asserting a woman's right to refuse an unwanted match, conduct literature also fails to acknowledge how women's personalities are formed within prevailing liberal ideals, how women 'are interpellated as gender,' as Wendy Brown observes.[41] Brown contends that liberalism's oppositions determine not only role but personality: the masculine liberal subject is 'autonomous' and 'unencumbered,' whereas liberalism's women are 'socially constructed to be encumbered by family reponsibilities, and naturally dependent on men.'[42] Rights therefore apply to a subject for whom connection with others is unnecessary and meaningless when he is within the public sphere (where the public aspect of marriage is negotiated), whereas needs correspond to a subjectivity embedded in the recognition of our relationships to one another. This certainly held true for women of the eighteenth and nineteenth centuries: the social and psychological pressures to comply with a father's will were even more forceful than the economic ones, and certainly more important in considering the ethics of conduct. Yet, in advising a daughter of her rights, conduct literature fails to acknowledge the superior strength of fathers, not only materially, but even more important, by psychologically. Novelists, despite their awareness of the way in which married love theoretically grants women autonomy and rights, recognized this micro-politics of power and often thematized the ways in which subordination infiltrates subjectivity – this is the basis of Anne's repudiation of her 'rebellion.' But if *Persuasion*'s happy ending averts the potentially disastrous consequences of viewing the marriage choice in terms of rights, this is something Richardson had done already in *Clarissa*, which clearly shows the failure of rights to grant women any true power or autonomy. One of the many frustrations in this novel of many frustrations is Clarissa's refusal to go to her grandfather's farm, which would provide economic independence and hence sanctuary from the persecutions of both Lovelace and her father. Richardson must punish Clarissa for her flight with Lovelace, a true affront to patriarchal power. But Richardson's misogyny aside, such a course of action is out of the question, given Clarissa's sense of duty and propriety. From one standpoint, Clarissa's refusal to save herself indicates her superior morality (apart from the single error in judgment she makes in fleeing; indeed, her weakness for Lovelace is her tragic flaw). If Anne is 'almost too good' for Austen, Clarissa is too good for earth itself. But Clarissa's passivity also shows that her right to oppose her father by refusing an unwanted marriage with the odious Solmes is ultimately chimerical. Rights have no purchase within her system of values, values applauded within the context of the novel, even if (reading against the grain) they are distasteful to readers today.[43] Nor does the discourse of rights make much sense within the context of conduct books themselves. How can these texts advocate submission in every aspect of a woman's life, and then require some backbone when it comes to the marriage choice? The conduct-book formula of vetoes thus fails to provide a trustworthy method for resolving differences over the marriage choice. Not only can it lead to stalemate, it also fails to recognize the psychology of women's subordination, a psychology which these texts themselves obsessively inculcate.

If Austen chooses passion over reason in the dilemma between feelings and duty in order to advocate a particular vision of the good society, this vision conversely provides the answer to the initial dilemma. The key to resolving disagreements about the marriage choice in the most ethical way inheres in recognizing not rights, but needs, which sympathy addresses – in thinking not of what an individual is owed by the larger society, but imagining 'entitlement' in affective and relational terms. A theory of rights involves a consideration of what the individual is due according to her own merits, or what he is owed by the larger society. A discourse of rights cannot guarantee that a daughter's wishes will be respected because it is embedded in a legal, socioeconomic, and psychological culture that denies women such entitlements. But an ethic of sympathy imagines entitlement in affective and relational terms. Rights ask that people act according to what is abstractly correct; sympathy demands that they imagine the emotional consequences of their actions for themselves as well as for others, and that they alter their ways of seeing things when morally necessary. When Lady Russell disapproves of Wentworth the first time around, her thinking accords with the logic of rights: 'Anne Elliot, with all her claims of birth, beauty, and mind, to throw herself away at nineteen ... Anne Elliot, so young; known to so few, to be snatched off by a stranger without alliance or fortune; or rather sunk by him into a state of most wearing, anxious, youth-killing dependance! It must not be' (26–7). Motivated by 'pardonable pride,' Lady Russell decides for Anne according to the abstract criteria of wealth and status, thinking primarily of what is due to Anne. Although Lady Russell has Anne's best interests at heart, she is 'unsympathetic' to her wishes, and cannot, does not wish to view the marriage differently by acknowledging Anne's emotional needs. However, by forcing herself to overcome her aversion when Anne has a second chance for happiness, and, in the end, and 'to take up a new set of opinions and hopes,' Lady Russell is able both to see things from Anne's point of view and to prioritize feelings – and hence needs – above entitlement: 'if her second object was to be sensible and well-judging,' qualities which invoke the logic of rights, 'her first was to see Anne happy' (249).

Ungendering Ethics

To characterize Austen's criticism of liberal ideals in slightly different terms, *Persuasion* shows not only that a discourse of rights fails to address women's needs, but that the very divide between rights and needs is an artificial and untenable one to begin with, as many theorists today also aver.[44] For in the conflict between rights and needs, it is often difficult to tell which is which. What is Anne's right to veto Lady Russell's choice of a spouse but a way to protect her personal desires (her needs)? And what is Lady Russell's right to veto Anne's choice but an assertion of her desire (her need) to see Anne well-married? The impossibility of drawing a distinct line between rights and needs is similar to *Persuasion*'s rejection of a binary distinction between passion and reason. As we have seen, Lady Russell's 'reasonable' criteria for a wise marriage choice is motivated by feeling, and Anne's rejection of Wentworth is grounded in her love.

In rejecting categorization *Persuasion* ultimately rejects the essentialized view of gender that organizes it. This ungendering of concepts such as 'needs' and 'feelings' was crucial to legitimating a vision of a sympathetic society, for despite the connection between feeling and morality asserted by Hume and other philosophers of sentiment, the traditional characterization of emotion as feminine persisted. Austen's contemporary Thomas Gisborne asserts a common view when he invokes emotion to distinguish the 'character of the female mind' from 'that of the other sex': 'Were we called upon to produce examples of the most amiable tendencies and affections implanted in human nature, of modesty, of delicacy, *of sympathising sensibility, of prompt and active benevolence, of warmth and tenderness of attachment*; whither should we at once turn our eyes? To the sister, to the daughter, to the wife. These endowments form the glory of the female sex' [emphasis added].[45] Because of this feminization of ethical qualities, feeling, including sympathy, occupied a vexed position for men; it was thought to inspire virtue, but always with the danger of effeminacy. Men of feeling risked not being 'man enough.'[46] Austen's vision of a moral society, as well as Hume's, was open to being characterized as essentially feminine and therefore both untenable and inconsequential.

Austen's most forceful and direct resistance to the gendering of ethics, both individual and collective, inheres in her characterization of the navy. Because an ethos of sympathy could be easily dismissed in a man's world, Austen calls upon the navy to defend ideological as well as real territory. No one could accuse *Persuasion*'s intrepid and aggressive sailors of being less than manly. Yet, despite their very public role as defenders of England, they possess the 'feminine' 'private' capacity for sympathy that distinguishes Anne's character. They consistently make the effort to travel beyond the horizons of their own concerns, an epistemological flexibility emblematized by their constant mobility. They are all men of feeling, whose sympathy inspires them to care for others, even when this means extending the usual borders of social intercourse. Wentworth visits the poorer Harvilles in the same spirit as Anne visits her unfortunate friend Miss Smith. They are indeed the moral antithesis of Anne's solipsistic family, who are (with the exception of Anne) incapable of forming true relationships. Hume's list of qualities that constitute 'the good' (generosity, humanity, compassion, gratitude, friendship, fidelity, zeal, disinterestedness, liberality) might well have been written as a catalogue of their virtues.[47] Indeed, their difference in character from the selfish company Anne is forced to keep is expressed as a difference in modes of social interaction, which is also a largely feminine domain: Anne observes that Wentworth's naval friends possess 'a degree of hospitality so uncommon, so unlike the usual style of give-and-take invitations, and dinners of formality and display' (98). As Monica Cohen points out, *Persuasion* equates sailors and homemakers throughout, from Harville's loving attention to detail in his home to Wentworth's preoccupation with shipboard amenities.[48] The last line of the novel describes the naval officers as 'belonging to that profession which is, if possible, more distinguished in its *domestic* virtues than in its national importance' (252) [emphasis added]. The play on the word 'domestic' – as indicating both country and home – locates sympathy as the emotional and ethical territory of men as well as women. This characterization renders it impossible to relegate feeling and the institutions it authorizes to the private, domestic, feminine sphere.

The navy's crucial identity in *Persuasion* is in fact that of a social group which abides by proper ethical values, a self-selected society of men who have the 'right stuff.' We know of the importance of their military exploits, but these take place extradiegetically; what we see in the novel is that their worth, which derives from 'feminine' values, informs their actions. In a familiar, literary pairing, their capability is inextricable from good character; these men possess both 'worth and warmth,' as Louisa observes (99). The Dick Musgroves, deficient in both, inevitably fall by the wayside; for those like Wentworth, who become rich from plundering the enemy, hard-won success is simply virtue rewarded. However, these men are not, as has been argued, a rising class, nor a group of 'new men' in any socio-economic sense of the term, nor even a distinct social group with any permanence.[49] The navy epitomizes the just Humean society, in which private sentiments generate public benefits. To be sure, it is a shift for Austen to locate moral value in a military institution. As Alistair Duckworth observes, *Persuasion* is the only one of Austen's novels in which ethics and responsibility are dissociated from county property and leadership.[50] But this 'abandonment of the estate' is only temporary; the wars will end and the men of the navy will return. Captain Harville points to this inevitable future for other naval officers. And it is the probability of this re-entry into civilian life that holds the greatest hope for a better society. For if *Persuasion* is about renewal, a second spring for Anne Elliott, it is also about the possibility of moral regeneration for England's leadership. In this sense, it is more optimistic than Austen's earlier novels, where, despite the Pemberlys and the Donwells, England is far from uniformly ideal. If these landed estates represent centres of value, places where morality and justice organize the social order, their influence and power are limited. Opposed to the Mr Darcys and the Mr Knightleys are a corps of irresponsible and selfish aristocrats such as Lady Catherine de Bourgh and Sir John Dashwood, the spiritual kin of *Persuasion*'s Sir Walter. Pemberly might be a haven, but it is also a retreat. *Persuasion*, by contrast, offers the possibility of pervasive reform rather than utopian withdrawal. Through the rise of a true meritocracy, which is able to accrue sufficient social and economic status to infiltrate already existing social structures, England will become a great society, ethically as well as politically. The navy will facilitate such change. Its officers are already beginning to be accepted by the social elite of Bath, and they are certainly wealthy enough to purchase land. If Admiral Croft will not become the owner of Kellynch, he, or men like him, will probably own other estates. The navy therefore provides not only a model of just government and ethical relationships, but the pragmatic possibility of influence as well. Since it is only a possibility – a hope for reform – its fulfilment lies in the future. But this gesture beyond the boundaries of the text does not negate its significance; after all, *Persuasion* is a novel in which endings are characteristically beginnings. Austen leaves this chapter to be written by historians rather than novelists.

4

Feminism and Contract Theory in
He Knew He Was Right

Anthony Trollope wrote *He Knew He Was Right* from November 1867 to June 1868, years during which a bill to grant property rights to married women under common law was being fiercely debated in both Parliament and the press. The first Married Women's Property Act was passed in 1870. As an editor and writer for popular periodicals, as well as a politician manqué who stood for Parliament in November 1868, Trollope was certain to have been familiar with arguments both for and against this bill. *He Knew He Was Right*, an exploration of male authority and women's rights within marriage – core issues in arguments over married women's property – is Trollope's timely contribution to the debate about this and other issues concerning women's rights. Yet *He Knew He Was Right* reveals not only Trollope's personal views, more importantly, it illustrates how an ideal of married love intersected with the cultural discourse of contract, a fundamental mainstay of Victorian feminism. By articulating his belief in the necessity and dignity of married love, Trollope expressed opinions in accord with feminist activists of his day, who appealed to contract to argue for women's rights.

In the eighteenth century, the conceptualization of marriage as a version of the social contract had evoked the possibility of women's rights and autonomy, while defining love in appropriate ways had undermined the subversive potential that marriage accorded women as freely contracting agents. By the mid-nineteenth century, however, this ideological safeguard was becoming obsolete, as the fine distinctions between different modes of feeling that had guaranteed both proper women and proper marriages began to erode. The difference between representations of love in the eighteenth-century novel and the Victorian novel evinces this revision of earlier typologies of love. Love came to be seen less as an expression of rational choice and internalized social dictate and more as a personal, idiosyncratic, and unpredictable force, much as we view it in Anglo-American society today. This change enhanced the suggestion of autonomy for women that had been implicit from the start in a contractual ideal of love and marriage, causing married love to become even more volatile as an ideological element in Trollope's day than it had been in the previous century, and rendering the feminist appeal to the sanctity of marriage an especially effective rhetorical strategy. William Thackeray's *The Newcomes* shows with particular clarity the transformation in ideals of love from earlier times, while Trollope's *The Way We Live Now* underscores the relationship between these changing ideals and the implication of increasing autonomy and entitlement for women.

The Way We Ought to Live Now

In William Thackeray's *The Newcomes* (1853), the narrator Pendennis voices a bitter, ironical 'diatribe,' as he calls it, against the marriage of interest:

> This ceremony amongst us is so stale, and common that, to be sure, there is no need to describe its rites, and as women sell themselves for what you call an establishment every day, to the applause of themselves, their parents, and the world, why on earth should a man ape at originality, and pretend to pity them? Never mind about the lies at the altar, the blasphemy against the godlike name of love, the sordid surrender, the smiling dishonor. What the deuce does a *marriage de convenance* mean but all this, and are not such sober Hymneal torches more satisfactory often than the most brilliant love-matches that ever flamed and burnt out? Of course. Let us not weep when everyone else is laughing.[1]

Criticism of the loveless marriage had been a trope of the novel from its canonical origins with Richardson and Fielding. Novels of the eighteenth century frequently illustrated the conduct-book warnings against the marriage of interest: it is immoral and unchristian, a profanation of holy matrimony, a socially condoned form of prostitution, and perjury before God. In the passage cited above, Thackeray, speaking through his narrator Pen, condemns the loveless marriage on similar grounds.

But further on in the chapter, we see that Pen-Thackeray differs from his predecessors of the previous century on two essential points. First, he urges that loveless marriages ought to be avoided at all costs, even if this entails filial disobedience. He therefore thinks that his friend Jack Belsize should do everything possible to rescue his lover Clara from the marriage of convenience into which her parents are forcing her to enter. Apostrophizing Jack in his imagination, Pen urges him to 'tear her out of yon carriage, from the side of yonder livid, feathered, painted, bony dowager [her mother]! Place her behind you on the black charger; cut down the policeman, and away with you!' Pen is being ironic, for he cannot really expect his friend to act in this histrionic fashion. But the very fact that such behaviour would be inappropriate, even ludicrous, in his day and age – the archaic language of the passage highlights the anachronistic nature of such gallantry – points to the shortcomings of Pen's own society. In an unheroic world, heroic action becomes merely melodramatic.

Second, companionate love, which comprises friendship and esteem, and which was openly endorsed as a superior category to passion by Richardson and his contemporaries, is viewed by Pen as a sad, second-best alternative to the unreflective immediacy of 'true love.' Although for Thackeray, passion is best when it is grounded in recognition of the worth of another, even unreflecting romance is better than lukewarm regard, for its immediacy ensures that it is genuine. Although Ethel Newcome so greatly esteems her cousin Lord Kew 'that the sum of regard which she could bestow upon him might surely be said to amount to love,' Pen concludes that there is another sort of love that is 'ten thousand times more precious' (220).

How do we account for Thackeray's forceful, almost panicked insistence on married love; for his disregard of established authority, figured as both parents and the police; and for his forceful valorization of passion, which the majority of authors through Jane Austen's time had been so anxious to qualify or moderate? Austen's own work both epitomizes and explains the shift in values that registers so stridently in Thackeray's novel. In *Sense and Sensibility*, Austen follows Richardson in advocating warm friendship, that is, companionate love, as a motive for marriage, and in carefully distinguishing between good and bad forms of desire. But by the time she writes *Persuasion*, she has shifted ideological ground. Although her heroine Anne loves wisely, Austen's emphasis is not on distinguishing between kinds of love, but rather on asserting the ethical validity of passion as opposed to interest. Strong and immediate feeling is not only a better guide than prudence in the individual's choice of a spouse, more importantly, it is the best guarantor of an ethical society. The excesses of passion are shown to be less dangerous than the errors of prudence, which can easily devolve into a destructive solipsism that threatens the fundamental bonds of sociality.

Expressing an insight that became a truism of the age, the nineteenth-century novel associates this solipsism with materialism, showing that what Carlyle calls the 'Gospel of Mammonism' leads inevitably to the commodification of human relationships. Carlyle warns in *Past and Present*, 'We have profoundly forgotten everywhere that *Cash-payment* is not the sole relation of human beings.'[2] Marx later similarly observes throughout *Capital* that capitalism commodifies social interaction, transforming relationships between people into relationships between things.[3] To put this in Marxist terminology, the logic of capitalism relies on exhange-value rather than use-value; people, practices, and things are valuable only for the money they can accumulate, or for the economic value produced by their labour, rather than for any intrinsic worth; practices and things are of value only for the price they bring. Moreover, the momentum of capitalism is unstoppable as it permeates the various layers of social life.[4]

Because of the status of marriage as a Christian sacrament, as well as its identification with domestic ideology and therefore with the literal and ideational space where business does not take place, the novel conventionally figures marriage as the moral opposite of the marketplace. The marriage of interest therefore violates the true and essential character of marriage itself, substituting exchange-value – the most common transaction in the marriage market trades wealth for status – for use-value, love of the inherent and untranslatable worth of another.[5] The right kind of marriage, however, one grounded in love, functions as the antidote to the depersonalization of capitalism – it is one connection that valiantly defies the logic of commodification, the impulse to see everything for the price it brings. Even a novel such as *Little Dorrit*, in which marriage is not the symbolic centre, deploys the conventional figuration of marriage as a trope for purity and disinterestedness, the violation of which underscores the opposition between true and false forms of value. Arthur Clenham's marriage to Little Dorrit is founded in these characters' mutual recognition of each other's worth, a value that cannot be corrupted by the world in which their marriage provides a sanctuary for both themselves and others.[6] Conversely, Fanny's marriage to Edmund Sparkler, which is motivated by her desire to outdo Mrs Merdle, transfers the values of capitalist competition to the realm of personal relationships; Fanny's ambition, dishonesty, and disregard for others parallels the goals and tactics of Merdle himself.

Trollope's novel *The Way We Live Now* (1869) reveals the relationship between the Victorian novel's critique of capitalism and its valorization of passion. Trollope claims to have written this novel as a criticism of his society's 'dishonesty': 'dishonesty magnificent in its proportions, and climbing into high places, has become at the same time so rampant and so splendid that there seems to be reason for fearing that men and women will be taught to feel that dishonesty, if it can become splendid, will cease to be abominable ... Instigated, I say, by some such reflections as these, I sat down ... to write *The Way We Live Now.*'[7] The narrative itself reveals that this dishonesty consists primarily in the hegemony of exchange-value rather than use-value as the measure of worth, and hence, the increasingly abstract and unreal nature of value itself as embodied by credit, which the novel represents as the proliferation of signs without referents. The company that Melmotte sponsors claims to be building a railroad, but this is a pure fiction, as Melmotte and his dishonest cohorts know: '[t]he object of Fisker, Montague, and Montague was not to make a railway to Vera Cruz, but to float a company,' and the directors are 'indifferent whether the railway should ever be constructed or not ... fortunes were to be made out of the concern before a spadeful of earth had been moved.'[8] When Melmotte fails to pay for the house he has purchased from the Longestaffe family (the error that will lead to his downfall), he appeases Mr Longestaffe with empty words of reassurance, words whose value lies in Melmotte's reputation – his credit – as a great man of business. The narrator, in a moment of sardonic moral repulsion, sums up this sign of the times: 'As for many years past we have exchanged paper instead of actual money for our commodities, so now it seemed that, under the new Melmotte regime, an exchange of words was to suffice' (1:423).

Melmotte's attempt to force his daughter Marie into an advantageous marriage mirrors his shady (both nefarious and insubstantial) commercial dealings. Here as in the business world, the real exchange proposed for Marie and her intended has nothing to do with the purported nature of the transaction, for the marriage Melmotte plans involves not a mutual sharing of hearts and bodies but the usual course of marriage à la mode: 'Rank squanders money; trade makes it; – and then trade purchases rank by re-gilding its splendour' (2:59). This characterization of the interested marriage is totally conventional;

what makes the thematization of marriage distinctive in this novel is that it reveals the relationship between the status of married love as a trope for legitimate value and the revision of eighteenth-century categories of love. The subplot concerning the love triangle between Hetta Carbury, her cousin Roger Carbury, and Paul Montague foregrounds an association that for the most part remains tacit, although central, in the genre.

In *The Way We Live Now*, as in Thackeray's *The Newcomes*, companionate love is shown to be an unacceptable alternative to passion. Hetta feels affectionate friendship and respect for Roger, who is deeply in love with her. Indeed, so strong are her feelings of gratitude and esteem that she is tempted to accept him, and almost does so one of the many times he proposes. The narrator comments, '[h]ad he seized her in his arms and kissed her then, I think she would have yielded. She did all but love him' (1:184). Roger's failure to embrace his beloved signals not a lack of his own passion, which is abundant, rather, it is a displacement of Hetta's inability to reciprocate, indicated by the phrase 'all but love.' It is this lack that Paul supplies, and she feels for him the romantic passion that she cannot feel for Roger. As she later tells her lover, 'she did not think that she could ever have loved anybody but him ... as to Roger ... no; it was not the same thing' (149).

Hetta's story departs from conventional representations of love in the eighteenth-century novel not only in its dismissal of companionate love but in its characterization of Hetta's lover as well. For despite Hetta's own impeccable character and moral judgment, she loves the less worthy of her suitors, a character who would be an unacceptable husband for most eighteenth-century heroines.[9] Paul has many moral failings. Above all, he is weak and susceptible to temptation, as we see most markedly in his continued relationship with a woman to whom he was formerly engaged, and whom he still finds attractive. Roger, on the contrary, is faultless, and yet 'though his [Paul's] rival were an angel, he could have no shadow of a claim upon her, – seeing that he had failed to win her heart' (2:150). Hetta's love is purely romantic, in the 'Hollywood' sense of the word we use today. It is not a passionate response to the inherent worth or decency of another person – the eighteenth-century paradigm – but rather pure emotional responsiveness that cannot be broken down into its logical determinants. Such an irrational basis for feeling is crucial because it separates Hetta's love from the least possible taint of calculation, thereby diametrically opposing it to the logic of exchange-value. There is no self-interest in

Hetta's choice, not even a thought for her emotional (rather than financial) security; Hetta's love is totally careless of any benefit to herself.

Hetta's conflict with her mother shows why, in terms of thematics of the novel, Hetta's feeling must be essentialized in this way. Lady Carbury urgently wants Hetta to accept Roger's offer, for this marriage would guarantee her daughter's financial future. It would also secure Roger's help for the rest of the family, especially Hetta's reprobate brother, who is draining the family's financial and emotional resources. Lady Carbury's matrimonial ambitions for Hetta are grounded in her character and view of the world. Her life has been and continues to be based on the logic of commodification, through her eager participation in markets of different kinds. Her marriage, which was motivated by the material considerations of the marriage market, was unhappy, yet that did not inspire her to change her attitude or way of doing things. As a widow, hoping to succeed in the literary world, she writes mediocre books that she attempts to sell by virtue of her social connections. The narrator points out repeatedly that Lady Carbury hopes to achieve success 'not by producing good books, but by inducing certain people to say that her books were good' (1:17). Trading on her charms as an attractive woman to gain a literary renown and financial remuneration, Lady Carbury, like Melmotte, builds on the illusion of value, a chimerical foundation that will ultimately disintegrate. But the difference that gender makes is that Lady Carbury's wiles border on prostitution, which is precisely the problem with the loveless marriage made for wealth or status – 'women sell themselves for what you call an establishment every day,' as Thackeray's Pen observes. In her view, there is nothing wrong with selling yourself; that is how the world works. It is therefore telling that Lady Carbury is bothered even more by Hetta's motives in refusing Roger than by the material consequences of that refusal: 'But that which pained her most was the unrealistic, romantic view of life which pervaded all Hetta's thoughts. How was any girl to live in this world who could not be taught the folly of such idle dreams?' (2:385). This overt antipathy to Hetta's motives rather than merely to the object of her affection makes clear what had always been true of struggles between parents and children over the marriage choice: such disagreements are not merely about differing personal predilections, more importantly, they are about fundamentally different definitions of value.

Differences between parents and children over the marriage choice are also about freedom and entitlement for women. I have suggested in earlier chapters that married love implied an ideal of liberal, contractual subjectivity that theoretically accorded women the rights and liberties that were denied to them by law and custom. When, in the course of the eighteenth century, marriage for love became widely accepted, marriage was newly conceptualized as a relationship entered into voluntarily for the happiness and benefit of the lovers, rather than as a strategic alliance between families. Marriage was therefore a contract like all the other contracts that held society together. According to political theories that were contemporaneous with the emergence of this new ethic of marriage, legitimate contracts implied certain protections and freedoms for both parties. Locke, as we have seen, had argued that valid contracts do not violate a base line of rights and liberties: people cannot contract their liberty away altogether; a self-destructive contract is not valid; and if either of the parties to a contract violates its terms, their agreement is dissoluble. With these parameters of contract subtending her argument, Wollstonecraft invoked an ideal of married love in support of women's rights, a strategy that would be widely deployed by feminist activists in the following century. *The Way We Live Now*, as well as many other novels, expresses this logic by associating a woman's right to choose her spouse with her independent selfhood. Indeed, it is only through Marie Melmotte's desire to marry the man she loves, and her opposition to her father on this issue, that she finds her sense of her own personhood, 'an identity of her own in the disposition of which she herself should have a voice' (1:38). We will see this connection even more pointedly in *He Knew He Was Right*, a novel in which the relationship between married love and feminism becomes the explicit focus.

I discuss *The Way We Live Now* because it shows that the erasure of distinction between different forms of passion that we find in the Victorian novel, as well as the genre's decidedly inferior valuation of friendship in contradistinction to love, emphasizes the contractual implications of married love for women. By shifting the balance in the marriage choice towards feeling and away from prudence – even the internalized prudence that expresses itself as passion ('sentimental love') – nineteenth-century definitions of love intensified the argument for women's freedom implicit in a liberal, contractual ideal of marriage. *Sir Charles Grandison* and other eighteenth-century novels demonstrate that distinctions between kinds of love theoretically preserved the hierarchical structure of middle- and upper-class society by ensuring that women's passion always directed itself towards partners from the right socio-economic circles. Although in this light the typology of love might appear to be concerned primarily with class, it had just as much to do with gender: men's domination of women was always crucial to securing the proper, legitimate transmission of property. Women who chose correctly, who were guided by 'rational' motives to make socially and economically acceptable marriages, even when such motives coincided with and were masked by their own 'passion,' still behaved in accordance with men's desire and authority. But when passion was unmoored from its rational determinants, women's choices became more autonomous and potentially more dangerous. Once desire itself was no longer constituted by patriarchal objectives, women were less subject to the control of men. Hetta's passion is significant not only because it signals her own freedom, which is authorized by an ethic of married love (as is conventional in the novel), but, just as importantly, because her inappropriate choice represents a total rejection and undermining of her mother's patriarchal objectives to maintain the honour of the family by assuring a secure future for its heir. If nineteenth-century reworkings of earlier typologies of love undergirded a moral vision of society that opposed the dehumanizing forces of commerce and industry, like many ideological 'solutions' to social 'problems,' this new way of thinking had consequences beyond the scope of its original purview: it emphasized the freedoms of the contractual subject that an ideal of married love had already, problematically, invoked.

Contract Theory and the Reform of Marriage Law

The disruptive implications of married love were politically significant in this period because the institution of marriage was the focus of much nineteenth-century feminism. Although writers and activists addressed a wide range of issues for women, including education, employment, and suffrage, the amendment of marriage law was fundamental to all their concerns. It was an urgent target for reform, since women married to abusive husbands had almost no means to protect themselves. Common law, the primary system of laws that governed in default of other judicial arrangements, consigned a woman completely to her husband's power. A married woman had no separate legal identity and was compelled to cede all property, including wages, to her husband.[10] Poorer women could not afford to apply to the divorce courts for even the limited relief that had been made available by the Divorce Act of 1857. And in any case, women rarely petitioned for divorce successfully.[11] Most women trapped in abusive marriages therefore faced the choice of putting up with their situation or becoming destitute. Upper- and middle-class women might have the means to separate from abusive or profligate husbands if separate property had been settled on them under the legal system of equity – if the terms of a woman's settlement specified no restrictions on her ownership (although the property per se was always nominally under the guardianship of trustees), she could use her property free from common law liabilities. But settlements that granted a woman this degree of independence were extremely rare, and more often than not a woman had no access, or very limited access, to her fortune. As Susan Staves has demonstrated, the purpose of separate property was to keep estates intact for posterity by protecting them from profligate husbands, rather than to grant women property or independence; as a result, a body of legal practices developed that prevented women's access to their separate property.[12] Yet however inadequate settlements within the courts of equity might have been as a means of protection for affluent women, the law hit poor and working women the hardest. Indeed, it was Parliament's growing recognition of the unfairness of the discrepancy between common law and equity, rather than their support of women's rights, that motivated many legislators to support reform of marriage law.[13]

In addition to promising to ameliorate conditions for many women, the reform of marriage law held immense theoretical purchase in the struggle for a broad spectrum of women's rights, since legal recognition of the 'personhood' of women, including wives, was fundamental to feminist activism of any kind. Reform of marriage law promised to recognize the autonomous contractual selfhood of women, which was implied by the contractual nature of marriage itself. Activists therefore strategically alluded to liberal principles to argue that English common law violated the 'law' of contract. Even when they did not refer explicitly to contract theory per se, they relied on its assumptions in defining entitlement and personhood. For instance, in *Two Treatises of Government*, Locke had averred that all but lunatics, idiots, and children were guaranteed the God-given rights inherent in the State of Nature, rights that were also protected by the social compact and all other legitimate contracts. In arguing that a woman's ability to think and act for herself entitled her to certain liberties and protections, not least of which was the recognition of her separate legal and economic identity even after marriage, feminists relied on this Lockean definition of legal and civic competence. When Frances Power Cobbe objected that the law treated women like 'lunaticks, idiots, and minors' rather than competent adults, she may or may not have been conscious of her citation of Locke,[14] but Locke's criteria for legal identity and protection were nonetheless at the heart of Cobbe's arguments for extending women's rights.

Because ideals of love and marriage were historically and theoretically interwoven with theories of contract, endorsing married love also meant confronting the implication of women's autonomy and rights. We have seen that Richardson attempted to dissociate the threat of women's independence from married love by his treatment of Charlotte Grandison, while Austen accepted the connection between the marriage for love and women's autonomy. It was, of course, possible to assert that married love implied wifely dependence rather than liberty, and this position was taken by various members of Parliament who opposed laws that granted married women separate property from their husbands. One opponent of married women's property acts argued that 'it was a most important thing toward preserving the institution of marriage that the identity of interests between the parties and the control of the husband over the joint property should be maintained as far as possible.'[15] Another feared that 'unless you put the whole property of a married couple in the hands of the husband ... there is no chance of concord and harmony in the marriage state.'[16] Others contended that such laws were needed only in exceptional cases. Since wife abuse was so exceedingly rare, and because the abuse that did occur was almost always limited to the lower classes, there was no need to change the law in order to give women the security of separate property: 'this was exceptional kind of legislation; it was legislating for a certain class to the disregard of the interests of the greater portion of the population.'[17] Another maintained: '[Y]ou have a building raised up by the labour of a great number of years; it existed as a whole – one great and entire edifice, but ... if it [the bill] were passed in its present form, under the pretext of interfering with a few bricks or repairing a few rents, it would pull down the whole structure.'[18] However, because marriage had already been positioned within a Lockean discourse of contract, these comments contradicted fundamental, hegemonic beliefs about love and marriage. Voluntarism, including married love, had by this time become inextricably associated with rights and autonomy. Thus when Trollope chose specifically to address the relationship between married love and women's rights in *He Knew He Was Right*, he became, as N. John Hall notes, 'a feminist in spite of himself.'[19] To show what Trollope was up against – the force of the discursive current in his time – I would like first to turn to John Stuart

Mill's *The Subjection of Women* (1869), in which the Victorian feminist discourse of contract finds its fullest articulation.[20]

Marriage, Contract, and Progress in the *The Subjection of Women*

The assumption that a loving marriage is a relationship that both recognizes and authorizes a woman's independent, contractual subjectivity is the organizing principle of *The Subjection of Women*. Mill focuses, however, not on spelling out the relationship between married love, contract theory, and women's rights. Rather, he asserts their interrelatedness by analysing the negative consequences of his society's failure to grant women the freedoms and entitlements that enable them to become good wives, and which, conversely good wives deserve because they are loving companions and partners. This failure not only damages individual marriages, it also negatively affects the institution of marriage itself and the ethical quality of society as a whole.

In accord with feminist, liberal discourse of his day, Mill points out the discrepancy between the marriage contract and other contracts. While the law recognizes marriage as a legal compact, in practice, marriage belies the basic principles of contractual relationships:

> The most frequent case of voluntary association, next to marriage, is partnership in business: and it is not found or thought necessary to enact that in every partnership, one partner shall have entire control over the concern, and the others shall be bound to obey his orders. No one would enter into partnership on terms which would subject him to the responsibilities of a principal, with only the powers and privileges of a clerk or agent. If the law dealt with other contracts as it does with marriage, it would ordain that one partner should administer the common business as if it was his private concern; that the others should have only delegated powers; and that this one should be designated by some general presumption of law, for example as being the eldest. The law never does this: nor does experience show it to be necessary that any theoretical inequality of power should exist between the partners, or that the partnership should have any other conditions than what they may themselves appoint by their articles of agreement.[21]

Apart from the injustice of this arrangement for individual women, this distortion of the marriage contract undermines the companionate nature of marriage itself. Mill claims that because 'the principle which regulates the existing social relations between the two sexes' is 'the legal subordination of one sex to the other' (125) (i.e., unequal partnership), marriages often lack the openness and mutual confidence that is essential for true companionship: 'It often happens that there is the most complete unity of feeling and community of interests as to all external things, yet the one has as little admission into the internal life of the other as if they were common acquaintance. Even with true affection, authority on the one side and subordination on the other prevent perfect confidence ... [I]t may be confidently said that thorough knowledge of one another hardly ever exists, but between persons who, besides being intimates, are equals' (151–2). This lack of trust is due largely to the fact that a wife is likely to be reluctant, perhaps without even knowing it, to display her true inner self to one who wields so much power over her: 'there is an unconscious tendency to show only the best side, or the side which, though not the best, is that which he most likes to see' and therefore the 'position of looking up to another is extremely unpropitious to complete sincerity and openness' (152). Disparity in education also contributes to the failure of companionship between spouses by creating unbridgeable differences in character and interest, so that 'while women are brought up as they are, a man and a woman will but rarely find in one another real agreement of tastes and wishes as to daily life' (232). Even benevolent wifely influence, so lauded by conservatives, cannot be very useful if women lead such limited existences. In short, if a wife is properly submissive, a man gains not a true friend and partner, but 'an upper servant, a nurse, or a mistress' (233). A few enlightened and fortunate people might manage to achieve 'that union of thoughts and inclinations which is the ideal of married life' (231), but such an ideal, desired by all, is unattainable by most married couples under existing legal and social institutions.

For Mill, contract is the mark of human progress. As Locke and other contractarians had described the beginnings of civil society, men voluntarily left the anarchic freedoms of the State of Nature to enter into a consensual government that would protect their property, liberty, and happiness. The social compact, or the formation of various social compacts of this kind, provides the earliest instances of moral development: 'The ancient republics, being mostly grounded from the first upon some kind of mutual compact, or at any rate formed by an union of persons not very unequal in strength, afforded, in consequence, the first instance of a portion of human relations fenced round, and placed under the dominion of another law than that of force' (133). *The Subjec-*

tion takes these founding moments as its paradigmatic model, characterizing all subsequent human development as a shift in the governing principle of relationships from force to consent. This is true both for individuals and countries. Once societies begin to function according to consensual moral law, people succeed through their talents and abilities, rather than their physical strength. Moreover, the most enlightened forms of government, such as that which exists now (i.e., in Mill's day) in England, allow the individual a degree of liberty bounded only by the need to protect the rights of others. The social compact is therefore part of a familiar Victorian narrative, the march of progress, which, throughout *The Subjection*, implicitly opposes another popular narrative, that of evolution. Sovereignty rooted in mere physical force, be it of bodies or armies, belongs to the world 'red in tooth and claw' – that is, to the story of the survival of the fittest (or strongest), rather than to the narrative of the growth of modern institutions and relationships. The diachronic story of civilization becomes a synchronic paradigm for further advances.[22]

This model of progress argues the necessity of laws that prevent the tyranny of husbands, for 'the law of force,' which has been replaced by 'moral law' (134) in enlightened societies and institutions, still holds sway with respect to marriage. While the widespread belief in marriage for love – a contractual ethic – is certainly evidence of moral development, people are misguided in thinking that 'all is now as it should be in regard to the marriage contract ... [and] that civilization and Christianity have restored to the woman her just rights' (158). Allowing women to choose their spouses is a small step towards making marriage progressive and truly contractual. Marriage is still a barbaric institution precisely because it is a contract that abandons its contractual nature; once entered into, marriage for women is not consensual, but is grounded in force rather than moral law. Men originally dominated women because of their superior physical strength, and English law continues to perpetuate this barbaric condition in the institution of marriage. Marriage is therefore simply 'the primitive state of slavery lasting on ... a monstrous contradiction to all the principles of the modern world' (130, 217). *The Subjection* underscores the benightedness of marriage by repeatedly analogizing existing marriage law with political Absolutism (see, e.g., 135, 137, 163, 215). Just as seventeenth-century contractarians defeated this retrograde vestige of past relations, so nineteenth-century feminist contractarians will work to make marriage conform to the law of contract.

Much is at stake in their success. It is impossible to have a fully just society while injustice persists within the family, and moral progress begins at home. As marriage now constitutes relationships between men and women, 'the family is a school of despotism' (174). This is so for two reasons. First of all, when children are brought up in families that naturally assume the greater entitlements of fathers and sons, they are educated to believe that rights are not inherently guaranteed, and that success depends on birth and strength rather than merit: 'Think what it is to a boy, to grow up to manhood in the belief that without any merit or any exertion of his own, though he may be the most frivolous and empty or the most ignorant and stolid of mankind, by the mere fact of being born a male he is by right the superior of all and every one of an entire half of the human race' (218). If women are inferiors, why not stigmatize other populations? Women's subjection thus teaches lessons contrary to English law and the English constitution, as they have developed through the centuries to expand rights for all others but women. The harmful effects of such training does not end with childhood, but extends throughout our lives; women's oppression demands that we live a contradiction, one that must inevitably impede our development as a nation and as a species: '[S]o long as the right of the strong to power over the weak rules in the very heart of society [i.e., marriage and gender relationships], the attempt to make the equal right of the weak the principle of its outward actions will always be an uphill struggle; for the law of justice, which is also that of Christianity, will never get possession of men's inmost sentiments; they will be working against it, even when bending to it' (220).

In order for marriage to be truly contractual – mutual, reciprocal, and companionate – England must commit to making radical social and legal changes that will grant women freedom, power, and opportunity. If married love epitomizes the moral and progressive character of an ethos of contract, marriage itself must be made to live up to its best and truest nature, both for the happiness and benefit of individuals and for the collective health of society. To believe in married love is to concede to women the basic rights and opportunities which allow that love to flourish.

He Knew He Was Right and the Discourse of Contract

Through its depiction of the dissolution of a marriage, *He Knew He Was Right* explores the boundaries of patriarchal power and a wife's entitlements. The quarrel between the Trevelyans begins when Louis Trevelyan forbids his wife Emily to see Colonel Osborne, an aging but flirtatious family friend. By this prohibition, he casts aspersions on her honour and bullies her in a way considered unacceptable among people of their class. Although Emily resentfully complies with her husband's orders, Trevelyan finds he cannot master his wife's spirit; she refuses to submit gracefully to his command, for to do so would be to countenance the insult. As Trevelyan becomes progressively more obsessed with his right to 'mastery,' the quarrel escalates, and they separate. He eventually goes mad, demanding that his wife confess to her 'infidelity,' which he has come to allege in his disordered condition. In the end, debilitated by mental illness, Trevelyan dies, freeing both himself and his wife from his monomania. Yet this escape is not a victory for Emily in moral terms; it merely saves her from the harsh consequences of having lost the quarrel due to the iniquity of marriage law. As a married woman, she was not only unable to divorce or even legally separate from her husband, she also had no right to custody of their child, despite Trevelyan's obvious inability to care properly for the boy.

At stake in the quarrel is the definition of marriage itself. In Trevelyan's view, Emily's insubordination threatens the very foundation of their union; in her view, his orders undermine their loving partnership. Trollope had of course written about marital unhappiness in earlier novels such as *The Bertrams* (1859) and *Phineas Finn* (1869), while the theme of women's independence had been the focus most famously in *Can You Forgive Her?* (1864–5). But in no other novel did he concentrate so fully on the relationship between a husband's authority and the legal and social institutions that undergird that authority, and on the implications of marriage as a contract.

That this and other of Trollope's novels centre on 'the woman question' is obvious to critics, and many of their discussions of his challenges to patriarchal ideals reflect a wish to claim Trollope for feminism. Yet despite the progressive tendencies in Trollope's novels, particularly those of the 1860s, they still, as Jean Nardin observes, evince so many 'elements that resist feminist readings' that even those most eager for a feminist Trollope must confess that his position with respect to women's roles and entitlements is contradictory. *He Knew He Was Right* clearly exemplifies such self-division. The logic of the exceptional case can be seen to support an antifeminist interpretation of the novel. Read against its subplots, which show happy couples able to resolve whatever problems they encounter, the Trevelyans' sad story is an aberration and does not justify changing a law that works for most. Marriage is 'a risk,' says the narrator, 'but what excitement is there in anything in which there is none?'[23] But the Trevelyans' story is equally appropriable to a feminist point of view. The sympathetic representation of Emily's troubles, including her devastation when Trevelyan kidnaps their child; the narrator's repeated assertion of Trevelyan's incompetence, culminating in his bleak post-mortem assessment, 'the maniac was dead' (928); and the exasperation of trustworthy characters, who can do nothing to control Trevelyan's abuse of his family, all suggest that society does not do enough to protect women who encounter exceptional circumstances. Moreover, that Trevelyan subjects Emily to what we would now call 'mental cruelty' argues for a complex and subtle definition of abuse, one that exceeds even the feminists' demands for the legal redress of tyranny.

The status of sexual difference in *He Knew He Was Right* also reveals Trollope's inconsistency. Sexual difference was traditionally the ground for denying women both equality and access to the public sphere. By claiming that men and women were completely different – what Thomas Laqueur calls a 'two-sex' model of conceptualizing differences between men and women – opponents of women's rights argued that women necessarily belonged entirely in the domestic sphere, where they complemented a man's public role. They had no need for or right to a man's civic prerogatives or public opportunities. Thus, when the American minister, an unpleasant and abrasive character with 'advanced' views, endorses Mill's ideal of 'perfect equality between the sexes,' another more trustworthy character replies, 'Can he [Mill] manage that men shall have half the babies?' (521). This quip refutes equal opportunity for men and women. Yet nature and motherhood also argue the feminist position in this novel, since the law is portrayed as deficient in allowing Trevelyan custody of his son. As one character says, 'He can't suckle 'em: can he?' (555).[24] And even though Trollope had opposed women's education and employment in his 'Higher Education For Women,' arguing the conservative position that unmarried women were exceptional cases and that society ought not to change to accommodate them, the novel's sympathetic portrayal of the bleak lives of single women, many of whom lack sufficient incomes and outlets for their talents and energy, suggests the contrary: that these women ought to be allowed to lead meaningful, busy lives that render them economically self-sufficient.[25] Such inconsistencies show that, at the very least, Trollope is ambivalent. He even confessed that *He Knew He Was Right* betrayed his principles and intentions. He was unable to portray Trevelyan sympathetically despite having begun the novel with a wish to do so: 'I do not know that in any literary effort I ever fell more completely short of my own intention than in this story.'[26]

Trollope's writing is conflicted not merely because of personal indecision but rather because, as I have suggested already, married love was part of the discourse of liberalism that implied a contractual subjectivity for women. With this in mind, we see that Trollope's 'feminism' in this novel has less to do with his attitude towards women than with his attitude towards marriage. By wholeheartedly endorsing marriage for love, an endorsement that constitutes the major theme of his *oeuvre*, and by following through on the contractual implications for women of that endorsement Trollope writes a different story than he intended, one paradoxically at odds with many of his own views. Like Richardson, however, Trollope attempts to reassert patriarchal ideals and to undermine the progressive implications of his belief in married love. In particular, he tries to redefine masculinity in order to make a husband's authority compatible with his role as a loving companion, and to ward off the threat to masculinity that such redefinition might entail. But unlike Richardson, Trollope is true to the companionate ideal itself. We have seen that Richardson uses strategies of displacement to dissociate women's independence from love. In doing so, he simply denies the connection between the voluntarism of love and the independence such voluntarism implies. But Trollope allows the contradiction to play itself out, imaginatively following through on the idea that marriage grants certain entitlements to women, even if these are not legislated. Despite Trollope's mockery of Mill and his supporters, Mill's constellation of married love, personal happiness, contract, and the progress of civilization provides an explanatory framework for this novel.

As in all Trollope's novels, *He Knew He Was Right* asserts as its fundamental moral premise the belief that for those fortunate enough to find love in the world, marriage is a joy as well as a duty. Conversely, marrying without love is a sin. When Hugh Stanbury, the novel's hero, deliberates about whether to marry on his small income, he views marriage as an ethical expression of selflessness: 'there came upon him some dim idea of self-abnegation, – that ... the poetry of his life, was, in fact, the capacity of caring more for other human beings than for himself' (237). Nora Rowley, the woman he loves (and Emily Trevelyan's sister) reaches a similar conclusion, rejecting a brilliant match with the future Lord Peterborough because she does not feel strongly about him. Characters who use marriage for economic or social advancement, such as the French sisters, come in for heavy punishment. It is better to lead the lonely life of a spinster, like Hugh's aunt, Priscilla Stanbury, than to marry without love.

If marriage for love is a duty, it is also a right – a right that even justifies a woman's rebellion from patriarchal authority – as the stories of Nora Rowley and Hugh's sister Dorothy Stanbury show. Marriage for love, in other words, legitimates a woman's desires and choices, recognizing the very personhood and autonomy of which the law would deprive her after marriage. Although Nora's parents forbid her engagement to Hugh, she firmly insists both that she will marry the man she loves and that it is her right to do so: 'There is a time when a girl must be supposed to know what is best for herself, – just as there is for a man' (658). Her sister Emily's story suggests that such knowing what is best continues even after marriage. Dorothy Stanbury also asserts her right to choose her husband freely. When her aunt and adoptive guardian, Miss Stanbury, informs her that plans have been readied for her marriage to Mr Gibson, a local clergyman, Dorothy refuses because she is not in love. Miss Stanbury is shocked that Dorothy, with her meager fortune and poor prospects, would dare to reject such an offer, which includes the two thousand pounds that she herself will contribute as a dowry: 'An offer from an honest man, with her friends' approval, and a fortune at her back as though she had been born with a gold spoon in her mouth! And she tells me that she can't, and won't, and wouldn't and shouldn't, as though I were asking her to walk the streets' (342). But Miss Stanbury is indeed asking Dorothy to 'walk the streets' insofar as she is asking her to prostitute herself – to negate her desires (Dorothy shudders when she thinks of embracing Mr Gibson) and to commodify herself, exchanging her person and devotion for a good establishment. Not only does Dorothy refuse Miss Stanbury's choice of a husband, she later engages herself to the man she loves, despite her aunt's disapproval.

He Knew He Was Right shows, as Mill also contends, that although the right of choice in marriage had not always existed, denying it now is impossible given contemporary mores, and that this in itself is evidence of moral progress. Miss Stanbury clearly associates Dorothy's refusal of Mr Gibson with the changing role of women. 'I don't know what has come to the young women; – or what it is they want' she says, after Dorothy rejects her arranged marriage. When Nora's father finds she is determined to marry Hugh, he threatens to curse and disinherit her, like the unyielding Mr Harlowe in *Clarissa*. But his wife points out the absurdity of such a threat in the modern world by imagining it within the context of their everyday lives: 'On the stage they do such things as that ... and, perhaps, they used to do it once in reality. But you know that it's out of the question now. Fancy your standing up and cursing the dear girl, just as we are all starting from Southampton!' (844).

Like Nora's father, Trevelyan wants to exert masculine control in an autocratic and inflexible manner, 'to achieve empire' (743), but unlike Mr Rowley, he fails to realize the impracticability and error of such methods. His main difficulty is that he cannot change with the times, and his inability to accept the changing role of women is what drives him mad.[27] While Mr Rowley eventually acknowledges his place as a modern father, compelled by the morals and customs of the times to grant approval of his daughter's lover, Trevelyan clings to his outmoded ideas about male authority, becoming in the end, just like a figure 'on the stage.' The melodramatic, histrionic course his madness takes – his gaudy colours of dress, exaggerated gestures, and citation of Shakespeare's *King Lear* (another madman) – all signal his removal from the everyday world. Long before he is mad, he is shown to be nostalgic, longing for a past when, in his view, the exercise of authority was more straightforward, and methods of social control were more direct and forceful. He laments the fact that '[a]s wives are managed nowadays, he could not forbid to her [Emily] the use of the post office' (254). Because Trevelyan is unable trust to contemporary modes of exercising power, he cannot put his faith in the moral law of self-discipline and resorts instead to the 'rigours of surveillance' (254): unwilling to trust his wife to police her own behaviour, he hires an ex-policeman to do it for her, although this course of action is degrading to himself and insulting to her. As to his rivalry with Colonel Osborne, he believes that in an earlier age, his problems would have been quickly solved by a duel: 'Gentlemen of old, his own grandfather or his father, would have taken such a fellow as Colonel Osborne by the throat and have caned him, and afterwards would have shot him, or have stood to be shot. All that was changed now' (254).

Trevelyan's longing for a mode of autocratic rule over his wife that is no longer appropriate is at the heart of their quarrel, and later, of his insanity. Literary precedent suggests that Trevelyan's suspicion of his wife's adultery causes his madness – critics have noted the parallels between Trevelyan's story and *Othello*. Traditional attitudes towards women's sexuality also authorize his association of independence with adultery; in this view, famously expressed by Rousseau, women's subordination is justified by the possibility that independent women will be unfaithful to their husbands, thereby deflecting the legitimate descent of property. Trevelyan similarly imagines a connection between his wife's autonomy and her unfaithfulness, just as the conservative Lord Penzance opposed granting married women property rights because he feared that a married woman with economic independence might go into business with a lover-partner.[28] However, in Trevelyan's case, the usual causality of suspicion and control are reversed: Trevelyan does not want to control his wife because he fears her faithlessness; he suspects her of infidelity because he cannot control her. As the omniscient narrator reveals, Trevelyan never believes wholeheartedly in Emily's adultery, nor seriously questions the respectability of her relationship with Colonel Osborne; his 'desire to achieve empire' over his wife has led to the 'sorrows which had come upon him in his unsuccessful struggle' (743). Trevelyan is unable to allow his love for his wife to temper his need for mastery, although he knows he ought to do so in order to resolve the quarrel.[29]

Yet if Trevelyan is wrong to tyrannize over his wife, this does not mean that Trollope abandons his belief in men's sovereignty. In *He Knew He Was Right*, he attempts to make such patriarchal ideals accord with his progressive views of women's entitlements by presenting what we might call 'gentle patriarchy,' a milder form of domination, as a successor to a tyrannical version of male power. While a husband still ought to retain supreme authority in his household, such authority should manifest itself through persuasion rather than force. Thus Hugh tells Trevelyan that rather than insulting his wife by forbidding her Colonel Osborne's company, he ought to have hinted his disapproval (184). Trevelyan himself, on the brink of madness, hears the internal voice of a better, saner self, which urges this form of exercising authority: 'A man should be master in his own house, but he should make his mastery palatable, equitable, smooth, soft to the touch, a thing almost unfelt' (44). Such a view receives official sanction within the novel when Dorothy reads aloud from Jeremy Taylor's sermon, *The Marriage Ring* (486), which advocates the exercise of a husband's power in precisely this way.[30]

Yet, Trollope's attempt to square the contractual freedoms implied by the marriage choice with the continued and unquestioned domination of the husband after marriage is doomed to the failure of contradiction. Gentle patriarchy cannot resolve any real differences of opinion between husband and wife, just as the conduct-book right of both parents and children to veto the marriage choice could not resolve their disagreements in a productive manner. In the case of a true clash of opinions, one or the other must prevail, just as Nora and Dorothy win the battle with their guardians. Gentle patriarchy cannot mediate between women's entitlements and men's authority because it ultimately assumes the same patriarchal premises as Trevelyan's 'mastery.' It is not a resolution of contradictory principles, but a mystification of power. A husband can only assert his authority in muted ways when he can depend on his wife to know what is expected of her.

Such scrupulous attention to the rules on the part of both husband and wife exemplifies the self-policing that is always the mark of well-regulated society in Trollope's novels, as D.A. Miller has demonstrated.[31] Indeed, Emily's problems are due in part to the fact that as a colonial, she has incompletely internalized the rules of English etiquette, which are always the first defence against more serious breaches. Her failure to play by the rules unmasks the fact that the relationship between husband and wife is grounded in force. However 'wrong' Trevelyan might be about the seriousness of Emily's transgression, and however inept he is at dealing with her misconduct, his reactions disclose the extent to which gentle patriarchy depends on a wife's ability to shape her behaviour to accord with the commands and wishes of her husband. If she fails to do so, law and convention are on his side, as we see when Trevelyan takes their child and runs away to Italy, and the lawyers can do nothing about it. That Emily does not fare worse is due to Trevelyan's fundamental decency rather than to any protections English law or society afford. Gentle patriarchy is just plain patriarchy after all.

However inadequate we might deem Trollope's solution as a means to accord women rights and protections within marriage, it was progressive enough in Trollope's time to threaten traditional ideals of masculinity. Despite the continued attempts to revise such ideals, attempts that we can trace through Puritanism, Christian moral discourse of the eighteenth century, and evangelicalism, the identification of masculinity with insensitivity and force was deeply engrained within English culture. As a result, assertions of Christian manliness are often accompanied by defensive justifications of one kind or another. We have seen how, in *Sir Charles Grandison*, libertine duellists are characterized as fopish and effeminate, while the chaste and peaceable Sir Charles possesses the strength and power they lack. In a similar fashion, Trollope aligns true masculinity with gentle deployments of authority, while suggesting that blustery displays of men's sovereignty signify impotence rather than power.

Thus Trevelyan, who exemplifies an older model of masculinity, is shown to be somewhat effeminate. Inhabiting the domestic rather than the public sphere, he leads a life much like that of an educated, middle-class Victorian woman. Although he has the option of working at a profession (unlike the poor spinsters), he chooses to lead a life of leisure, pursuing his intellectual interests in a dilettante fashion. He is unusually domestic; unlike most other men of his class, he takes no joy in being able to dine at his club or in any similar 'release from the constraint imposed by family ties'; on the contrary, he is 'one ... to whom the ordinary comforts of domestic life were attractive and necessary' (174). Even Trevelyan's madness is the sign of an inherent effeminacy; Elaine Showalter points out that women were supposedly more susceptible to insanity than men because 'the instability of their reproductive systems interfered with their sexual, emotional, and rational control.'[32] And when he loses his sanity, his extravagant dress expresses the lack of manliness that makes him susceptible to the illness to begin with.[33] Trevelyan has problems with 'mastery' of his wife because he is not 'man enough,' as Hugh makes clear when he reproaches his friend for his inept handling of the quarrel: 'You have only to bid her to come back to you, and let bygones be bygones, and all would be right. Can't you be man enough to remember that you are a man?' (310). It is telling that Hugh, who is manly where Trevelyan is lacking, with an active, civic public life and a taste for male comaraderie, offers the proper solution to Trevelyan's problems.

In the end, Trevelyan, the most domestic of men, ironically destroys his home. For the very concept of home as a refuge and haven, the kind of dwelling which Trevelyan holds dear and which was generally idealized, is at odds with his intolerant style of mastery. Such a home depends on respect, complaisance, and above all, trust. As Emily points out, 'A wife does not feel that her chances of happiness are increased when she finds that her husband suspects her of being too intimate with another man' (100). Trevelyan's story inevitably endorses the connection between companionate marriage and greater freedom for women, which Trollope's contradictory version of patriar- chy cannot successfully undermine.

Contradiction and Progress

Like Trevelyan, Dorothy's spinster aunt, Miss Stanbury, hates being forced to change with the times. 'I'm too old to change and I don't mean to try' (112), she tells Dorothy. In her view, political reform entails 'murder, sacrilege, adultery, treason, atheism ... every kind of nastiness under the sun' (206). Yet whereas Trevelyan is overwhelmed by a changing world, Miss Stanbury provides a successful model for coping with the stress of social progress.

That Miss Stanbury's story is to be read dialogically with Treve- lyan's, as offering an alternative response to similar problems, is evi- dent from the many parallels between the two.[34] Although she never marries, Miss Stanbury enters into an implicit contract with her niece, in which, like a marriage, they agree to share love, a home, and mate- rial possessions. As in a marriage, only one of the partners is economi- cally self-sufficient, and her power derives to great degree from this advantage. Miss Stanbury, like Trevelyan, brings all the wealth to this relationship, and her knowledge of her economic power reinforces her already well-established sense of her right to control her niece, just as Trevelyan thinks his penniless wife should be especially obedient because of the material advantages she has gained from her marriage. They are also similar in that Miss Stanbury, like Trevelyan, 'likes to have her own way' (60), a quality that results in several 'separations' between herself and other characters.

For Miss Stanbury, as for Trevelyan, the most upsetting change brought by the modern world is the increasing autonomy of women. After Dorothy refuses the suitor her aunt has chosen for her, Miss Stan- bury endures a long illness, which parallels Trevelyan's madness. The doctor interprets her inability to recuperate as a failure of will; she, like her counterpart, is also depressed, if not actually mad. And like Treve- lyan, Miss Stanbury sees a connection between women's increasing independence and sexual laxity. When Dorothy becomes engaged against her aunt's wishes, Miss Stanbury accuses her of 'immodesty' (544), a serious charge for a respectable young lady. As in the main plot, this intolerable insult causes the last and most serious of her sepa- rations, this time from Dorothy.

But unlike Trevelyan, Miss Stanbury is strong enough – as strong as a man and therefore stronger than Trevelyan – to allow her great love for her niece to get the better of her destructive rigidity. Relenting from her sternness and implicitly retracting the insult, she eventually approves the marriage between Dorothy and her lover. Miss Stanbury realizes that the happy home she has found with her niece will be destroyed if she persists in her rigid and authoritarian attitude, and that the love and comfort her niece has brought to her lonely life depend on her yielding. Her relationship with her niece even causes her to re-evaluate her aversion to change itself: 'She would still scorn the new fangles of the world around her, and speak of the changes which she saw as all tending to evil. But, through it all, there was an idea present to herself that it could not be God's intention that things should really change for the worse, and that the fault must be in her, because she had been unable to move as others had moved' (839). Miss Stanbury is able to learn that change is the way of the world, and once she accepts this, she emerges from her depression. The moral here is that those who cannot adapt do not survive.

Miss Stanbury's acceptance of change does not, however, involve a complete transformation of her character and beliefs. It is in fact fraught with contradiction; she concedes the necessity and benefit of change without altering her antipathy to it ('she would still speak of the changes which she saw as all tending to evil'). Her life story demonstrates similar paradoxes. Despite her conservative politics and identification with county society, her own wealth derives from 'new money' – beer, trade, and railways.[35] She believes that men should be the masters, but has never yet allowed a man to master her, as her falling out with her supposed spiritual guide, Mr Gibson, illustrates. Although she does not think her niece should choose a husband for herself, as a young girl Miss Stanbury had engaged herself to a man of whom her family disapproved. Her story is only one of this novel's many indications that, in Trollope's view, conflict and contradiction are endemic to change, and that the ability to live with such division, both in one's own life and in society as a whole, is a necessary skill. People must be able to 'contain' contradiction in both senses of the word – to embody paradoxical beliefs and to bracket the distress of living in a world that does not entirely make sense.

In his *Autobiography*, Trollope suggests that the injunction to live with contradiction applies collectively as well as individually. For Trollope, contradiction is at the very heart of social progress, a necessary if illogical step in the advance of civilization. In a discussion of his political views, Trollope asserts that the conservative opposition to change retards the liberal desire for improvement; this ensures that social development will be productive, a measured advance of betterment for all, as opposed to a destructive forward rush of beliefs and events. Trollope therefore observes that the liberal who advocates diminishing inequality between men is nevertheless glad that his conservative opponent regards such 'diminution as an evil': '[H]e [the liberal] knows that he must be hemmed in by safeguards, lest he be tempted to travel too quickly [towards the lessening of social distance between men]; and therefore he is glad to be accompanied on his way by the repressive action of a Conservative opponent. Holding such views, I think I am guilty of no absurdity in calling myself an advanced Conservative-Liberal.'[36]

Trollope exemplifies this division of stances within his own thought in the *Autobiography*, where, in a discussion of the condition of the working classes, he expresses both progressive and reactionary views. While advocating amelioration of conditions for the working classes, he also strictly qualifies the degree and kind of change that is desirable. Similarly, he supports the diminution of inequality even while asserting that equality is 'offensive' and that social 'distances are of divine origin.'[37] Trollope's own political analysis thus embodies the conservative check to progressive tendencies that he sees as a desirable regulatory social mechanism, and which he captures in his paradoxical description of himself as an 'advanced Conservative-Liberal.'

The unresolved contradictions in *He Knew He Was Right* stem from the conflict within Victorian middle-class society between a belief in men's absolute power and the challenges to that power posed by married love and Christian manhood. But the *Autobiography* suggests yet another, unconventional way to read the representation of such conflicts: as instantiations of the mechanism of progress itself. Reading *He Knew He Was Right* in light of *An Autobiography* reveals it to be an argument for social change made through a demonstration of the contradictory, dialectical method by which such change occurs. The novel's very ambivalence in its attitude towards women's rights once again ironically aligns Trollope with the feminists he so often opposed and ridiculed. Like Miss Stanbury, Trollope appears to be perfectly able and willing to absorb this and other paradoxes. To do otherwise, to be disturbed by the contradictory nature of social relationships and cultural ideals – that way madness lies.

5

Margaret Oliphant's Women Who Want Too Much

What marriage may be in the case of two persons of cultivated faculties, identical in opinions and purposes, between whom there exists that best kind of equality, similarity of powers and capacities with reciprocal superiority in them – so that each can enjoy the luxury of looking up to the other, and can have alternately the pleasure of leading and of being led in the path of development – I will not attempt to describe. To those who can conceive it, there is no need; to those who cannot, it would appear the dream of an enthusiast. But I maintain, with the profoundest conviction that this, and this only, is the ideal of marriage.

John Stuart Mill, The Subjection of Women[1]

Despite the joyful celebration of marriage here articulated, a description, surely, of Mill's own relationship with Harriet Taylor, *The Subjection of Women* (1869) laments the failure of many couples to attain this blissful union. One of the central insights of *The Subjection* is that inequality between men and women distorts relationships between the sexes. Because of inequitable laws, institutions, and customs, men fail to respect women adequately; this precludes the kind of loving and reciprocal marriage that Mill eulogizes in this passage, and which was an ideal for both feminists and their opponents. Mill's insight, a fundamental premise for other feminists, is not often found in novels of this period, where the teleological drive of narrative is the happy, heterosexual union. Although some novelists concede the limiting nature of marriage for women, most stop short of suggesting that such restraint might affect the personal quality of the marital relationship itself. For the most part, even those novels that address 'the woman question' tend to suggest that a woman is indeed likely to make a happy marriage provided she chooses wisely, and that marriage can provide adequate emotional compensation for the restrictions on women's lives. In *Middlemarch*, for example, Dorothea ultimately narrows the scope of her vision and benevolence, neither fulfilling her personal potential nor realizing her desire to make a significant difference in the world at large. Despite these constraints, she finds love, companionship, and happiness with Ladislaw, and she continues to better the lives of those within her limited reach. Margaret Oliphant, however, rejects the notion that marriage, for a woman such as Dorothea, can compensate for other deprivations; rather, the same laws and institutions that limit women's opportunities distort marriage itself. Oliphant's novels repeatedly reveal a view of relationships similar to that found in *The Subjection*'s grimmest moments.

Mill and Oliphant might appear to be strange allies to readers aware of Oliphant's reputation as an opponent of women's rights.[2] It is therefore worth taking some time to look more closely at her writings about feminism. As Merryn Williams contends, Oliphant's reputation as a conservative vis-à-vis women's issues is a misconception, due largely to the selective publication of her views by her original editor, her niece Annie Coghill. Oliphant's opinions were 'neither conservative, nor, over a career of nearly fifty years, consistent.'[3] She was often ambivalent, as we see in her review of Mill's *Subjection*, written in 1869, seven years before she published *Phoebe Junior*, the first of the novels considered below. Oliphant expresses several traditional, antifeminist opinions in this review. She states that it is impossible for a woman to have both career and family, a belief that was likely rooted in her own difficult experience as a working wife supporting an unsuccessful husband, and subsequently as a widow responsible for a large, extended family. A man might pursue his career with the singularity of focus necessary to success, whereas a woman's profession would always be subject to the interruptions of childbearing and childrearing, which divide the attention in ways damaging to both work and family.[4] Moreover, biology determines a woman's subordination within marriage as well as her exclusion from the workplace. Because the man works outside the home to support his family, it is only natural that a woman run the household and serve him when he returns (585). Nor could this arrangement be altered significantly. Oliphant contends that if all the laws subordinating women were suddenly to vanish and humanity to start afresh, the natural arrangement of men's public life and women's domestic one, of male work and women's service, would emerge once again (599). It follows from these beliefs that married women ought not to vote: the franchise was allocated by a consideration of households rather than individual civic entitlement, and Oliphant believes that only one person should represent a household politically (589). Given his natural participation in the public sphere, this person should be the husband.

Oliphant thus differs with Mill on three important issues: married women's entry into the public sphere; the subordination of women within marriage; and women's suffrage, one of Mill's most sacrosanct goals. In accord with predominant antifeminist discourses of the day, her judgments about all of these points of contention are based on what she believes to be the immutable and irrevocable laws of sexual difference. Because marriage and the gendered division of labour it necessitates are institutional and structural manifestations of biology, the relationship of husband and wife must be complementary rather than equal. Yet even in this review, Oliphant's points of agreement with Mill are significant. Above all, both agree that women are as intellectually capable as men, a view that becomes abundantly clear in Oliphant's novels (582). Both agree that women have a right to education (595).[5] And both support the Married Women's Property Act and assert that existing marriage laws are an insult to women (579, 585).[6] Whatever their differences in opinion about opportunities for wives, both agree that single women ought to have access to careers, and to the training necessary for professional competence (599).

Oliphant's article 'The Grievances of Women,' published eleven years later, reveals that her political views on women had become increasingly progressive. Like Mill, she now asserts that men's physical strength rather than their essential superiority is responsible for women's subordination. (They draw opposite conclusions on this last point: Mill believes that civilization can supersede mere 'force' as a criterion for such superiority; Oliphant disagrees.) She admires and is grateful to feminists, despite having 'very mixed feelings' about some of their views, for braving the public insults and ridicule of men in order to agitate for their cause; she feels that she would not have been able to do the same.[7] Like Mill, she wonders why men are so anxious to deny women equal opportunities; if they are so superior, 'the weaker vessel' should offer little competition and men need not be threatened (700).[8] She now believes that 'independent and self-supporting women who head households,' such as herself, ought to be allowed to vote:

'My opinion on this point resolves itself into the very simple one, that I think it is highly absurd that I should not have a vote, if I want one – a point upon which I am much more uncertain' (708–9).

Oliphant's most significant point of congruence with Mill in 'Grievances,' and the one that is most pertinent to her novels, is her contention that men's lack of respect for women, as indicated by their undervaluation of women's work, has a negative influence on marriage. Oliphant observes, as feminists would argue a good many years later, that men perceive women's labour as invisible, despite their own and society's dependence on such labour for the maintenance of daily life:

> To keep the world rolling on, as it has been doing for all these centuries, there have been needful ... two types of creatures, the one an impossibility without the other. And it is a curious thought, when we come to consider it, that the man, who is such a fine fellow and thinks so much of himself, would after all be a complete nonentity without the woman whom he has hustled about and driven into a corner ever since she began to be. Now it seems to me that the first, and the largest, and most fundamental of all the grievances of women, is this: that they never have, since the world began, got the credit of that share of the work of the world which has fallen naturally to them, and which they have, on the whole, faithfully performed through all vicissitudes. It will be seen that I am not referring to the professions, which are the trades of men, according to universal acknowledgment, but to that common and general women's work, which is, without any grudging, acknowledged to be their sphere. (701)[9]

To illustrate such obtuseness, she recounts an incident on a train. A husband, noticing his wife's shabby gloves, exclaims, 'One would think ... that I could not afford to buy you gloves' (705). By characterizing his wife as a total dependent, who must look to and be indebted to him for an item as basic as gloves, the husband obscures her contribution to the marriage in actual monetary terms, through the dowry she brought, and more importantly, the contribution she makes through the value of her labour. This husband is no different from most men: self-importance – 'the strong sense of superiority which exists in the male bosom from the age of two upwards' (707) – and the private, dutiful nature of a wife's work lead men to ignore such contributions, despite the fact that if a husband had to hire a 'stranger' to do his wife's job, 'that stranger would have been highly paid and a very independent person indeed' (706). Such stories are the norm: more often than not, even a good husband will consider his wife as a passive object of his bounty, indebted to him for a living, and with 'no right to anything, not even to her gloves and bonnets, her share of the living which she so largely helped to earn' (706). Such an attitude is not conducive to 'perfect understanding and good intelligence' between a couple, for it leads a man to regard his wife as a 'child' rather than a friend (705–6). Oliphant, like Mill, here suggests that marriage is inherently demeaning to women. Just as Mill, in the epigraph to this chapter, invokes the rhetorical figure of occupatio to emphasize the positive side of marriage, Oliphant utilizes this figure to assert the negative: 'Whatever women do, in the general, is undervalued by men in the general, because it is done by women. How this impairs the comfort of women, how it shakes the authority of mothers, injures the self-respect of wives, and gives a general soreness of feeling everywhere, I will not attempt to tell (710).

If Oliphant refuses to 'tell all' in her non-fiction, she does so in her novels, where men's injustice towards women is shown to originate in a lack of respect. Even when men are not tyrants, their undervaluation of women precludes the truly companionate marriage, a relationship between friends who provide emotional and intellectual fulfilment for one another. The happiest marriages in this *ouevre* are between men who think and women who feel, for whom such reciprocity of mind is neither expected nor missed. These relationships are amicable, loving, and symbiotic, but they are not friendships in the sense extolled in novels and elsewhere. There are no Elizabeths to provide witty and mocking rejoinders to their Mr Darcys. Given existing laws and institutions, marriage can almost never be what it is meant to be, in Mill's view, a union between 'two persons of cultivated faculties, identical in opinions and purposes, between whom there exists that best kind of equality.' In her review of *The Subjection*, Oliphant had criticized Mill for apocalyptic and dire views on marriage, for viewing a husband and wife's 'mutual relations with one another' not as 'that sentiment which inclines one soul towards the other and knits between them the closest and most subtle of all bonds, but a brutal sense of superior strength and determination to subjugate and oppress' (575). Yet Oliphant's novels show that she is, in the end, the truer pessimist. Her scepticism about the possibility that men and women will form such 'subtle' bonds leads her not only to criticize instances of men's injustice to women, but also to radically challenge fundamental assumptions about gender and heterosexual relationships.

Oliphant's novels further demonstrate that the support of opportunities for single women expressed in 'Grievances' stems from this negative view of marriage. Invoking the sanctity of marriage to argue for rights for single women was a familiar strategy for feminists, including Mill. One of the best-known examples of this argument can be found in Frances Power Cobbe's 'What Shall We Do With Our Old Maids?' Cobbe points out that in England women outnumber men by 'four or five percent' and as a result, 'thirty percent of women ... never marry, leaving one-fourth of both sexes in a state of celibacy.'[10] Because very few of these single women have sufficient financial resources to support themselves for a lifetime, and since women are barred from most professions (writing was an exception), they are doomed to a life of inactivity, uselessness, and shabby gentility, or even penury. Moreover, the old maid is often a figure of ridicule within the culture, as Oliphant's Mr Copperhead makes painfully clear in *Phoebe Junior*. Cobbe thus argues for the necessity of finding sources of money, activity, and respect for single women. Such reform, however, is essential not only for the financial well-being of women themselves, but for the sanctity of marriage as an institution. Cobbe contends that the lack of alternatives to marriage leads women to view marriage as a necessity and to ignore the personal, moral, and psychological cost of a loveless union to themselves and their spouses. Cobbe thus argues in terms of dominant beliefs about marriage. If marriage should be a union of hearts and minds, it should not be entered into for interested motives:

> When we make the assertion that marriage is good and virtuous, do we mean a marriage of interest, a marriage for wealth, for position, for rank, for support? ... Such marriages as these are the sources of misery and sin, not of happiness and virtue ... There is only one kind of marriage which makes good the assertion that it is the right and happy condition for mankind, and that is a marriage founded on free choice, esteem, and affection – in one word, on love ... Is it not to the conclusion that to make it a woman's *interest* to marry, to force her, by barring out every means of self-support and all fairly remunerative labour, to look to marriage as her sole chance of competency, is precisely to drive her into one of those sinful and unhappy marriages ... When we have made it *less* women's interest to marry, we shall indeed have less and fewer interested marriages, with all their train of miseries and evils. (595–6)

While many novelists confront the problem of 'old maids' by showing that young women faced economic and social pressure to marry, and some even represent the unpleasant consequences of remaining single, few go so far as to argue for alternative careers for women. Instead, more often than not, they rescue their heroines through marriage, a device Oliphant herself referred to as 'the sudden "good marriage," which is the one remaining way in which a god out of the machinery can change wrong into right,' without offering a structural solution to the problems confronting single women in general.[11] And women who marry for money or status, no matter how desperate their situations, are in general portrayed unsympathetically. Oliphant, in contrast, depicts with compassion women who marry because they have few other options, such as Clarence's mother in *Phoebe Junior*. Her novels also frequently show the rightness and necessity of allowing opportunities for single women. Yet her reasoning goes beyond an appeal to the sanctity of marriage or a consideration of demographics: her claims are ultimately more radical. Oliphant's novels suggest that there ought to be alternatives to marriage for women not only because economic need interferes with the possibility of true companionship between husband and wife, but because such companionship is difficult to attain for 'exceptional women' in any case. Marriage, by its very nature – because of the restrictions and the inequities it almost inevitably fosters – is incapable of providing fulfilling relationships for capable, intelligent women. And in any case, some women need more than marriage, even a good one, to be satisfied.

Phoebe Junior, *Hester*, and *Kirsteen* express progressively somber views of marriage as a means to fulfilment for strong and proficient women. In these novels the happiness or unhappiness of Oliphant's heroines becomes increasingly detached from the issue of who, or if, they marry. Their satisfaction depends rather on whether or not they can find a sufficient outlet for their energy and capability, a definition of well-being conventionally associated with men.

Oliphant re-envisions cultural expectations about the gendering of personality through a reworking of novelistic convention. In earlier chapters, I have shown how the multiplot form allowed the novel to explore alternative, often contradictory, representations of love and marriage. This remains true in many of Oliphant's novels; for instance, in *Phoebe Junior*, Ursula May's story represents a different kind of marriage from that of Phoebe. But for Oliphant, what we might call a 'shadow plot' is just as important a device for offering alternative cultural ideals. Each of these three novels invokes a conventional courtship story at the outset, only to radically rework it in terms of Oliphant's views on marriage and women.[12] This shadow plot, which we recognize from our reading of countless other novels, hovers at the edges of the text we are given, playing on our expectations of well-known generic paradigms.

A Different Kind of Marriage

Phoebe Junior initially follows a conventional narrative pattern for the courtship novel, the choice between suitors. This decision often represents a choice between competing kinds of love, as we have seen in *Sir Charles Grandison*. It can also represent a choice in judgment and values, as in *The Newcomes*, where Ethel's suitors Clive and Lord Farintosh represent her own ambivalence about whether to allow love or ambition to guide her marriage choice. *Phoebe Junior* follows this second paradigm, but with a twist: Phoebe's choice of lovers is indeed a choice between love and ambition, but not of the usual kind. Phoebe's ambition is not directed towards money or status, as is usually the case in the novel, but rather towards utilizing her abilities. Moreover, *Phoebe Junior* reverses the usual novelistic moral: ambition rather than love offers happiness.

While in *Phoebe Junior* Oliphant is not as pessimistic about the possibility of companionship between men and women as she is in some of her later novels, she nevertheless suggests that marriage in traditional domestic terms cannot provide fulfilment for a woman of Phoebe's talents and energy. Phoebe consistently demonstrates intelligence, self-possession, and deft social skill. She knows how to say and do the right thing, abilities that enable her to orchestrate the novel's many social gatherings as well as her encounters with individuals. While, as Elizabeth Langland points out, these are qualities are required of all capable middle-class women, who manipulate the signs and conventions of their social world in order to advance their husband and family's position, Phoebe's abilities transcend those of even the most skilful domestic manager.[13] For, in addition to her social intelligence, and her ability to strategize (qualities requisite to business and politics as well as domestic management), she possesses a decidedly unfeminine nerve and tenacity. Throughout her adventures, Phoebe draws on an inner strength of character that enables her to pursue her goals in the face of contradiction and intimidation.[14] Moreover, she possesses an understanding of business and public affairs that extends beyond the social world in which women's intelligence normally operates.

Phoebe's difference from other women is underscored in two early scenes in the novel. When Phoebe's parents see her off on the train for her visit to Carlingford to care for her ailing grandmother, they comment on her self-sufficiency: 'Her fond parents accompanied her to the station and placed her in a carriage, and fee'd a guard heavily to take care of and watch over her. 'Not but that Phoebe might be safely trusted to take care of herself anywhere,' they said. In which expression of their pride in their daughter, the observant reader may see a proof of their own origin from the humbler classes. They would probably have prided themselves on her timidity and helplessness had they been a little better born.'[15] This closing comment on the narrator's part concerning the class-inflected differences in expectations of womanhood points us towards Ursula May, the novel's other heroine, whose behaviour in public situations is characterized by just such timidity and helplessness, and who is indeed 'better born.' Yet despite the class snobbery inherent in a phrase like 'better born,' the passage as a whole is tonally and ideologically unstable: does the narrator adhere to the opinions of the better born or merely ventriloquize them? Is being better born actually better? Such ambiguity is typical of Oliphant's ambivalence towards new money and status, as well as traditional gentility.

A later passage clearly questions the value of such better-born timidity, which leaves women helpless, while also indicating the narrator's admiration for Phoebe's independence. Even before Phoebe leaves for Carlingford, where her intelligence and resourcefulness will be tested to the limit, she tells her mother: '"... I am myself whatever happens; even if poor dear grandmamma's habits are not refined ... that does not make me unrefined. A lady must always be a lady wherever she is – Una," she continued, using strangely enough the same argument which has occurred to her historian, "is not less a princess, when she is living among the satyrs"' (75). Although this passage makes gentle fun of its heroine, it ultimately endorses her judgment and applauds her strength. The narrator's admission that this 'argument has occurred to her historian,' that is, herself, identifies her with Phoebe and her beliefs. Yet the ironic distance between the real situation – Phoebe's visit to Carlingford – and Princess Una among the satyrs, points to the inflated views that Phoebe has of herself, her position, and her heroism. Indeed, it is precisely Una's noble birth that Phoebe lacks, which in romance (such as the story of Princess Una), is always the source of the princess's worth. Such obtuseness separates her from a narrator who is intensely conscious of social position, and in this light, the narrator's claim to have thought of the same argument becomes satirical, distancing rather than aligning character and narrator. And yet, a moment later, Phoebe herself says, 'Of course, I am not like Una – and neither are they like the wild people in the wood' (75), so that her initial hyperbole is undercut by her wry realization of her inflated notions and rhetoric. This consciousness testifies to an ability to distance herself from events and social interactions that again suggests her identification with the narrator, and hence, with a reliable point of view, this time seriously rather than ironically. Moreover, the fact that later events prove her observations to be true in spirit – it is indeed Phoebe's ability to remain conscious of her identity as a lady that sustains her through her ordeals at Carlingford – undercuts the mockery of the passage altogether.

Perhaps it is not so wrong for Phoebe to think of herself as a princess, if the criteria for being a princess is merit rather than birth. This definition gains in credibility when we recall that in *The Subjection* John Stuart Mill refers to 'princesses' as providing proof that women possess the same capabilities as men: '[P]rincesses, being more raised above the generality of men by their rank than placed below them by their sex, have never been taught that it was improper for them to concern themselves with politics; but have been allowed to feel the liberal interest natural to any cultivated human being, in the great transactions which took place around them, and in which they might be called on to take a part. The ladies of reigning families are the only women who are allowed the same range of interests and freedom of development as men; and it is precisely in their case that there is not found to be any inferiority' (189). Phoebe's lack of better breeding thus indicates not simply, or even primarily, her lack of polish, but rather the fact that she has not been inculcated with the passivity and helplessness that other, 'better-born' women absorb from infancy. Her family's plural and mobile social status ensures that she has, to a great extent, 'the same range of interests and freedom of development as men,' which helps to make her so competent.

During her visit to Carlingford, where most of the novel takes place, Phoebe is suddenly thrust into a social milieu much inferior to her own, and must come to terms with the disparity between her identity and upbringing as a lady and the humiliating status of her family. For while Phoebe has been aware that her 'self-made' parents have risen in social status, she does not know the extent of their departure from their origins. When she arrives to care for her ailing grandmother, she discovers not merely that her grandfather was in trade before retiring, but that he had actually owned a shop for many years, that he was indeed no more than the local butterman.[16] This discovery is a shock and a disappointment, but Phoebe is able to negotiate its threat to her self-image and to her standing in the community with skill and grace: she remains honest about her grandparents' identity while gaining acceptance and respect, even in elite circles, by a continued demonstration of the signs of her middle-class status and breeding. By asserting her own value and refusing to display shame or weakness, Phoebe shapes others' perceptions of herself despite the prejudices of a rigidly stratified social hierarchy. What sets Phoebe apart, therefore, is not merely her ability to utilize the signifying system of the middle classes with consummate skill, but the strength and tenacity with which she insists that others accept her interpretation of herself. She stands her ground and refuses to capitulate to the shame or weakness suggested by her position, and which she feels in private.

In the novel's two climactic crises, such strength enables her to confront others as well as to sustain herself. Phoebe is perspicuous and astute enough – indeed, she possesses the business sense – to realize that Mr May has forged her grandfather's signature on a bill, and to save him from ruin and disgrace through her quick thinking; she hides the bill so that there is no evidence. She later gets the best of her furious grandfather, who suspects she has undermined him, refusing to be intimidated even when he threatens violence. Similarly, when Mr Copperhead threatens to disown his son Clarence for his engagement to Phoebe, she holds her own as he tries to bully her into giving up the relationship. Mr Copperhead usually gets what he wants through intimidating others. Only Phoebe is strong enough to stand up to him.

Phoebe's ability to elicit the best and get the better of those around her distinguishes her as an accomplished politician. Indeed, Phoebe has all the requisite qualities for a brilliant public career – except the right gender. As a woman, her options are either to marry or to become a spinster and endure the unpleasant attendant social and economic debilities of remaining single. The Dorset sisters illustrate what this would mean for a woman of Phoebe's class. The elder, Anne, an altruistic, almost saintly woman with few personal desires or ambitions, looks forward to caring for her brother's children with no expectation of reward. Yet despite her capacity for nurture, which domestic ideologues such as Sara Lewis and Sara Ellis characterize as the hallmark of the devoted wife and mother, Anne has no desire to marry. She is fulfilled as long as she can be useful and busy. Her sister Sophia is also single, although not by choice; she had been jilted and is therefore unmarriageable. Unlike Anne, she does not accept her position calmly or gently; she longs for a husband and children, and is bitter and cynical as a result of her experience.[17] But whatever the cause of their failure to marry, both realize the difficulties of their position. Even the saintly Anne knows that her path will not be an easy one, a fact brought to her attention as well as the reader's early in the novel. As the Dorsets and their cousin Ursula walk through the streets of London, Anne sees a carpet she wants for the drawing room, but her father vetoes the purchase, saying that the existing carpet will last for his time and after that her brother 'will prefer to please himself' (39). He thereby reminds Anne of what she knows already, that her brother's wife will some day be 'mistress in the old house' (39), thereby displacing herself. Whether or not Anne will be poor, she will certainly be demoted from a position of relative security and honour to become one of England's 'useless' old maids. Her father's statement 'brings a little cloud' to her usually placid face and she no longer takes pleasure in window shopping, which evokes 'painful feelings' (40). Introducing and closing the novel, the narrative of the Dorset sisters frames the narratives of Phoebe and Ursula both structurally and thematically. It suggests alternative stories for both heroines, looming as a threat at the beginning of the story, and reminding us of a course fortunately averted at the end. Anne and Sophy's marginality suggests that marriage is the prerequisite for a young lady's success – for being a central character – both in novels and in 'real life.'

Despite her unusual abilities, Phoebe's choice, then, is not between marrying and remaining single, but in deciding what kind of marriage to make. For the novel's other heroine, Ursula, this decision is not difficult; she follows her heart without question, marrying her suitor Reginald Northcote, who, true to the genre's romantic strain, has fallen in love with her at first sight. This is a fortunate marriage for her, because Northcote is wealthy and Ursula's family is poor.[18] In the context of Oliphant's other fictions, Ursula's story is markedly traditional – yet another instantiation of the novelistic wisdom that marriage is the greatest good that can befall a young woman. Through this unsurprising narrative, Oliphant emphasizes that conventional marriages suit conventional women, for whom a life centred exclusively on home and family will be fulfilling. Ursula epitomizes the ideal of feminine womanhood familiar to us from both novels and the ideologues of domesticity; sweet and good and pretty, she is not particularly intelligent or independent or resourceful. In this sense, she is the antithesis of Phoebe.

In contrast to this utterly pedestrian story, Phoebe's narrative departs from the usual expectations and values about womanhood. As I mentioned earlier, *Phoebe Junior* revolves around the choice of suitors and of corresponding marital motives. But it is organized not by the traditional conflict between love and other considerations such as money, status, or prudence. These oppositions assume that marriage is the best of all possible worlds, and that a respectable heroine will have no greater desire than to be a wife. This is not to say that *Phoebe Junior* ignores these familiar factors in the marriage choice. On the contrary, by creating a social panorama that extends from self-made millionaires to impoverished gentry, and from Dissenters to ministers of the established Church, Oliphant represents a more extensive and complicated hierarchy than we find in many of the novels of her contemporaries, and therefore provides a more detailed picture of the nuances of attraction and advantage – or disadvantage – in the marriage choice for each of her main characters. But for Phoebe, these oppositions are coloured by her knowledge of the limitations of a woman's position. Phoebe's awareness that marriage is a respectable woman's only option, and that she is limited to the private, domestic sphere, at least insofar as appearances are concerned, determines her decision.

For Phoebe, then, the marriage choice is between love and ambition, but ambition with a difference – Phoebe strives not to acquire wealth or social position, but an opportunity to employ her considerable talents. Reginald May, 'a true lover' (272) offers Phoebe the chance of a conventional love match. Although Phoebe is not in love with him, she is touched by his confession of feeling with an emotion that is a precursor to love. She is aware of the true value of what Reginald offers, and there is 'a sense in her mind that perhaps she had never touched so close upon a higher kind of existence, and perhaps never again might have the opportunity' (272). But she nevertheless prefers what Clarence has to offer, the profession, which, as a woman, she cannot openly have:

He [Clarence] was not very wise, nor a man to be enthusiastic about, but he would be a career to Phoebe. She did not think of it humbly like this, but with a big capital – a Career. Yes; she could put him into parliament, and keep him there. She could thrust him forward (she believed) to the front of affairs. He would be as good as a profession, a position, a great work to Phoebe. He meant wealth (which she dismissed in its superficial aspect as something meaningless and vulgar, but accepted in its higher aspect as an almost necessary condition of influence), and he meant all the possibilities of future power. Who can say that she was not as romantic as any girl of twenty could be? Only her romance took an unusual form. It was her head that was full of throbbings and pulses, not her heart. (234)

The choice Phoebe makes is thus between head and heart, career and love. This would become a familiar decision for the 'odd women' of a slightly later time, but it is highly unusual here, and even more so because Phoebe's choice is not between marriage and other options, but between options within marriage itself. For what Phoebe attains by marrying Clarence is not the mere influence over her husband that impacts on public affairs in a highly mediated way, as advocated by Lewis, Eliot (at the end of *Middlemarch*), and others, but an active political career: by the end of the novel, she is writing Clarence's parliamentary speeches. This arrangement of course determines the quality of the marriage Phoebe makes, for she could not have had this opportunity with an intellectual equal. But Phoebe is not a feminist or an advocate of women's entry into the public sphere. Indeed, she is as divided as the author who created her, a division reflected in her reading matter, which includes both the novels of the conservative antifeminist Charlotte Yonge, which repeatedly assert women's limitations and the propriety of a domestic woman's separate sphere, and 'Mr Mill's dissertations.' Phoebe's maverick response to the limits of women's lives is not the product of feminism or any other systematic belief, but rather the personal response of a prodigiously capable woman to the restrictions imposed on her by society.

While Phoebe is able to find a way to circumvent the limited scope allowed to women in her society and to lead the kind of active, assertive life that she finds so necessary and fulfilling, her quirky path to happiness does not provide a structural solution to the problems facing women. Indeed, although her unusual toughness and independence render her choices not only tolerable but satisfying, they would not be tenable to Oliphant's other, more sensitive heroines. Phoebe does not appear to be disturbed by marrying a man who is crass and stupid, and who cannot possibly provide intelligent companionship, the foundation of the traditional happy marriage. As long as she can have her career, she is content. Oliphant thus softens her mordant critique of the culture of heterosexuality in *Phoebe Junior*. Although she suggests that the kind of active career that Phoebe wants is not possible within a conventional marriage, the novel's happy ending undermines the inference that such a culture leads to unhappiness for most capable women.

Hester's Hobson's Choice

Hester (1883) asserts the pessimistic conclusion that *Phoebe Junior* avoids: that true companionship between men and women is nearly impossible and that capable women need more than marriage. Because Hester seeks not only a way to employ her talents and energies, but also emotional fulfilment and companionship from her personal relationships, Phoebe's solution would not suit her. Like *Phoebe Junior*, *Hester* invokes and revises the traditional courtship plot, the heroine's choice of suitors. But for Hester, Phoebe's decision is transformed into a Hobson's choice, for none of her suitors respects her as a friend and peer, and therefore none can provide the friendship and reciprocity that most intelligent women find requisite for a happy marriage. *Hester* clearly shows Mill's contention that inequities between men and women preclude loving reciprocity, that 'even with true affection, authority on the one side and subordination on the other prevent perfect confidence' (151–2). The limitations inherent in heterosexual relationships lead Oliphant to two radical conclusions in *Hester*: that for capable women, work is much more likely to provide satisfaction than marriage, and that emotional fulfilment is much more likely to be found in relationships with other women than in relationships with men.

Hester's suitors are all unsatisfactory both because they have traditional ideas and expectations about women and because they display the kind of self-centredness that both Mill and Oliphant attribute to men raised in a misogynistic culture. Harry, a kinder, more polished version of Clarence, is in some ways the best of Hester's prospective husbands. Honest and true, he refuses to slight Hester or her mother at their wealthy cousin Catherine's social gatherings, whereas his rival Edward is frightened to acknowledge Hester's existence. But Harry is perceived by all as being slow and unexciting. '[H]e'll never set the Thames on fire,' says Catherine; less charitably, his cousin Edward characterizes him as 'a big idiot – a nonentity.'[19] He is certainly no soulmate for the quick-witted and passionate Hester. But lack of intelligence is not Harry's primary fault; his condescending attitude is the more significant deterrent to a loving relationship. For, although Harry's respect for Hester's abilities is flattering, and although it promises, as in Phoebe's marriage, to accord her greater power in their relationship than is typical for a woman, he still regards himself as Hester's superior rather than as her friend.

To begin with, Harry's awareness of his own deficiencies does not prevent him from being arrogantly confident that Hester will accept his proposal. Harry believes 'his suit was a wonderful chance for his distant cousin; that Hester had no right to look for such good fortune as that of being the object of his affections. He knew that he was bringing in his hand everything a girl need wish for' (97). Everything a girl who considers marriage a business proposal might wish for, that is. In fact, Harry sees his proposal as a business transaction as far as Hester is concerned, and his method of acquiring a wife is similar to Catherine's acquisition of younger business partners: both are forms of patronage. What is significant for Oliphant about Harry's easy acceptance of the loveless marriage is not that it ignores the obligations of the Christian marriage in accord with the mercenary ethos of the time – the basis of criticism for most contemporary novelists – but that it reveals that Harry does not consider Hester's feelings. In Harry's marriage bargain, *his* feelings are the only ones that matter. His obtuseness also indicates how little true reciprocity Harry expects. Such attitudes reveal a fundamental sense of superiority that, in his case, can be based only on the entitlements of masculinity.

Edward, whom Hester does come to love, also fails to acknowledge her as a friend and partner. Although Edward realizes that she will marry only for love, and that she disdains the thought of marriage as a practical necessity, he greatly underestimates Hester's complexity and intelligence. This is because he thinks of women as alien and inferior to men. When Catherine expresses her annoyance with Hester's arrogance at their first encounter, Edward reveals his disdain of women: 'Don't you think you have given too much importance to the nonsense of a girl?' he asks. 'I know ... what girls are. I have six sisters. They are strange beings' (40). Later, when he himself has fallen in love with Hester, he assumes, like Harry, that she reciprocates his passion, and although this is eventually true, he anticipates it as a certainty long before he has a right to do so (220). When he repeatedly ignores Hester at Catherine's parties because he is afraid of what Catherine will think, he assumes that 'the little shrug with which he pointed her attention to his bondage would have an attraction even greater than had he been always at her side' (239). But he is wrong, and she is offended. Worst of all his sins is his refusal to take Hester into his confidence after they have become lovers. He wants and expects docile and unreflecting support from his partner, rather than intelligent participation in his concerns. When Hester urges him to share his burden with her (i.e., his anxiety about speculating with the bank's money), Edward refuses: '"Hester," he said, "that is not what a man wants in a woman; not to go and explain it all to her ... What he wants, dear, is very different just to lean upon you – to know you sympathise, and think of me, and feel for me, and believe in me, and that you will share whatever comes ... My only love! under-standing is nothing; it matters nothing; another fellow, any man ... would understand. I want your sympathy. I want – you"' (400–2).

Hester's third suitor is Roland Ashton, a stockbroker, whose obtusensess is so extreme that he almost parodies the other two. His inability to recognize women's individuality and intelligence takes the form of compulsive flirting: Roland regularly trots out his repertoire of seductive mannerisms, such as soft eyes, a melting voice, a sympa-thetic manner. As with rakes of an earlier era, who also denied women's individuality and autonomy, all women are fair game, and Roland never really means anything by his behaviour; indeed, he never distinguishes one woman/object from another. It follows that (like Edward), Roland believes that women should not 'step out of their sphere' (331). When Hester talks to him about her desire to work, he counters by articulating the doctrine of influence, one of the most prominent antifeminist arguments against women's rights: 'Pardon me; but don't you think that [working] is far less than what you have in your power? You can make others do; you can inspire ... and reward ... But there is nothing a man might not do, with you to encourage him' (330–1).[20] Moreover, he, like the others is all too sure of himself, and assumes Hester's susceptibility long after his allure has faded. In short, all three of these men are self-centred and self-important; all view women in stereotypical and demeaning ways; and all assume a sense of their inevitable superiority. None sees Hester as she really is or appreciates her truly distinctive qualities.

The story of Hester's elderly cousin Catherine suggests that for intel-ligent women like Hester, work is likely to provide greater satisfaction than marriage. Jilted as a young woman by yet another of the novel's disappointing men, she begins her career when her former lover embezzles funds from the family bank, nearly destroying the fortunes of his entire family. Catherine repairs the damage and takes over as the bank's director, discovering in the process that she has a talent for business. Although Catherine's bitterness at romantic disappointment leaves her cynical and disdainful of others, for over thirty years, she leads a life that is both exciting and fulfilling. Hester's own romantic tendencies never preclude her desire for a similar life. Like Phoebe, she longs for a 'career,' in her case, to establish a school for teaching foreign languages: 'It was not a little money that Hester wanted, but work of which something good might come' (331). When Hester is forbidden to work, ironically by Catherine, she languishes in a world of petty feminine accomplishments that leave her perpetually dissatisfied.

Hester's longing for productive labour explains in part the unusual intensity of her feelings for Catherine: Catherine represents what she would like to become. For although *Hester* establishes the familiar paradigm of the romantic triangle, in which Harry and Edward compete for Hester's love, the true affective focus of the novel is towards a competing triangular relationship: that of Catherine, Hester, and Edward. Although Hester initially believes that she is in love with Edward, the truth is that her feelings for Edward are primarily a displacement of her feelings for Catherine.

In *Deceit, Desire and the Novel*, René Girard formulates an account of this kind of triangulation, which is a common trope of the genre of the novel. A character, whom Girard calls the 'vaniteux,' desires something because another character, the 'mediator,' covets or possesses it. The true fascination of the 'vaniteux,' the person who desires, is not with the ostensible object of his or her desire, but with the mediator, the person who possesses or controls this object. As Girard explains, 'The impulse toward the object is ultimately an impulse toward the mediator ... Fascinated by his model, the disciple inevitably sees, in the mechanical obstacle which he puts in his way, proof of the ill will borne him. Far from declaring himself a faithful vassal, he thinks only of repudiating the bonds of mediation. But these bonds are stronger than ever, for the mediator's apparent hostility does not diminish his prestige but instead augments it ... The subject is torn between two opposite feelings toward his model – the most submissive reverence and the most intense malice. This is the passion we call *hatred*.'[21]

Hester experiences such 'hatred' for Catherine. From their very first mutually hostile encounter, Hester is resentful yet fascinated; she remarks (of Catherine), 'I shall either love or hate her. I have not made up my mind which' (49). And actually, she will do both, as is always the case with such Girardian 'hatred.' It is not accidental that Edward becomes Hester's lover; it is because he is Catherine's chosen 'mate' (son, live-in companion, protegé), that he is the object of Hester's desire. This is evident in the dynamic of their relationship: Edward's attraction consists in his reticence – his being 'hard to get' – and this reticence is due to his fear that acknowledging their friendship would mean his ruin with Catherine. For Hester, winning Edward thus means the ultimate triumph over her rival. Moreover, it is Catherine who generates the sense of communion that Hester feels with Edward. Catherine has them both in thrall as objects of her will and charity, and this inspires them both with intense resentment and a restless desire for freedom. It is clear that even their most personal and intense desires, including the desire for one another, depend on Catherine.

The triangle between Hester, Catherine, and Edward is not an ontological fact of relationships – one possible inference of Girard's work, since his account lacks a developed sense of causality or history. That is to say, Hester's desire is historically specific, grounded in the circumstances of women's lives at the time Oliphant was writing. Eve Kosofsky Sedgwick's critique and extension of Girard's theory explains this specificity. In *Between Men: English Literature and Male Homosocial Desire*, Sedgwick argues that Girard's dialectic of power is embedded in both 'masculine/feminine' and 'sexual/nonsexual' dichotomies, since 'the placement of [these] boundaries in a particular society affects not merely the definitions of those terms themselves ... but also the apportionment of forms of power that are not obviously sexual. These include control over the means of production and reproduction of goods, persons, and meanings.'[22] Certainly, the middle-class society to which Hester belongs defines work as something men do; therefore, men, for the most part, have control over goods and persons – that is to say, they possess economic and political power, which they continue to ensure will be divided along lines of gender. That Catherine defies the gendering of empowerment largely constitutes her attraction for Hester; Hester is drawn to what Catherine represents, the possibility of a 'Career,' and hence of her own efficacy and independence. Hester's fascination with Catherine is an expression and displacement of her intense desire for 'work of which something good might come.' Indeed, for Hester, strong homosocial feelings for other women are always bound up with her ambitions. Hester's short-lived crush on her beautiful cousin Ellen, for instance, is inspired by Ellen's promises to help her set up her school. Although Ellen promptly forgets this off-the-cuff remark, Hester dwells on it, going to her room to 'recollect all that had passed, and to go over it again and again as lovers do' (70). For Hester, true lovers are people who empower. In the end, she discovers that these are never men.

If a dialectic of gender and power accounts for the component of attraction in Hester's complex feelings for Catherine, it also accounts for her hostility. Hester's feelings about Catherine are ambivalent because Catherine inhabits a doubly gendered subjectivity. As head of the Vernon family, she becomes its patriarch (definitely not its matriarch). The novel emphasizes her masculine role and qualities; she articulates and practises the patriarchal values that keep Hester imprisoned, and these include her paternalistic charity as well as her refusal to let Hester work, despite her own example. But if Catherine inhabits a masculine and masculinist subjectivity, she is still a woman – a woman who, through her actions and capability, repudiates the very system she supports. Hester's recourse to triangulation and displacement is therefore not a structural fact of life, but a justifiably ambivalent response to Catherine's duality. If Hester's attraction originates in intense admiration for this extraordinary and unfeminine cousin, her resentment is a response to the patriarchal Catherine, who upholds traditional values. Yet paradoxically, such a multiple identity also constitutes part of Catherine's attraction for Hester, tipping the balance of her feelings towards admiration rather than resentment. For the very fact of Catherine's doubly gendered identity challenges the binariness it seemingly instantiates. By wielding power in a masculine mode Catherine performatively rearticulates that power, opening up possibilities for women and challenging the culture she consciously supports. As Judith Butler contends, a heterosexist, misogynist culture enacts its own empowerment by performative reiterations of that culture, which, in her view, are articulated through the formation of individuals' psychic sense (construction) of their bodies and egos. Yet for any sociopsychological structure (social or psychic, individual or collective) to replicate itself, it must reiterate its significations. And where there is reiteration, there is the possibility of subversion. Butler explains this process within a Lacanian theoretical framework:

The phantasmatic moment in which a part suddenly stands for and produces a sense of the whole or is figured as the center of control, in which a certain kind of 'phallic' determination is made by virtue of which meaning appears radically generated, underscores the very plasticity of the phallus, the way in which it exceeds the structural place to which it has been consigned by the Lacanian scheme, the way in which that structure, to remain a structure, has to be *reiterated* and, as reiterable, becomes open to variation and plasticity. When the phallus is lesbian, then it is and is not a masculinist figure of power; the signifier is significantly split, for it both recalls and displaces the masculinism by which it is impelled.[23]

Catherine possesses the 'lesbian phallus' in just this divided and subversive way, splitting and thereby challenging the signification of the 'masculinism' – the phallic masculine power – that she wields.

It is not accidental that Oliphant reverses the gender norms of triangulation. Sedgwick characterizes triangulation between men as an essential, identificatory element of patriarchal cultures, which traffic in women to negotiate male homosocial relationships. Such relationships are obviously the important ones with regard to affect as well as men's control of social and economic resources. By regendering this trope of the novel, Oliphant suggests that despite her culture's obsessive emphasis on marriage for women, the truly important relationships that women negotiate are those with other women – that these are the relationships that matter in women's lives. Triangulation between women, as between men, therefore functions in two registers, both as power and as feeling. Thus, Hester is drawn not only to what Catherine represents, but to the woman herself. For Hester intuitively realizes that only another capable, intelligent woman can provide the understanding and companionship of which her masculinist lovers are incapable. It is only Catherine's hostility that keeps this relationship from flowering early on, as Hester makes clear in a conversation with Edward: '[S]he has taken the trouble ... to humiliate me ... But you: she has been kind to you ... she has loved you ... If she were fond of me I should be proud ... Hester's eyes were shining with eloquence and ardor' (243).

Edward's embezzlement and subsequent flight unmask the illusions of triangulation, bringing about the circumstances necessary for homosocial bonding between Catherine and Hester. When Edward asks Hester to abscond with him, it is finally revealed to her that they are not soulmates, for it is not in her loyal, honest nature to repudiate the bonds of family and community. With Edward's flight, Catherine becomes the true rather than the displaced object of Hester's affection; they unite initially to save the bank, and then remain devoted companions until Catherine's death. During this brief time, each finds understanding and friendship with the other, as opposed to the hollow and illusory bond each has had with Edward. For these women, the homosocial rather than the heterosexual relationship is revealed to be the truly important one.

But with Catherine's death, Hester is once again alone, circumscribed by the limits of her culture. The novel ends with an ironic query which points to the impossibility of true love or fulfilment for a woman such as Hester: 'And as for Hester, all that can be said for her is that there are two men whom she may choose between [Harry or Roland], and marry either if she pleases – good men both, who will never wring her heart ... What can a young woman desire more than to have such a possibility of choice?' (495). What indeed!

A Career Beyond Marriage: *Kirsteen*

Kirsteen (1889) answers the narrator's question in *Hester* as to what a woman might desire beyond the prospect of marriage. Another of Oliphant's capable women, Kirsteen neither marries to find happiness in an unconventional relationship, like Phoebe, nor is she thwarted, like Hester, by limitations with respect to both the opportunities and relationships that women face in her society. Oliphant once again marks the singularity of her heroine through a reworking of generic plots, a departure from conventional narrative that she openly foregrounds: 'Kirsteen was one of those who make a story for themselves,' the narrator tells us early on.[24] While *Phoebe Junior* and *Hester* revise the version of the courtship plot that addresses a choice in suitors, *Kirsteen* reworks two other traditional kinds of narrative. The first, another courtship plot, concerns disagreement over the marriage choice between parents and children, such as we see in *Clarissa* and *Persuasion*. The second is the tale of the hero's progress, exemplified in novels such as *David Copperfield*, *Great Expectations*, and *The Heir of Redclyffe*.[25] These respective narratives are almost always gendered: women disagree with their parents about the marriage choice while men go off to make their fortunes. Oliphant's innovation is to reject the gendered limitations of women's lives by appropriating the second, 'male' plot for her heroine, while at the same time altering its essentially masculine characteristics. This new narrative of the heroine's progress replaces the first courtship plot, the traditional woman's story.

Kirsteen's tale begins by invoking its gendered shadow plot, disagreement over the marriage choice. Kirsteen is the daughter of Drumcarro, an impoverished but noble and fiercely proud lord of the Douglas family, who lost their lands and wealth after the failed rebellion of Bonny Prince Charlie in 1745. Her father is a patriarch in the most patriarchal sense, a tyrant who terrifies his invalid wife (her bodily weakness figures her moral defeat) and treats his daughters as worthless appendages, despite their substantial contribution to running his household and providing for his daily comfort. Although he ordinarily forces these young women to live in obscurity, seeing few outsiders and acquiring what little education they can on their own, Drumcarro decides to send his two older daughters to the duke's ball, both for the dignity of the family name, and in the remote hope that one of them will find a husband. This plan succeeds with unexpected alacrity, for Glendochart, an older man, falls in love with Kirsteen. But such a marriage is impossible, for unbeknownst to her family, Kirsteen and her lover Ronald have already pledged their troths on the night before he left for India to make his fortune. Although the engagement is secret and must remain so for the time being, in the young lovers' eyes, they are already married. Drumcarro is enraged when Kirsteen will not agree to marry Glendochart; like all misogynist tyrants, he dismisses the issue of her consent to the marriage. 'You're not of the least importance' (81), he tells her. While Kirsteen knows that the kindhearted Glendochart would not force her to marry, nor would he want her if she did not love him, Kirsteen fears that her father will literally strike her dead if she refuses. She flees his house in terror.

With Kirsteen's flight, the second narrative, 'the hero's progress,' begins. Relying on the help of the family servant Margaret, Kirsteen travels to London to Margaret's sister, Miss Jean, a successful dressmaker. Kirsteen convinces Miss Jean to let her enter the business, despite the latter's misgivings about employing an aristocrat in trade. It is precisely Kirsteen's genteel status that makes her story so unusual; for a working-class woman like Miss Jean, it was socially acceptable to own a business. The social problem in this and other of Oliphant's novels is finding independence and occupation for middle- and upper-class women. Kirsteen's unusual circumstances allow her opportunities denied to other women of her station, and she makes the most of them. Kirsteen turns out to have a genius for fashion and a keen business sense. She transforms Miss Jean's establishment into the most sought after and respected of its kind in London.

In the chapters that portray this period, the courtship plot and the story of the hero's progress overlap. Kirsteen waits for her lover to return from India, when she will leave business to become his wife (the courtship plot), but continues to work in the meantime (the hero's progress). But when her fiancé is killed in battle, the latter plot displaces the former. The novel conveys this displacement not only through narrative, but by using literary diction to signal that what Kirsteen thinks of as an 'episode' (213) in her life, her dressmaking career, will become her true story, while her romance will be relegated to the status of just that, a romance.[26] Kirsteen's expectation of a domestic rather than a business career turns out to be the digression, the 'episode.' Thus, with her lover's death, literary terminology begins to be applied to Kirsteen's life as a bride to be, rather than as a businesswoman: 'Life was over for Kirsteen [after Ronald's death]; and life began. No longer *a preparatory chapter*, a thing to be given up when the happy moment came – but the only life that was to be vouchsafed to her in this earth so full of the happy and the unhappy' (228) [emphasis added]. The parallel structure of the sentence ['life was over ... life began'] indicates that one life will replace the other, while the reference to the first life, the time when she expects to marry, as a 'chapter' enacts its dissolution into unreality, a point that is underscored by various comments on the fictive nature of Kirsteen's romance throughout the novel. Kirsteen's Scottish acquaintances who come to Miss Jean for dresses are fascinated by Kirsteen's past: 'So interesting – like a story out of a novel' (69), comments one. 'So dramatic! It might go on the stage' (69), says another.' Kirsteen herself refers to this part of her life as 'an old story' (219). Most important, later in Kirsteen's life, this romantic episode has become almost completely illusory to her:

> In the times which are not ancient history, which some of us still remember ... there lived in one of the most imposing houses in one of the princeliest squares of Edinburgh a lady who was an old lady, yet still, as may be said, in the prime of life. Her eye was not dim nor her natural force abated; her beautiful head of hair was still red, her eyes still full of fire. She drove the finest horses in the town, and gave dinners in which judges delighted and where the best talkers were glad to go. Her hospitality was almost boundless, her large house running over with hordes of nephews and nieces; her advice, which meant her help, continually demanded from one side or other of a large and widely extended family. No one could be more cheerfull, more full of interest in all that went on. Her fig-

ure had expanded a little like her fortune, but she was the best-dressed woman in Edinburgh, always clothed in rich, dark-colored silks and satins, with lace which a queen might have envied. Upon the table by her bed-head there stood a silver casket [containing the handkerchief she had given Ronald, embroidered with her hair] without which she never moved; but the story of which the records were there enshrined sometimes appeared to this lady like a beautiful dream of the past, of which she was not always sure that it had ever been. (323)

Kirsteen's own romantic past has become as unreal as a 'story' or a 'dream,' while the time and life she leads at the moment, which she has created by her own industry and genius, is a reality she inhabits to the fullest.

The appropriation of the hero's plot to a heroine's story is initially signalled by the novel's invocation of the traditional narrative that it usurps. *Kirsteen* begins with what appears to be a conventional hero's progress narrative, the story of her brother's departure for India (along with her lover). This thread of 'male' narrative, which is soon abandoned, serves as a point of comparison for Kirsteen's own flight. In particular, the image of the road, and the description of the brother's and sister's journeys (at least in its initial stage for Robbie), predominate in both narratives; these are familiar tropes of the genre.[27] The novel initially focuses on this ultimately irrelevant story of Robbie in order to establish the congruence between sister and brother: Robbie leaves to make his fortune; Kirsteen later departs to make hers as well. Yet while equating the two stories to characterize Kirsteen's masculine path, the novel also emphasizes the unusual nature of Kirsteen's undertaking. When she tells Miss Jean that she plans 'to work for [her] living – and make [her] fortune, if [she] can' (149), Miss Jean replies, 'That's all very well in a lad – and there's just quantities of them goes into the city without a penny and comes out like nabobs in their carriages – but not women, my dear' (149).

But that is precisely what Kirsteen does. Indeed, her extraordinary success as much as the nature of her enterprise constitutes the novel's most significant appropriation of male narrative. Drumcarro sends all Kirsteen's brothers away as they reach manhood, both to obtain a living for themselves and, more important in his view, to attempt to make some money that can be put towards re-establishing the family economically. When Glendochart takes an interest in Kirsteen, the family hope that she will contribute to this effort in a woman's way, by bringing some of her husband's prosperity to them. The promise of easier times is suggested from the start of Glendochart's courtship by his pleasant tokens of affection for the whole family, such as chocolate and oranges, luxuries in the impoverished highlands. The only remorse that Kirsteen feels in running away is that she has ruined the chance for a better life for her mother and siblings. But she vows to compensate, to become 'the staff of her family.' And this is just what she does. While her brothers all achieve a modicum of success, Kirsteen's accomplishment is the most dramatic; it is she who restores the family to its proper economic and social standing, not her brothers. In fact, when the heir returns from his work abroad, he is surprised to find that he owes the restoration of his lands to his sister. Kirsteen enjoys the independence, money, power, and status usually reserved for highly successful and competent men – men who possess the energy and aggression needed to compete successfully in the marketplace.

As in the case of Oliphant's other heroines, an unusual life suits an unusual woman. Although as a young woman Kirsteen longs for the safe return of her lover above all else, the life she dreams of is actually inappropriate for a woman of her talent and intensity. While her life as Ronald's wife would have been less oppressive and more eventful than her life at home before she goes to London, Kirsteen's longing for adventure suggests that any life confined to the purely domestic would not be enough for her. On the eve of her brother's departure, she complains, 'I cannot settle to work ... I'm not just a machine for darning stockings. I wish I was Robbie, going out into the world' (23). Later, her dissatisfaction with the pettiness of domestic life is revealed by her intolerance of her sister Anne's inability to see beyond the concerns of her husband and children. Viewing her sister with her family at home, 'Kirsteen stood and looked upon them all with a flash of scorn. Was this the effect of marrying and being happy, as people say? The little plump mother, with her rosy face, no longer capable of responding to any call outside of her own little circle of existence The prosaic interior, the bondage of all these little necessities, the loosening of all other bonds of older date or wider reach, was this what happiness meant?' (239–40). Once Kirsteen follows Robbie's path, she has no regrets. Kirsteen decides early on that 'even if there was no Glendochart she would not now go back. She would stay and work and make her fortune' (150).

Yet, while Kirsteen achieves a man's aims, she does so by relying on women and womanly concerns. To obtain positions for his sons,

Drumcarro calls on a network of male friends and acquaintances. When Kirsteen sets out on her journey, she appeals to an alternative network of female contacts, which includes innkeepers, her sister Anne in Glasgow, Margaret, Miss Jean, and the acquaintances in London who flock to her shop and help to establish her sovereignty as a designer in fashionable circles. It is through dressmaking, a woman's concern, that she builds her social and financial dominion. Kirsteen's story thus not only appropriates a male narrative, but revises it with respect to both gender and genre so that it is neither exclusively a woman's nor a man's story. Such refiguring creates a narrative that cannot be divided along the usual lines of gender and empowerment, thereby forcefully rejecting patriarchal restrictions and mandates. Like Catherine Vernon's assumption of masculine and feminine subjectivities in *Hester*, Kirsteen's story disrupts the binary logic of men's supremacy.

The novel's rejection of male authority and women's subordination is emblematized through Kirsteen's name. When she becomes Miss Jean's partner, she refuses to use her family name, calling herself 'Miss Kirsteen' instead, ostensibly in order to avoid sullying the Douglas name by associating it with trade. However, her avowed intention in using her first name is undermined within the text, for despite Kirsteen's ambivalence about the relationship between her aristocratic heritage and her career, the novel ultimately shows her choice to have been a noble and proper one. In the end, Kirsteen's rejection of the name of the father, especially the name of this particular father, figures the refutation of patriarchal authority that she enacts by going into business and therefore needing to put her name on a plate. The novel emphasizes the significance of Kirsteen's self-naming by calling our attention to it repeatedly: when she enters into a partnership with Miss Jean (174); in conversation with her father, to reassure him that she has not sullied his aristocratic heritage (280); and significantly, at the very end of the novel, whose last sentence reminds us that 'her name had appeared on a neat plate in conjunction with the name of Miss Jean Brown, Court Dressmaker and Mantua-Maker, as Miss Kirsteen' (324).[28] As she has made her way in the world, so she has chosen her name.

6
Liberalism and Feminism: The End of the Line

I conclude with Oliphant because she represents a founding moment in the critique of liberal feminism with which we are so familiar today; Oliphant rejects the belief that married love holds the promise – or the threat – of equity for women in their relationships with men. I have argued throughout this study that this belief came about as changes in the ideology of marriage contributed to an emergent feminism in the eighteenth and nineteenth centuries. Implicit in the companionate ideal was an extension of the principles of liberal theory to women as well as men, above all the individual's right to freedom and self-determination. This is because once marriage was viewed as an agreement between lovers rather than families, it situated women within the liberal discourse of contract, thereby theoretically guaranteeing certain inalienable rights, rights that were at odds with both law and custom. Feminists in this period therefore invoked liberal contract theory, especially that of Locke, to argue that a woman who was capable of making the proper ethical marriage choice and who was expected to enter into a marriage of her own free will possessed an autonomous subjectivity – a 'contractual subjectivity' – that challenged a wife's subordination. Moreover, the threat of equality inherent in a woman's role as friend and partner also challenged beliefs about sexual difference, a fundamental premise of women's subordination, as we see in the writings of both feminists and their opponents in this period. Finally, by suggesting that women and men ought to be companions as well as lovers, an ideal of married love revised ideas about masculinity, as well as ideas about womanhood, undermining many traditional markers of manliness.

Focusing on particularly legible examples, I have looked at how the novel as a genre enables us to trace the logic of this argument. In *Sir*

Charles Grandison, Richardson accepts the challenge of defending paternal absolutism from the challenge that was implicit in granting women freedom in the marriage choice. While in accord with a Christian ethic of consensual marriage, this novel actively endorses the virtues of marriage for love throughout its seven volumes, at the same time, it disarms the potentially disruptive, liberal implications of this ideal through its various plots. *Grandison* defines appropriate forms of love against volatile alternatives which might undermine established socio-economic as well as gender hierarchies through Sir Charles's 'double love' for two women, which is played out through the bifurcation of the novel's primary narrative. This enables the dual endorsement of companionate love, a form of friendship, and sentimental love, a blend of reason and passion, both of which guarantee marriage choices likely to accord with a father's judgment. Other narrative lines demonstrate the rejection of romantic love and lust, subversive modes of feeling in that they cannot be trusted to lead to appropriate marriage choices. Richardson's strategic characterization of Sir Charles's sister Charlotte in the most important of the novel's subplots dissociates women's contractual subjectivity from consensual married love, linking 'feminism' and its dangers with passionlessness rather than feeling: Charlotte, the novel's sole advocate of women's rights, appears to be incapable of falling in love. But this apparent invulnerability brings its own dangers, threatening to undermine sexual difference, for women are supposedly more susceptible to the 'tender passion.' Richardson escapes this double bind by suggesting that Charlotte is like other women after all; she loves, but her love is an incestuous passion for her own brother, which she cannot admit, even to herself. *Grandison* also addresses the threat to sexual difference posed by the 'new husband' by revising the terms of masculinity itself: Sir Charles shows that true manliness consists of virtue and feeling, while aggression, the mainstay of traditional masculinity, is in reality the sign of effeminacy.

Austen also focuses on the problem of the marriage choice, exploring the contradictions in conduct that followed from the new ethic of married love. How was a daughter to marry for love while obeying her parents? How was she to marry at all if each continually vetoed the other's choices? *Persuasion*'s two stories, of Anne in the past and Anne in the present, both reveal the costs and benefits of filial obedience in the marriage choice. However, through the cumulative meaning of individual scenes, *Persuasion* moves beyond the indecision it reflects in its structure, ultimately validating passion over prudence as a superior ethical motive for marriage. This conflict, and the alternatives it presents, affects not only the interests of daughters but the moral quality of society itself. As Hume contends in his *Treatise of Human Nature*, society depends upon sympathy, the ability to transcend the boundaries of self-interest and to identify imaginatively with others. At its best, passion, including love, is an intensified form of such sympathy (i.e., sentimental love), even if it can sometimes be a destructive force for both individuals and families. Prudence, in contrast, while it can take benevolent forms, is perpetually on the brink of collapse into self-interest, which threatens to dissolve the bonds of civilized society altogether. Implicit in this grammar of values is a critique of the theory of rights, which is the basis of conduct-book advice that attempts to avert crises over the marriage choice. Austen thus anticipates feminist critiques of liberalism in our own day.

Austen's endorsement of passion instantiates a shift in values for the novel as a genre. While the difference between constructive and harmful forms of love that we see in *Grandison* continued to be recognized in the nineteenth-century novel, it became much less important than the contrast between love and interest. Victorian writers on the whole followed Austen's identification of strong feeling, whatever its motive or origin, as the guarantor of an ethical society: in these later novels, passion is often a trope for purity and disinterestedness, qualities which oppose the calculated and heartless materialism that was believed to be one of the primary moral evils of the time. In novels of this period, married love often stands for Christian values such as piety, mercy, empathy, and decency, which many believed were being neglected by an England caught up in an addictive and corrupting capitalist machine. The elision of distinctions between kinds of love exacerbated the 'problem' of women's autonomy, for if such distinctions encoded the exclusivity of England's elites, they also encoded the patriarchal objectives of marriage. For Victorian novelists, then, the association between married love and women's rights became even more volatile.

This linkage is especially clear in the work of Anthony Trollope, whose novels obsessively inculcate the value of marriage for love as an index of England's moral and spiritual health. *He Knew He Was Right* explores the subversive implications of the marriage choice for women, taking up the issues Mill addressed in *The Subjection of Women*. *The Subjection* claims that marriage laws, which placed a wife under the complete legal and financial control of her husband, flout the logic of contract implicit in an ideal of married love. Through narrative rather than exposition, by juxtaposing a primary plot in which a wife's demand for a reasonable amount of autonomy leads her husband to suspect her of adultery and a subplot in which a young woman angers her guardian by becoming engaged without permission, *He Knew He Was Right* thematizes the contradiction between Victorian domestic ideals and marriage laws – between a vision of marriage as a loving partnership and a legalized version of gender relations that denied women's separate personhood altogether. However, Trollope was not a feminist, and he publicly criticized women's rights. He therefore attempts to mitigate the progressive implications of his novel by redefining masculinity as authoritative, yet not oppressive, as Richardson had done. Yet Trollope's attempts at ideological backpedalling are unsuccessful; he lacks the casuistical ingenuity (or perhaps disingenuousness) that we see in Richardson. Such a failure renders *He Knew He Was Right* part of the feminist discourse of its time, a fate which was probably not entirely surprising to its author, viewed in light of his meditations on the necessarily paradoxical nature of politics in his *Autobiography*.

With Oliphant's novels, the happy union of liberalism with feminism begins to unravel. Richardson and Trollope feared that the companionate ideal implied an extension of the priciples of liberal theory to women; Austen suggested that there might be psychological impediments to embracing such freedom, but did not question the probability of finding loving and workable partnerships through marriages that defied paternalism and inequality. Oliphant, however, shows that the freedom to follow one's heart is often a worthless privilege.

The truth about marriage for love, as demonstrated in *Phoebe Junior*, *Hester*, and *Kirsteen* is that it is never sufficiently liberating or fulfilling, for intelligent, proficient, ambitious women. Within English society, both men and women are positioned (socially, economically, psychologically) in gendered roles that obviate the possibility of companionate marriage. A woman cannot be a true partner within marriage, given that marriage is part of a culture that denies the possibility of such partnership through its legal and social institutions. In this sense, Oliphant has much in common with liberalism's feminist critics of today, who argue that the liberal subject is tacitly a man, and thus women are excluded from the parity that liberalism ostensibly guarantees. Oliphant's novels also suggest that for truly capable women, marriage is simply not enough. The gendering of private and public spheres, which some theorists argue is an ineluctable feature of liberalism, also typifies Victorian ideology about work and marriage. Oliphant's unusual women thrive on this public dimension, conventionally denied to women.

Insofar as Oliphant would never have argued for the kinds of radical changes in society that would eliminate inequities for women, her feminist insights lead to a dead end (although to be fair, how could anyone have imagined the agendas of feminists of the following centuries?). But the quietistic pessimism of her observations does not negate the fact that she grasped the problems women face in a culture that genders both roles and personalities from an androcentric perspective. More hopefully, her work also suggests that in performing and reiterating these personas, there is always the chance of slippage between prescription and reality; the capable woman emerges in the interstices of conventional expectations.

Oliphant herself inhabited this ideological no wo/man's land. All her adult life, she supported her family through her writing. Yet although she wrote in the service of her family, this was not her only, or even her primary, motive. Like her own capable heroines, the domestic was never enough, no matter how intensely caring and dedicated she was to her loved ones. And like many women today who want both career and family, she felt divided and inadequate. Although she would never have relinquished the responsibilities or the pleasures (fleeting towards the end of her life) of family life, she nevertheless felt it keenly that her work suffered from her inability to devote herself completely to literature. She was resentful and jealous of George Eliot, whose writing was not impaired by the stress of a divided identity. In *The Autobiography* she writes, 'No one will even mention me in the same breath with George Eliot. And that is just. It is a little justification to myself to think how much better off she was, – no trouble in all her life as far as appears, but the natural one of her father's death – and perhaps coolnesses with her brothers and sisters, though that is not said. And though her marriage is not one that most of us would have ventured on, still it seems to have secured her a worshipper unrivalled.'[1]

While the handicaps of domestic life might not have been primarily to blame for Oliphant's inability to equal Eliot's accomplishment as a writer, the fact that she believed this to be true is telling.[2] The autobiographical assertion expresses her perception of the inevitable frustrations that accompany women's attempts to exceed the bounds of their subordinate identity and constricted lives. Only women who 'become' men, as did Eliot, with her adoring spouse and few encumbrances, will be able to fulfil their potential. Whether the promise of equity takes the form of work, through succeeding to the fullest possible extent in a man's world, or of marriage, through a companionate ideal that promises true partnership, it can never be achieved as long as people are 'interpellated as gender' in hierarchized and inequitable ways. With Oliphant's work we see that although the equity implied by consensual married love might have been an enabling fiction, it was ultimately destined to be unmasked as more fictitious than enabling.

Notes

Introduction

1 Brathwaite, *The English Gentlewoman*, 344. In *A Midsummer Night's Dream* (I.ii. 93–4), Lysander uses the same gag line.
2 Austen, *Northanger Abbey and Persuasion*, 246.
3 'Structure of feeling' is Raymond Williams's term, by which he means a 'cultural hypothesis' that enables us to define individual perception within a given period of culture without reducing it to either the individual or the collective. 'The term ... feeling is chosen to emphasize a distinction from more formal concepts of "world-view" or "ideology" ... [W]e are concerned with meanings and values as they are actively lived and felt, and the relations between these and formal or systematic beliefs.' *Marxism and Literature*, 132. I find Williams's definition especially useful because it embraces thought, feeling, and theory, thereby epitomizing the way in which liberal ideals permeated both public and private life.
4 In subsequent chapters, I explain that categories of love unacceptable to middle-class ideology were lust and romantic love, while permissible ones were 'companionate love' (friendship) and 'sentimental love' (virtuous passion). Because the terminology is already in place within the critical and historical literature about love and marriage, I use the phrase 'companionate marriage' or the 'companionate ideal' to refer more generally to the belief that love ought to be an important component of the marriage choice, while also using the term 'companionate love' to refer to a specific mode of feeling. The lack of distinction within this terminology indicates that literary critics and historians have often missed the complexity of ideals of love. Lawrence Stone discusses the categories of 'romantic' and 'companionate' love but does not recognize their crucial synthesis in sentimental love. *The*

Family, Sex and Marriage in England, 217–53. Joseph Allen Boone also neglects this category, viewing romantic love as the motive for companionate marriage. *Tradition Counter Tradition*. Jean H. Hagstrum shows how sentimental love includes both passion and friendship, but fails to account for the historical and ideological factors that generate these categories. *Sex and Sensibility*, 160–85. Erica Harth astutely analyses sentimental love but does not distinguish it from companionate love, which serves a crucial function within the very terms of historical analysis that underpin her discussion. 'The Virtue of Love: Lord Hardwicke's Marriage Act.'

5 Congreve, *The Way of the World*, 86.

6 Perry, 'Women in Families,' 120.

7 Barrett Browning, *The Letters of Elizabeth and Robert Browning*, 31.

8 Barrett Browning, 'Letters on Aurora Leigh,' *Aurora Leigh*, ed. Reynolds, 334.

9 Whatever their differences, most historians of the novel writing after the publication of Ian Watt's *The Rise of the Novel* (1957) agree that the genre articulated and disseminated middle-class values. Scholars of a post-Watt generation, however, tend to emphasize that the novel does not merely reflect middle-class identity, but also helps to produce it. See Armstrong, *Desire and Domestic Fiction*; Brown, *Institutions of the Novel*; Hunter, *Before Novels*; Mayer, 'Did You Say Middle Class? The Question of Taste and the Rise of the Novel'; McKeon, *The Origins of the English Novel, 1600–1740*; and Warner, *Licensing Entertainment*.

10 This point is fundamental to both McKeon and Armstrong.

11 This famous phrase appears in a letter from Samuel Richardson to Aaron Hill dated 5 January 1746/7. Richardson, *Selected Letters*, 76. It also appears in the title of an anonymous pamphlet, *Essay on the New Species of Writing founded by Mr Fielding*. The author's preface and half of the essay is reprinted in *Novel and Romance 1700–1800*, 150–9. Henry Fielding uses the term 'new Province of Writing' to signal that *Tom Jones* constitutes a deliberate departure from other traditional genres: 'For as I am, in reality, the Founder of a new Province of Writing, so I am at liberty to make what Laws I please therein.' *The History of Tom Jones, a Foundling*, 77.

12 This belief was so pervasive that I will not attempt to pinpoint an originary moment. Books that address this issue at some length include Flint, *The Woman Reader*; Langbauer, *Women and Romance*; Pearson, *Women's Reading in Britain*; Taylor, *Early Opposition to the English Novel*; Todd, *Sensibility: An Introduction*, 132–7; and Warner, *Licensing Entertainment*.

13 Warburton and Blair, *On Fictitious History* (1726), 123. Cited by Warner, *Licensing Entertainment*, 11. Taylor points out that 'the standard preface of

the eighteenth-century novel contains dual protestations to fidelity of fact and moral aim' (88). However, as a century of sophisticated reflection on the issue has shown, there is no simple or stable ontological way of defining realism. For a survey and analysis of theoretical issues associated with realism, see Shaw, *Narrating Reality.* Although the claim to realism on the part of novelists of the classical period might be naive, this does not render it any less useful as an index of their concerns and objectives.

14 Samuel Johnson, '*Rambler* 4, Saturday, March 31, 1750,' *Samuel Johnson: Rasselas, Poems and Selected Prose,* 69.

15 Warner, *Licensing Entertainment,* 6.

16 It is telling that as feminist attitudes towards liberalism have become more problematic, literature has begun to articulate the negative implications of sexual contracts for women. See, for instance, Morgenstern, 'The Afterlife of Coverture: Contract and Gift in The Ballad of the Sad Cafe,' forthcoming.

17 Garrett, *The Victorian Multiplot Novel,* 15, 20.

18 There are exceptions. See note 4 above.

19 Watt argues that the individuation of character, one of the distinguishing features of the novel, depends on liberal notions of epistemology, especially those of Locke and Hume, as well as on the liberal emphasis on individual rights. McKeon extends Watt's account, showing why those elements of the novel resistant to Watt's theory, such as the presence of non-realistic, romance elements, continued to be a significant feature of the genre. Kay, in *Political Constructions,* draws primarily on Hobbes's writing to argue for the influence of contemporary political thought on the novel. Irene Tucker looks to the genre to discuss the relationship between liberalism and national identity. *A Probable State.* Armstrong concentrates on gender, arguing that modern, middle-class ideals of subjectivity were essentially feminine ideals. Liberal theory is important to her analysis as we see in her evocation of contract theory to discuss the way in which the sexual contract, implicit in marriage, allegorizes class alliance and class conflict. None of these studies, however, addresses the relationship between liberalism and women's subjectivity.

20 Langland, *Nobody's Angels,* 7.

21 Mill, 'The Subjection of Women,' *Essays on Sex Equality,* 168–9.

22 Trumbach, *The Rise of the Egalitarian Family.*

23 Okin, 'Women and the Making of the Sentimental Family,' 65 and 88.

24 In following Okin on this point, I do not espouse a simplistic notion of separate spheres that positions women as entirely powerless. Studies such as Langland's clearly document the ways in which women wielded cultural power in this period, power which accorded them control over many of the

material as well as the social aspects of their world. But it is nevertheless true that wives lacked legal identity, and that most also lacked economic self-sufficiency, as well as access to education or the professions. To overestimate the reach of the middle-class woman's power is, ironically, to subscribe to a version of the doctrine of influence, which nineteenth-century opponents of women's rights believed could compensate wives for their lack of legal and economic authority. I discuss this more fully in the following chapter.

25 Staves, *Married Women's Separate Property*. See also Okin, 'Patriarchy and Married Women's Property in England: Questions on Some Current Views.' Okin observes that the practice of strict settlement, which gave landed property to the eldest son while also specifying financial provisions for daughters, probably did give daughters greater freedom in the marriage choice. But, as Staves emphasizes, it is important to remember that increased freedoms for women were a by-product of practices designed to preserve the property of families.

26 Okin, 'Patriarchy and Married Women's Property' and Staves, *Married Women's Separate Property*, chap. 5.

27 In discussing this debate, I draw on two essays that I believe best epitomize pro- and anti-liberal feminism, even though the essays do not directly address one another. See Brown, 'Liberalism's Family Values,' and Nussbaum, 'The Feminist Critique of Liberalism.' Subsequent references to these essays appear in the text. The feminist literature both for and against liberalism is extensive. Selected writings include Eisenstein, *The Radical Future of Liberal Feminism*, *Feminism and Sexual Equality*, and *The Color of Gender*; Harstock, *Money, Sex, and Power*; Hampton, 'Feminist Contractarianism'; Hirschman, *Rethinking Obligation*; Jagger, *Feminist Politics and Human Nature*; MacKinnon, *Toward a Feminist Theory of the State*; Noddings, *Caring*; Okin, *Justice, Gender and the Family*; Pateman, *The Sexual Contract* and *The Problem of Political Obligation*; Pateman and Grosz, eds., *Feminist Challenges*; and Tronto, *Moral Boundaries*.

28 Brown, however, maintains that this very dichotomy is itself part of the hierarchical gendering of subjectivity.

29 Crittenden, *The Price of Motherhood*.

30 I here allude to Eisenstein's pioneering work, *The Radical Future of Liberal Feminism*. While this study made an important contribution to feminist theory, it reveals some of the problems with taking liberal theory at face value. Anticipating aspects of Brown's argument, Eisenstein recognizes that liberal theory is inherently patriarchal because it enforces hierarchical binary divisions between men and women by defining subjectivity as autonomous

(191). Yet she locates the promise of progress and change – of true equality for women – within this very autonomous liberal subjectivity, contending that the radical future of liberalism for feminists inheres in the conflict of women's identity as mothers with the reality of women as wage earners, a contradiction that will ultimately force women into consciousness and political action. The subordinate place of women in the workplace, and their lack of access to truly equal opportunity, has proved this prediction to be misguided: although there are more women wage earners today than in any other time in Anglo-American history, the continued domination of liberal ideology in the workplace has resulted in the replication of the division between work and private life within the workplace itself. Crittenden shows that mothers (or others, including men, who assume the care of children) who attempt to accommodate work to family life in any way consistently face discrimination, resulting in lower wages and less 'successful' careers in terms of both salary and position. Workers are still largely expected to be autonomous (i.e., liberal subjects) – free of responsibilities other than their jobs. If women, and especially mothers, are to receive truly equal opportunity, there needs to be a radical restructuring of social and economic life that classic liberal theory cannot accommodate. In subsequent work, Eisenstein addresses this problem by theorizing ways in which a revised form of liberalism could lead to such development. In *The Color of Gender* she suggests that liberalism's shortcomings might be corrected by imagining the liberal subject not as a white male, but rather as a woman of colour. Such a shift in focus would enable us 'to reinvent the universality of this discourse [liberal democratic rights discourse] by locating its specification in gender, race, and class' (4) and to 'distinguish ... between liberal individualism, which pictures an atomized and disconnected person in competition with others, and a post-patriarchal individuality that recognizes the capacities and diversity of individuals, although as part of a community that can either enhance or constrain their development' (34).

31 See Langland, *Nobody's Angels*, 1–20 for an analysis of how cultural characteristics constitute an essential component of class as a category.

32 See, for instance, the revisionist historian Dror Wahrman, *Imagining the Middle Class*.

33 Defoe, *Robinson Crusoe*, 9.

34 Perkin, *The Origins of Modern English Society*, 23.

35 Grossmith and Grossmith, *Diary of a Nobody*. Lawrence Stone and Jeanne C. Fawtier Stone maintain that well into the nineteenth century, despite 'the homogeneity of cultural values and behaviour among the landed classes, the wealthier merchant and banking patriciates, and the gentrified "mid-

dling sort" ... the whole of this genteel society was sliced and sliced again into extremely thin status layers, subtly separated from each other by the delicate but infinitely resistant lines of snobbery.' *An Open Elite?*, 423.

36 McKeon, *Origins of the English Novel*, 164. For an account of the middle class in eighteenth-century England, see Paul Langford, *A Polite and Commercial People*, 61–8 and passim.

37 Although scholars of the Victorian period in particular often argue for the originality of its beliefs, those who work in earlier periods as well tend to acknowledge important precedents and roots for supposedly Victorian phenomena. Shifts in belief between the mid-eighteenth century and the Victorian era are often a matter of degree rather than kind. On the continuity of ideals between the eighteenth and nineteenth centuries see Vickery, 'Golden Age to Separate Spheres?.'

38 Individual motives have always been overdetermined and subject to self-deception and displacement. But, as Susan Staves argues, relying on texts to tell us the truth about real marriages is likely to be misleading. Eighteenth-century texts are untrustworthy guides for a variety of reasons: there were multiple, often conflicting, discourses about marriage (conduct books differ from gossip columns); many pronouncements about marriage came from interested parties, such as adversaries in court proceedings; such pronouncements were subject to tacit rules about what could and could not be said; individuals' accounts of their own feelings were often influenced by literary representations; and conventions of expression differ from one age to the next. 'Where Is History But in Texts? Reading the History of Marriage,' 132 and 125–43.

39 Harth, 'The Virtue of Love,' 124. See also Skinner, 'Women's Status as Legal and Civic Subjects,' 92.

1. Married Love and Its Consequences

1 Lawrence Stone writes extensively about the rise of an ethic of married love in *The Family, Sex and Marriage*. While Stone was criticized for being too sanguine about the positive effects of this ideological shift, especially on women's lives (see my discussion in the Introduction), his contention that beliefs about marriage changed in this period is generally accepted.

2 Margo Todd argues that marital love had been forcefully advocated by Renaissance humanists, especially Erasmus, and that the Puritans, who are often viewed as the originators of this ideal, inherited their ideas from earlier humanist writers. *Christian Humanism and the Puritan Social Order.* Tilney's *The Flower of Friendship* (1573), exemplifies the Renaissance com-

panionate ideal of marriage that Todd identifies. Kathleen M. Davies questions the identification of Puritanism with married love from another standpoint, arguing that this ideal stems more generally from the bourgeoisie. Yet identifying married love as either an exclusively middle-class or Puritan ideal becomes problematic when we consider the overlap between these two groups. 'The Sacred Condition of Equality.' On this point see also Gillis, *For Better, For Worse*, 105. In any case, while marital love might not have been the invention or the exclusive intellectual property of the Puritans, they arguably had the widest influence on novelists via Milton's appropriation of some aspects of Puritan doctrine. For Milton's belief in married love see, for instance, the famous apostrophe to wedded love in *Paradise Lost* (bk 4, ll 750–75) and 'The Doctrine and Discipline of Divorce,' *Complete Prose Works of John Milton*, 2:235 and passim.

3 Although there were other many kinds of guides, I discuss texts that concentrate on morals and behaviour rather than on practical skills; these include sermons and dialogues. The conduct book became a recognizable and popular genre in the eighteenth century, but examples of the literature of conduct can be found both earlier and later.

4 On the consistency and stability of the ideology of marriage in conduct literature, see Jones, 'Introduction,' *The Young Lady's Pocket Library*, xvii.

5 Armstrong and Tennenhouse, eds., *The Ideology of Conduct*. While some of the earlier texts I discuss were Puritan guides, these were also middle-class texts.

6 Jones, 'Introduction.' xii.

7 Cleaver, *A Godly Forme of Household Government* (1598 London: Thomas Man, 1603), chap. 1, first page (no page numbers given in this edition).

8 Whatley, *A Bride Bush, or a Wedding Sermon* (1619), 32.

9 Ibid., 42.

10 Snawsel, *A Looking Glass for Married Folk* (1610), 4.

11 *Court of Good Counsell* (1607), chap. 6, second page of chapter (no page numbers given in this edition).

12 Ibid., chap. 6, first page of chapter.

13 Ibid., chap. 1, first page of chapter.

14 Ibid., chap. 6, second page of chapter. This is a familiar observation and can be found in many types of literature, including the romance and other genres that do not necessarily advocate love as a marital motive. In Madame de La Fayette's *The Princess of Cleves*, for instance, the heroine, who enters into an arranged marriage, later falls in love with another man. However, this text does not criticize her parents for forcing her to marry. In *The New Atalantis* (1709), Delarivier Manley expresses the typical English view of a slightly

later date, which is much more aggressively moralistic: 'Were marriages not the result of interest but inclination? Were nothing but generous love! the fire of virtue! and the shine of merit! consulted in that divine union, guilty pleasures would be no more.' *New Atalantis*, 133–4.

15 Allestree, *The Ladies Calling*, 178.

16 Ibid., pt 2, 177, 220.

17 Defoe, *Conjugal Lewdness*, 101.

18 Pennington, *An Unfortunate Mother's Advice*, 66.

19 Ibid., 76.

20 Gregory, *A Father's Legacy to his Daughters*, 108–9.

21 Fordyce, *Sermons to Young Women*, 1:73. Fordyce also comments, 'The parents of the present generation, what with selling their sons and daughters in marriage, and what with teaching them by every possible means the glorious principles of Avarice, have contrived pretty effectually to bring down from its former flights that idle, youthful, unprofitable passion, which has for its object personal attractions, in preference to all the wealth of the world' (1:73).

22 For a survey of opinions in the eighteenth century regarding marital motives, and opinions about the quality of the relationship that follows marriage for love as opposed to the arranged marriage, see Hill, ed., *Eighteenth-Century Women*, 69–88.

23 For an account of several eighteenth-century marriages which show that marriage was never 'a clear-cut operatice choice between love on the one hand and lucre on the other,' see Vickery, *The Gentleman's Daughter*, 39–86.

24 Harth, 'The Virtue of Love: Lord Hardwicke's Marriage Act,' 133. My discussion of the marriage act is indebted to Harth, who shows how arguing for or against married love meant arguing for or against middle-class upward mobility.

25 *The Parliamentary History of England from the Earliest Period to the Year 1803* vol. 15 (London: Hansard, 1813), Sixth Session of the Tenth Parliament of Great Britain, col. 15.

26 Ibid., col. 3.

27 Ibid., col. 46.

28 Ibid., col. 68.

29 Ibid., col. 15.

30 Ibid., col. 18–19.

31 Ibid., col. 52.

32 For instance, Galley, in *Some Considerations upon Clandestine Marriages* (1750), and the anonymous author of *A Letter to the Public* (1753) both support the Marriage Act for a variety of reasons, but above all because it will

preclude fraud and ensure the legitimacy of all marriages as well as the
legitimacy of their issue. Both nevertheless aver the centrality of the issue of
class. Galley argues that if one family gains from upward mobility, another
must suffer, for 'no Advantage in this Way can be made by one Family, but
what must be, in the same Proportion, injurious to another Family.' If the
law must choose between advantage between those of superior and inferior
status, 'Society ought not to consider the Advantage of those, who are most
necessitious, preferably to the Advantage of those, who have most to lose.
For it would be contrary to all the Rules of good Policy, that Society should
shew a greater Regard to its less valuable, than to its more valuable Members' (129–30). Demonstrating more democratic sentiments, the author of *A
Letter* contends that intermarriage between social groups hurts all but the
lowest echelons of society: 'Nor is the Evil I am speaking of confined to
Minors of Rank and Condition; for the Child of an ordinary Tradesman
may marry with, at least, as much Probability of Ruin, as the Child of a
Duke. The Son of a Farmer may throw himself away upon a Prostitute, and
the Daughter of a Cottager be undone by a drunken, dissolute, and abandoned Soldier' (38). Henry Stebbing, who opposes the provision of the Act
that would annul the marriages of minors who marry without parental
consent on the grounds that it defies natural law and illegitimately
encroaches on individual liberty, also acknowledges the significance of
class in this debate, but reaches different conclusions. Stebbing argues that
such unequal marriages are rare even when children and minors are left to
their own devices, 'For look abroad into the World and what will you see?
Why (ordinarily) the Poor marrying among the Poor, the middle Rank
among the middle Rank, and the Rich and the Noble among the Rich and
the Noble.' Trying to prevent exceptional cases by force will lead to more
problems than it solves. *An Enquiry into the Force and Operation of the Annulling Clauses in a late Act for the better preventing of Clandestine Marriages, With
Respect to Conscience* (1754), 48. These tracts have been reprinted in *The Marriage Act of 1753: Four Tracts*.

33 For a survey of contemporary commentary on the Marriage Act, see Hill,
ed., *Eighteenth-Century Women*, 97–100. Hill also reprints Blackstone's codi-
fication of the law that resulted from the Act (99–100), which she cites from
Commentaries on the Laws of England 1:452 and 4:162.

34 Gillis, *For Better, For Worse*, 5.

35 Stone and Stone observe, 'it was the rise of the professions which confused
the status hierarchy more than any influx of low-born merchants.' *An Open
Elite?* 23.

36 Earle, *The Making of the English Middle Class*, 7.

37 Gillis observes that children were pressured into unwanted marriages primarily in aristocratic circles (*For Better, For Worse*, 21). Along similar lines, Stone and Stone contend that despite a widespread belief in the permeability of the English upper classes, social mobility by marriage into the highest ranks of society was extremely rare. That the arranged marriage was identified with the aristocracy well into the nineteenth century can be seen in Anthony Trollope's *Can You Forgive Her?* (1864), in which Lady Glencora is unduly pressured to marry Plantagenet Palliser. Trollope's novels generally show that young people determined to resist marriages desired by their parents, or determined to marry those whom their parents disapprove, get their way in the end. But these defiant sons and daughters are from the middle classes, as are most of Trollope's characters.

38 Habakkuk, 'Marriage Settlements in the Eighteenth Century.' Strict settlement entailed the family estate on the eldest son, thus prohibiting the sale of significant portions of landed property to raise cash and ensuring that landed wealth, especially the family seat, would descend intact through generations. Habbakuk notes that as political power was becoming more and more dependent on landed wealth rather than royal favour (as it had been in the sixteenth and early seventeenth centuries), wealth, both in the form of land and capital to acquire land, became a priority among England's landed elite. Marriage was one of the most efficient ways to increase the family fortune.

39 Temple, 'An Essay on Popular Discontents.' *Miscellanea. The Third Part.* (1701), 79–80. Temple also notes that 'this custom is of no ancient date in England' (79). Whether or not he is right, it is significant that Temple associates the practice of mercenary marriage with an increase in the commercial and professional wealth of the middle classes and with the rise of the legal practice of strict settlement.

40 Behn, *The Rover*, 45. Although Behn herself was not an aristocrat, her work articulates conventional attitudes of an aristocratic subject position.

41 This play is especially interesting with respect to issues of class and marriage. Sir Giles's attempt to enter the ranks of the nobility through his daughter is motivated by class antagonism. For him, interclass marriage is a form of class revenge: 'I will have her well attended, there are Ladies/ Of errant knights decay'd, and brought so low,/ That for cast clothes, and meate, will gladly serve her./ And 'tis my glory, though I come from the Cittie,/ To have their issue, whom I have undone,/ To kneel to mine.' Massinger, *A New Way To Pay Old Debts*, 29.

42 Sir Andrew Freeport in the 'Sir Roger de Coverly' *Spectator* papers, exemplifies this type of merchant, while Steele's *The Conscious Lovers* (1722) pro-

vides a particularly relevant example of this defensiveness. The themes of Steele's play are mercenary marriage and the virtuous character of respectable merchants. Cimberton, who aspires to a marriage of convenience with Lucinda, is loathesome, old, and ugly, providing a distinct contrast to the attractive merchant heroes of the play. Steele thus defends prosperous merchants from charges of mercenariness by scapegoating an inferior strain of their breed, a man willing to marry a woman sight unseen for money.

43 The concept of mutual hegemony relies on Antonio Gramsci's definition of hegemony as rule by consent in *Selections from the Prison Notebooks*, 5–231, and on Terry Eagleton's application of this concept to eighteenth-century studies. See his *Rape of Clarissa*, 1–5; *The Function of Criticism*, 9–27; and *Ideology of the Aesthetic*, 31–3. There is a consensus among historians and literary critics that in eighteenth-century England, middle-class values and representational codes displaced aristocratic ones. Studies that note this process include Armstrong, *Desire and Domestic Fiction*; McKeon, *The Origins of the English Novel*; Pollak, *The Poetics of Sexual Myth*; and Stone and Stone, *An Open Elite?*

44 Political leadership derived to a great extent from ownership of land, which still belonged primarily to the upper classes. On this point see Stone and Stone, *An Open Elite?*, 283, and Davidoff and Hall, *Family Fortunes*, 20.

45 Paul Langford maintains that by the late eighteenth century, 'peers had influence, but not power, let alone hegemony. The power that they continued to wield depended on their identity as 'a large propertied class, not a narrow oligarchy.' Although the primarily aristocratic and landed identity of those in positions of power suggests the continued rule of the upper classes, Langford's claims draw attention to the blurring of distinctions, based on mutuality of interests, between different social groups. *A Polite and Commercial People*, 30.

46 I owe this insight to Professor Rosemary Kegl of the University of Rochester.

47 On the middle-class appropriation of aristocratic customs see Stone and Stone, *An Open Elite?*, 409–10.

48 Pierre Bourdieu explains the relationship between symbolic capital and wealth: cultural 'practice never ceases to conform to economic calculation even when it gives every appearance of disinterestedness by departing from the logic of interested calculation (in the narrow sense) and playing for stakes that are non-material and not easily quantified.' *Outline of a Theory of Practice*, 177.

49 McKeon points out that the ideals of aristocratic ideology continued to be influential in the form he designates as conservative ideology, which admitted aristocratic tenets, but often with new justification (*Origins of The*

English Novel, 170). Birth makes a person better not because of inherited tendencies, but rather because it presents him/her with opportunities for self-cultivation not available to those born of lesser rank.

50 McKeon, *Origins of The English Novel*, 167.

51 *The Spectator*, 3:15–16.

52 Steele, 'The Tatler' 25, *Selections from The Tatler and The Spectator*, 86–7. See also *Spectator* 356 and 516. On the controversy about duelling, see Andrew, 'The Code of Honour and Its Critics,' 416–20. On the history of duelling see Kiernan, *The Duel in European History*. The last duel in England was fought in 1852. Burn, *The Age of Equipoise*, 257.

53 Terry Eagleton notes the importance of the *The Tatler* and *The Spectator* in creating an alliance between the upper and middle classes. See *The Function of Criticism*, 11.

54 On the levelling effects of ideals of virtue and sentiment see Todd, *Sensibility: An Introduction*, 132–3 and Markley, 'Sentimentality As Performance,' 218.

55 That identities exist not in isolation but rather in a dialectical relationship with one another is a generally accepted principle of feminist scholarship and cultural studies. My focus on marriage and liberal theory leads me to address the relationship between class and gender in particular.

56 Mill, 'The Subjection of Women,' 184.

57 Blackstone, *Commentaries on the Laws of England*, 1:430. Blackstone is also popularly believed to have said, 'in law a husband and wife are one person, and the husband is that person.' Cited by Holcombe, *Wives and Property*, 18.

58 The one exception in common law was real property, which a husband could not dispose of without his wife's consent, although he had a right to any income it generated. My information on marriage law is indebted to Holcombe, *Wives and Property*; Shanley, *Feminism, Marriage and the Law in Victorian England*; and Staves, *Married Women's Separate Property*.

59 As Staves points out, these settlements were generally made to protect property, not to give women freedom. See *Married Women's Separate Property*, chap. 5.

60 Property of any kind could be settled on a woman for her use under the guardianship of a trustee. If the terms of her settlement specified no restrictions on her ownership, she could use her property free from common law liabilities. She could sell it, will it to whom she pleased, use it to run an independent business, or even to leave an abusive husband.

61 Cobbe, 'Criminals, Idiots, Women and Minors: Is the Classification Sound?'

62 Wollstonecraft, *A Vindication of the Rights of Woman*, 113, 189. Subsequent references are to this edition and appear in the text.

63 Cobbe, 'Criminals,' 788, 790. Conversely, those opposed to feminism argued that granting women's rights would undermine the institution of marriage. One opponent of Married Women's Property contended that 'it was a most important thing toward preserving the institution of marriage that the identity of interests between the parties and the control of the husband over the joint property should be maintained as far as possible.' *Parliamentary Debates*, 3rd ser. vol. 192, 21 June 1870, col. 604. Another feared that 'unless you put the whole property of a married couple in the hands of the husband ... there is no chance of concord and harmony in the marriage state.' Ibid. (June 10, 1868), col. 1364.

64 Reid, *A Plea for Woman*, xxvii. Cited by Helsinger, Sheets, and Veeder, *The Woman Question* 14.

65 'The Lady's New-year's Gift: or, Advice to a Daughter,' in *The Works of George Savile Marquis of Halifax*, 2:363–406.

66 Victoria Kahn points out that supporters of the Stuart monarchy in the seventeenth century analogized the marriage contract with the social contract to 'naturalize and romanticize absolute sovereignty by making it seem that the subject, like the wife, was both naturally inferior and had consented to such inferior status out of affection.' 'Margaret Cavendish and the Romance of Contract,' 531–2.

67 'Interpellation' is Althusser's concept used to explain the way in which ideology constitutes subjects: *'all ideology hails or interpellates concrete individuals as concrete subjects.'* Althusser, 'Ideology and Ideological State Apparatuses,' 173; 170–7. But I employ his term more broadly, incorporating as well Foucault's contention that people perceive 'the truth' about themselves through the discourses that establish their conceptual boundaries. Foucault, *The History of Sexuality: An Introduction*, vol. 1. Liberal discourse in this period constitutes an important and definitional basis for identity.

68 Astell, in *The First English Feminist*, ed. Hill, 76.

69 Staves, *Married Women's Separate Property*, 4.

70 Thompson, *Appeal of One Half of the Human Race, Women*, 55–6.

71 Norton, *Selected Writings*, 4, 13. Cited by Poovey, *Uneven Developments*, 64.

72 Okin, *Women in Western Political Thought*; 'Women and the Making of the Sentimental Family,' *Justice, Gender and the Family.* Unlike Carol Pateman and Wendy Brown (see below), Okin believes that liberal rights and protections can be extended to women, although in *Justice, Gender and the Family*, she criticizes twentieth-century liberal philosophers and contemporary legal/social institutions for failing to do so.

73 Pateman, *The Sexual Contract*, 3.

74 Brown, 'Liberalism's Family Values,' 156.

75 Amanda Vickery summarizes these accounts in 'Golden Age to Separate Spheres?'

76 Ibid., 404.

77 Vickery, *The Gentleman's Daughter*, 1–12; Vickery, 'Golden Age to Separate Spheres'; Bannet, *The Domestic Revolution*, 123–59. It is also possible to argue that the concept of separate spheres is inaccurate because men did not cede control of their households just because they were identified with civil society. But this corrects only the most simplistic interpretations of this ideology. As Bannet points out, the attempt to make a woman's sphere truly her own by according her authority constituted the most important goal of one form of feminism.

78 Armstrong, *Desire and Domestic Fiction*.

79 Armstrong, *Desire and Domestic Fiction*; Langland, *Nobody's Angels*.

80 Bannet, *The Domestic Revolution*; Rendall, *The Origins of Modern Feminism*.

81 Brown, *Fables of Modernity*, 9.

82 Shevelow, *Women and Print Culture*.

83 *Eighteenth-Century Women Poets*, 40.

84 Ibid., 226.

85 Bannet identifies this group as 'matriarchal feminists.' They also belong in Marilyn Butler's tradition of Tory feminists, although certainly they were not all Tories politically. *Jane Austen and the War of Ideas*, xxii.

86 Filmer, *Patriarcha and Other Writings*. For a discussion of the development in the course of the seventeenth century of the conceptualization of marriage as a contract, see Shanley, 'Marriage Contract and Social Contract.' As both Shanley and Kahn explain, the analogy between the social contract and the marriage contract was invoked by Royalists to defend Absolutism, that is, loyalty to King Charles I rather than to Cromwell and the Commonwealth. According to this argument, the contract between king and subjects, like a marriage contract, is based on an initial act of consent. A king has sovereignty over his subjects thereafter, just as a husband has sovereignty over his wife, and once the contract has been agreed upon, it is irrevocable. But the analogy could work both ways. Some parliamentarians argued that the king was the wife rather than the husband, since he was 'created' to assist his people, just as the woman was created to be a helpmate to man. And just as a husband could divorce his wife for failing to fulfil her part of the contract by committing adultery, the subjects could dissolve their contract with the king if he failed to fulfil his contractual obligations. Henry Parker writes, 'When my Wife turneth adultress, my Convenant with her is broken, And when my King turneth Tyrant and continueth so, my Covenant with him is also broken.' Parker, *Jus Populi*, 1–2, cited by Kahn, 'Mar-

garet Cavendish and the Romance of Contract,' 533. Kahn also points out
that Milton, in the famous 'Preface to Parliament,' appended to the second
edition of *The Doctrine and Discipline of Divorce*, argued the case for divorce
by referring to the parliamentary argument for government by consent
(533). As I demonstrate, Locke deployed a somewhat different and more
complicated, contradictory logic.

87 Locke, *Two Treatises of Government*, ed. and with an introduction by Peter
Laslett (Cambridge: Cambridge University Press, 1988), 321. Subsequent
references are to this edition and appear in the text.

88 Laws in England at this time gave custody to men automatically.

89 This quotation concludes, 'but not a Political Power of Life and Death over
her, much less over any body else.' But as Locke himself recognizes, particularly in his discussion of slavery in the *Second Treatise* (esp. 284), authority
of this magnitude easily becomes absolute power. Locke's qualification at
the end of this passage, 'much less over any body else,' serves to distinguish the greater power a husband has over a wife from other hierarchized
relationships. In short, he suggests that women's subjection to men is even
greater than that of slaves to their masters.

90 'The *State of Nature* has a Law of Nature to govern it, which obliges every
one: And Reason, which is that Law, teaches all Mankind, who will but con-
sult it, that being all equal and independent, no one ought to harm another
in his Life, Health, Liberty, or Possessions' (271). As Peter Laslett points out
in his introduction to *Two Treatises*, this statement contradicts Locke's assertion in *An Essay Concerning Human Understanding* that we are born without
innate knowledge. The 'theory of knowledge in Locke's *Essay*' is inconsistent with 'the ethical doctrine of that work and the *Two Treatises*' (82). See
Locke, *An Essay Concerning Human Understanding*, 48–103.

91 Macpherson, *The Political Theory of Possessive Individualism*. It is through
possessive individualism that people can extend their possessions. A man
who is the first to increase the value of a piece of land through farming may
claim ownership of that land. Locke, *Two Treatises*, 285–302.

92 'And 'tis not without reason, that he [the man in a state of nature] seeks out,
and is willing to joyn in Society with others who are already united, or have
a mind to unite for the mutual Preservation of their *Lives, Liberties and
Estates, which I call by the general Name Property*.' Locke, *Two Treatises*, 350
[emphasis added].

93 'For all *Power given* [to the commonwealth] *with trust* for the attaining an
end, being limited by that end, whenever that *end* is manifestly neglected,
or opposed, the *trust* must necessarily be *forfeited*, and the Power devolve
into the hands of those that gave it, who may place it anew where they shall

think best for their safety and security. And thus the *Community* perpetually *retains a Supream Power* of saving themselves from the attempts and designs of any Body, even of their Legislators, whenever they shall be so foolish, or so wicked, as to lay and carry on designs against the Liberties and Properties of the subject. For no Man, or Society of men, having a Power to deliver up their *Preservation*, or consequently the means of it, to the Absolute Will and arbitrary Dominion of another; whenever any one shall go about to bring them into such a Slavish Condition, they will always have a right to preserve what they have not a Power to part with; and to rid themselves of those who invade this Fundamental, Sacred, and unalterable Law of Self-Preservation, for which they enter'd into Society.' Locke, *Two Treatises*, 367.

94 Pateman, *The Sexual Contract*, 66.

95 Poovey, *Uneven Developments*, 76–7. Poovey's analysis applies to middle- and upper-class women. Working women were of course subject to both forms of exploitation: their labour was alienable but they did not reap its meager benefits. They were workers at work, but wives at home.

96 Ruth Perry similarly observes that Locke's patriarchalism is evident in the juxtaposition of his theory of possessive individualism with the practices of his society. 'Mary Astell and the Feminist Critique of Possessive Individualism,' 452. Pateman briefly nods to the usefulness of contract theory in the past, but quickly dismisses it (*The Sexual Contract*, 90).

97 Gillis, *For Better, For Worse*, 101.

98 Johnson, *Journal of a Tour to the Hebrides*, 250.

99 My analysis of Rousseau here and elsewhere is indebted to Okin's *Women in Western Political Thought*. See esp. 101.

100 *Parliamentary Debates*, 3rd ser., vol. 192, 21 June 1870, col. 604.

101 The term is taken from Nancy Cott's pioneering article, 'Passionlessness: An Interpretation of Victorian Sexual Ideology, 1790–1850. See also Poovey, *Proper Lady*, and Todd *Sensibility*, 17–21.

102 For a discussion of this paradoxical view of women as both sexually pure and lascivious, see Poovey, *Proper Lady*, 19, 15. To take contemporary discourse at its word regarding female sexuality is to fall into the trap of Foucault's 'repressive hypothesis.' *History of Sexuality* 1:17–35.

103 Jenny Bourne Taylor and Sally Shuttleworth point out that 'passionlessness was not the only, or even the dominant, medical notion of female sexuality in the Victorian era.' *Embodied Selves*, 179. However, as John Tosh notes, 'the passionless woman was by now firmly established in respectable middle-class culture.' *A Man's Place*, 44.

104 For a summary of the association between virtue and feeling, see Barker-Benfield, *The Culture of Sensibility*, 105–14.

105 Paulson, *Representations of Revolution, 1789–1820*, 219–25.

106 On this point see Johnson, *Jane Austen*, xxii. In her subsequent book, *Equivocal Beings*, Johnson emphasizes that although the critique of strong feeling was utilized by both progressives and anti-jacobins, the critique of sentiment in particular was a crucial component of progressive discourse in the 1790s.

107 Burke, *Reflections on the Revolution in France*.

108 For a discussion of Burke's *Reflections* as a sentimental text, see Butler, *Jane Austen* 37–9, and Johnson, *Equivocal Beings*, 1–19.

109 Brissenden, *Virtue in Distress*, 39. On the physical basis of sentiment see Barker-Benfield, *The Culture of Sensibility*, chap. 1; Brissenden, *Virtue in Distress*, 39–48; Crane, 'Suggestions toward a Genealogy of The Man of Feeling,' 228–9; Todd, *Sensibility*, 7–8; and Van Sant, *Eighteenth-Century Sensibility and the Novel*, chaps. 5 and 6.

110 'Il y a un peu de testicule au fond de nos sentiments les plus sublimes et de notre tendresse la plus epuree.' Diderot to Damilaville (November 3, 1760), *Correspondance*, 3:216. Cited by Peter Gay, who also translates the quotation, in *The Bourgeois Experience, Victoria to Freud*, 52.

111 Kidder, *Charity Directed* (1676), 12. Cited by Crane, 'Suggestions,' 228.

112 Brent, *Persuasions to a Publick Spirit* (1704), 15–16. Cited by Crane, 'Suggestions,' 229.

113 Mackenzie, *The Man of Feeling*, 55.

114 Richardson, *Sir Charles Grandison*, 1:386.

115 Such arguments have been articulated repeatedly in the last two centuries and have survived into our own day, even though 'difference' has also been recognized as a complex and multifaceted phenomenon, likely to be invoked by feminists and other progressive thinkers as well as by their opponents.

116 Laqueur, *Making Sex*, 152 and chap. 5. Critics of the novel also observe an increasing emphasis on sexual difference in this period. See, for instance, Watt, *The Rise of the Novel*, 162 and Spencer, *The Rise of the Woman Novelist*, 15. For a discussion of how such changes influenced constructions of male sexuality, see Parker, *Sexing the Text*.

117 Moira Ferguson points out that Sophia probably wrote all three pamphlets and that the first and third feminist parts derive much from François Poulain de la Barre's *De L'Égalité des deux Sexes* (1673). *First Feminists*, 266. For an English translation that would have been available to Sophia, see *The Woman as Good as the Man Or, the Equality of Both Sexes*.

118 This and two other pamphlets in the debate (Sophia's opponent's response, which I discuss below, and another pamphlet by Sophia) were printed together as a trilogy titled *Beauty's Triumph*, which has been

reprinted on microfilm (New Haven: Research Publications, Inc., 1975). The quotation appears on page 10. Subsequent references are to the microform edition of *Beauty's Triumph* and appear in the text.

119 There are many such passages. Cf.: 'granting for a minute, that the organs of sense are as perfect in *Women* as in *Men* and yet more delicate; [one of Sofia's assertions] they are more liable to be thrown into disorder; and therefore the less to be depended upon ... as the mechanism of a watch, the more minute, gim, and delicate it is, the more is it subject to inconstancy' (110).

120 Sophia's answers in the third pamphlet, *Beauty's Triumph (Part the Third) Proving Woman Superior in Excellence to Man* (1740), for the most part reiterate her initial arguments. Yet it is interesting to note her increasing emphasis on education as the most significant influence in determining gendered differences. Her anonymous opponent had argued that women are not fit to educate their sons; Sophia rejoins that men ought not to find fault with women for doing a poor job educating children because men take sons from their mothers at a young age and prohibit women from raising daughters the way they want to. As a result, boys learn pride rather than good sense and virtue, while girls learn to be frivolous. If mothers were left to educate daughters in their own way, they would give them books instead of dolls: 'I am as much against putting a doll into a girl's hands, as I am for substituting books in the place of it' (202–3). The doll here figures feminine lightness and insignificance, a trope that becomes important in the 'dialogue' between Rousseau and Wollstonecraft discussed below.

121 Tosh observes of the Victorian period that '[p]robably the most reliable basis of companionate marriage – and also the clearest rebuttal of the two-sex theory – was shared cultural interests' (*A Man's Place*, 66). On the tensions between companionate marriage and patriarchy, see also Hammerton, *Cruelty and Companionship*, 73–85 and ch. 3.

122 For the persistence of this contradiction, see Davies, 'Continuity and Change in Literary Advice on Marriage,' in Outhwaite, *Marriage and Society*, 58–80.

123 Rousseau, *Émile*, 328. Subsequent references are to this edition and appear in the text.

124 In much the same way, sexual difference within the sexual act itself (at least as unimaginatively pictured by Rousseau) explains fundamental characterological distinctions between men and women: 'In the union of the sexes each alike contributes to the common end, but in different ways. From this diversity springs the first difference which may be observed

between man and woman in their moral relations. The man should be strong and active; the woman should be weak and passive; the one must have both the power and the will; it is enough that the other should offer little resistance' (322).

125 'She must find a way to make us desire what she cannot achieve unaided and what she considers necessary or pleasing' (350). At many points in his discussion, Rousseau attempts to cast women's gendered characteristics in terms of complementariness rather than evaluation – men are not better than women, but simply different. Thus, he characterizes 'cunning' as a morally neutral female talent that has been abused only because of the corrupting influences of civilization. But this is disingenuous, given the fact that cunning, especially women's cunning, is a suspect quality in most myths and narratives in the Western tradition (e.g., that of Eve). Even in male heroes such as Odysseus, cleverness has traditionally been viewed as a morally ambivalent quality, admirable but always somewhat dubious, and necessarily redeemed by more heroic and straightforward virtue.

126 Rousseau believes that the only motive for teaching a woman anything beyond 'the labours of her sex' (345) is that ignorance might make a woman vulnerable to seduction. Reason 'does not permit conscience to go astray and corrects the errors of prejudice ... [I]n this age of philosophy, virtue must be able to resist temptation; she must know beforehand what she may hear and what she should think of it' (345–6).

130 Okin, *Women in Western Political Thought*, 139.

127 Long before the chapter that explicitly addresses Rousseau's work 'Animadversions on Writers Who Have Rendered Women Objects of Pity' (chap. 5), it is clear that Rousseau is Wollstonecraft's implicit adversary. She cites long passages of *Émile* throughout the text, and most of her observations address and refute Rousseau's claims about sexual difference.

128 'Men have superior strength of body; but were it not for mistaken notions of beauty, women would acquire sufficient to enable them to earn their own subsistence, the true definition of independence; and to bear those bodily inconveniences and exertions that are requisite to strengthen the mind. Let us then, by being allowed to take the same exercise as boys, not only during infancy, but youth, arrive at perfection of body, that we may know how far the natural superiority of man extends' (185).

129 Cf. '[I]f woman be allowed to have an immortal soul, she must have ... an understanding to improve' (156).

130 See, for instance, *Julie ou La Nouvelle Héloïse: Lettres de deux amants habitants d'une petite ville au pied des Alpes, recueilles et publiées par J.-J. Rousseau,* 512–13.

131 By the late eighteenth century, even conservative writers such as Hannah More believed that education for girls was in need of reform. In her *Strictures on the Modern System of Female Education* (1799), More argued that girls needed education to suit them to lead virtuous, useful lives; for instance, they needed to be educated themselves in order to be able to teach and instil proper principles in their children. But even though More agreed with Wollstonecraft on this issue, she did not believe that boys and girls should study similar curricula, nor were her reasons for improving the education of girls the same as those of her progressive opponent – Wollstonecraft believed in education for a woman's own sake, not merely to enable her to serve others better. The same controversies extend well into the next century. Harriet Martineau, in *Household Education* (1849), likewise asserts that women need education to run their households well. But Margaret Mylne, who reviewed her essay in the *Westminster Review,* contends, like Wollstonecraft in *Rights of Women* and Mill in *The Subjection of Women,* that women should be educated for their own sakes, because they possess 'in common with him [man], a moral, rational, responsible, and, therefore, independent existence of their own.' Mylne, 'Woman and her Social Position,' 28. On these points, see Rendall, *Origins of Modern Feminism,* 117.

132 'Evangelicalism,' used broadly, refers both to evangelical Methodism and to the evangelical movement within the Established Church.

133 Rendall, *Origins of Modern Feminism,* 74. Rendall writes extensively on the relationship between evangelicalism and feminism. See esp. chap. 2.

134 Mermin, *Godiva's Ride,* xvi. See also Rendall, *Origins of Modern Feminism,* 106.

135 Helsinger, Sheets, and Veeder point out that Lewis's laudatory view of women was helpful to the feminist movement (*The Woman Question,* 20).

136 Lewis, *Woman's Mission* (London: John W. Parker, 1839), 30. Subsequent references are to this edition and appear in the text.

137 By such influence, women actually do participate in politics, 'as champions of the right in preference to the expedient' (52).

138 There are other, similarly deconstructive moments in Lewis's text. For instance, Lewis argues that men become selfish because they are taken from their mothers and put in the care of tutors or schools at an early age. This separation results in defects in their character: '[M]en are said to be more selfish than women. How can they help it? no pains are taken in

their education to make them otherwise' (28). However, in urging that women be allowed to perform this 'natural' duty, the education of their children, Lewis contradicts her assertion of their distinctive selflessness, which supposedly suits them for such work. If men can be taught to be unselfish, then selfishness is a matter of education rather than inherent character.

139 Laclau and Mouffe, *Hegemony and Socialist Strategy*, 105–14.

140 Patemen, 'Equality, Difference, Subordination: The Politics of Motherhood and Women's Citizenship,' in Bock and James, eds., *Beyond Equality and Difference*, 20. Cited by Skinner, 'Women's Status,' 105.

141 On this problem see Davidoff and Hall, *Family Fortunes*, 110; Barker-Benfield, chap. 2; and Rendall, *Origins of Modern Feminism*, 73–4.

142 On the feminization of feeling see, e.g., Barker-Benfield, *The Culture of Sensibility*, chap. 3. For a history of the gendering of feeling, see Lloyd, *The Man of Reason*.

143 It is important to remember that although women were increasingly identified with excellent powers of self-discipline, this characterization existed simultaneously with the belief that they lacked self-control to a far greater degree than men. Like women's 'passionlessness,' there is a fair amount of wishful thinking in the attribution of self-control to women. Thus, although the twists and turns of gender ideology generate these superior female powers, they are never truly superior. The concept of women's self-control is comprised by Armstrong's concept of female 'self-surveillance,' Pollak's 'myth of passive womanhood,' and Poovey's ideal of the proper lady (*The Proper Lady*).

144 Smith, *The Theory of Moral Sentiments*, 152.

145 Steele, *The Christian Hero*, 80.

146 Steele, *The Tatler* 25 in *Selections from The Tatler and The Spectator*, 87.

147 Steele, *The Spectator* 182 in *Selections from The Tatler and The Spectator*, 263.

148 Thomas Hughes, *The Manliness of Christ* (London, 1879), 2. Subsequent references are to this edition and appear in the text.

149 Steele, *Tatler* 25, in *Selections*, 86. For a detailed analysis of the ways in which the English periodical revised ideals of masculinity see Maurer, *Proposing Men*.

150 Stone, *The Family, Sex and Marriage*, popularized this term. See esp. chap. 7.

151 *The English Gentlewoman*, 344, 352.

152 Allestree, *The Ladies Calling*, 165–75

153 Pennington, *An Unfortunate Mother's Advice*, 47–8, 49, 76.

154 Gregory, *A Father's Legacy*, 126.

155 Fordyce, *Sermons*, 2:37–8.

2. Virtuous Libertines and Liberated Virgins

1 Harris, *Samuel Richardson*, 140.

2 Richardson, *Sir Charles Grandison*, ed. Jocelyn Harris, 3 vol. (London: Oxford University Press, 1972), 3:76. Future references will indicate volume and page of this edition and will appear in the text.

3 I use these terms anachronistically to describe eighteenth-century modes of feeling on the assumption that the categories they describe were cultural ideals even if contemporaries did not specifically identify them as such. Writers who have used these terms in our own day include Stone, *The Family, Sex and Marriage*, esp. chap. 8; Hagstrum, *Sex and Sensibility;* 162 and chap. 7; and Harth, 'The Virtue of Love: Lord Hardwicke's Marriage Act.'

4 With the rise of married love, there is a pronounced tendency within various traditions and genres that predate the novel to make distinctions among different modes of feeling. Most influential of all for the English novel, Milton's depiction of fallen and unfallen love in *Paradise Lost* contrasts salacious desire with pure desire ('founded in reason, loyal, just and pure'). *Paradise Lost*, 4, l. 755. French romances, which Richardson appropriated to his own ends, abound in discussions about the many forms and nuances of love. In the novel itself, the choice among kinds of love is often represented by a choice among suitors, as in *Grandison*. Another popular device of the courtship novel is to associate different characters and subplots with different kinds of love.

5 *Selected Letters of Samuel Richardson*, 193.

6 Sylvia Kasey Marks notes that *Grandison*'s influence is acknowledged by Jane Austen, George Eliot, Harriet Beecher Stowe, Thomas Babington Macaulay, and John Ruskin. *Sir Charles Grandison: The Compleat Conduct Book*, 16–17. See also Barker, *Grandison's Heirs*. For more detailed accounts of Richardson's influence on Austen, see Harris, *Jane Austen's Art of Memory*, chap. 4; Moler, *Jane Austen's Art of Allusion*, 77–81, 105–7, and 193–4; and Honan, 'Richardson's Influence on Jane Austen,' in *Samuel Richardson: Passion and Prudence*, 165–77.

7 Analysing the notion of multiplot in a different way, Lois A. Chaber suggests that *Grandison*'s alternative narrative possibilities, some of which take place and others of which are imagined, suggest 'the precariousness of human fate' that is appropriate to an 'orthodox providential world view.' '"Sufficient to the Day": Anxiety in *Sir Charles Grandison*,' 268–94.

8 For a discussion of the conflict between an ethic of married love and the dictates of patriarchy among Richardson and his correspondents, and the

thematization of this topic in his novels, see Gonda, *Reading Daughters' Fictions*, 66–110.

9 Redefining both love and masculinity is part of the middle-class project of altering aristocratic ideals. Indeed, Sir Charles himself, a very bourgeois gentleman in aristocratic clothing, is emblematic of this process. Marks observes that 'in many ways Grandison harks back to an older aristocratic tradition in which the nature of nobility, the formation of the young man, his education and recreation, and his larger responsibilities to his family and the state were important. At the same time, we see the emphasis on duty and on the responsibilities one has to one's superiors, peers, and inferiors found in the conduct books directed toward a more general [i.e., middle-class] audience' (*Sir Charles Grandison*, 70). In a psychoanalytically oriented reading of *Grandison*, Tassie Gwilliam observes that Richardson attempts 'to redefine masculinity for his era.' *Samuel Richardson's Fictions of Gender*, 133.

10 The majority of *Grandison*'s other subplots take up the issue of conflict between the marriage choice and filial duty, which Richardson had explored so thoroughly in *Clarissa*. But while this topic dominates nearly all Richardson's narratives, these narratives articulate different issues as well. For instance, as Kathryn Temple argues, the Clementina subplot establishes the supremacy of England and Englishness against Clementina's Catholicism, which still represented the threat of a Stuart invasion in Richardson's time. *Scandal Nation*. Albert J. Rivero suggests more generally that the function of Clementina's story is to expel the foreign and the romantic from Richardson's narrative. 'Representing Clementina: '"Unnatural" Romance and the Ending of *Sir Charles Grandison*.' I concentrate on Charlotte's story rather than on others because it is here that Richardson most fully and specifically addresses the connection between consensual love and female autonomy.

11 Harth, 'The Virtue of Love,' also discusses the ways in which defining love properly obviates undesirable alliances and facilitates alliances between the middle and upper classes. My analysis here is indebted to her article.

12 There are important exceptions. The literature of the Renaissance, where we find precedents for the seventeenth-century ethic of married love, also provides examples of the kind of typology Richardson constructs. For instance, Shakespeare's *As You Like It* formulates a schema of different kinds of love that is close to *Grandison*'s own. Touchstone marries Audrey out of lust and she reciprocates out of interest; Celia and Oliver marry for romantic love (as indicated by their love at first sight); and, best of all,

Rosalind and Orlando marry for sentimental love. Rosalind's disguise as a young boy enables them to build a solid basis of friendship which grounds their erotic attraction.

13 Defoe, *Conjugal Lewdness*, 105. Stone observes, 'Evidence of hostility to sexual desire as a basis for choice of a marriage partner can be found in every commentator of the seventeenth and eighteenth centuries' (*The Family, Sex and Marriage*, 281).

14 Restoration literature was more sanguine about the possibility of the reformed rake. Many comedies end happily with the rake's marriage, including William Congreve's *The Way of the World* and Aphra Behn's *The Rover*. Nevertheless, some Restoration literature questions the likelihood of such drastic changes in character. Most notable is Sir John Vanbrugh's *The Relapse*, written as a sequel to Colly Cibber's optimistic *Love's Last Shift*. Cibber's play ends with the rakish and erring Loveless's reform; as its title indicates, Vanbrugh's play reveals that this reform is temporary. Even writers who celebrated their reformed rakes usually ended their works at marriage, thus never having to prove that such conversions would last. The scepticism about reformed libertines is illustrated by Richardson in *Pamela Two*, where Mr B. falls into his former erring ways when he has an affair with a countess. In *Grandison*, the only truly reformed rakes are men whose poor health has taken a toll on their energy and spirits so that they are simply too weak (or impotent) to pursue a life of sin.

15 Pennington, *An Unfortunate Mother's Advice*, 86, 87, 88.

16 Mary Astell, 'Reflections Upon Marriage,' 97. Cf., Defoe: 'all the solemn Part is dropt out of our Thoughts, the Money and the Maidenhead is the Subject of our Meditations' (*Conjugal Lewdness*, 33). In his discussion of the popular novels of Mrs Manly and Mrs Heywood, John Richetti observes that 'lust ... is simply avarice transferred to the world of the emotions.' *Popular Fiction Before Richardson*, 152. Often lust and avarice are embodied in the same individual, thereby figuring avarice as a type of lust for wealth and lust as a form of eroticized greed. For instance, although Cimberton in Richard Steele's *The Conscious Lovers* intends to marry for money, lust becomes an added incentive to the match when he meets his prospective bride. Sir Thomas Grandison, who forbids his daughters from marrying for love because he wants to use them to make a personally lucrative marriage settlement, dies while he is in the midst of negotiating his own marriage to a beautiful sixteen-year-old peasant, whom he cannot resist. '[M]y girls will *keep*,' says Sir Thomas (1:329); use of the sexually suggestive word 'keep' with reference to his scheme to trade daughters for wealth implies the connection between lust and avarice.

17 Richetti points out that '[d]uring the first two decades of the century, the

production of original English amatory fiction was relatively small ... [The] great majority of amatory fiction consisted of translations, mostly from the French' (*Popular Fiction Before Richardson*, 179).

18 By grouping *Cassandra* and *The Princess of Cleves* in the same category, Richardson ignores important distinctions between the two. La Calprenède's work is a romance, a genre in which, as Ros Ballaster explains, women's love is depicted as ideal, pure, and lacking in sexual passion, while La Fayette's is a nouvelle and represents love as violent and irresistible, the woman as a victim of passion. Ballaster's analysis sheds light on why Richardson would ignore these differences: both novels are 'feminocentric' (despite the fact that La Calprenède is a man) in 'that they simultaneously address and construct an explicitly "feminine" or "feminized" realm' that privileges 'women's role in the production and consumption of art.' Romance was a woman's genre. *Seductive Forms*, 42. 66. Richardson's agenda was to discredit this body of feminocentric literature and to assert the difference and superiority of his own work. In this light, observing distinctions among these earlier texts was unimportant.

19 Laura Brown explains that libertine philosophy was identified with an aristocratic ethos by virtue of its most celebrated advocates, the Royalist cavaliers of the seventeenth century, who were for the most part '[a] segment of the youngest and most embittered members of the aristocracy [who] sought refuge in the advocacy of a loose social and philosophical system diametrically opposed to that of the increasingly prominent, often Puritan, bourgeoisie,' whom they perceived as a threat to their identity and way of life. *English Dramatic Form*, 40–1. The identification of libertinism with aristocracy continued throughout the eighteenth and nineteenth centuries. Lovelace is the novel's most famous rake and it follows, given the political origins of libertinism, that his feud with the Harlowe family is motivated to some degree by class antagonism.

20 *Grandison* tries to deflect attention from the fact that intelligence and virtue are distinct qualities by utilizing the concept of merit to include both. This formulation was attractive to middle-class ideology, which advocates meritocracy while also maintaining that virtue will lead to material success. In accord with *Grandison*, Adam Smith observes that '[i]n the middling and inferior stations of life, the road to virtue and that to fortune ... are, happily in most cases, very nearly the same.' *The Theory of Moral Sentiments*, 63. Margaret Anne Doody observes that '[t]he first edition of Smith's *Moral Sentiments* appeared five years after the last volume of *Grandison*, and might almost have been based upon it.' 'Identity and Character in Sir Charles Grandison,' 121.

21 Cf. Astell: 'But when a Woman marrys unequally and beneath her self,

there is almost Demonstration that the Man is Sordid and Unfair' ('Reflections Upon Marriage,' 107).

22 'It was permissible to trade status for money and marry your son to the heiress of a tradesman, but not to marry your daughter to the tradesman or even to his heir.' Stone and Fawtier Stone, *An Open Elite?*, 22.

23 This marriage is not quite as transgressive as some critics have mistakenly assumed. Pamela's education and deportment identifies her with the working middle class rather than the lower class, despite her role as a servant. McKeon, *Origins of the English Novel*, 365.

24 Although representations of sentimental love became prevalent in the novel, the concept of a reasonable passion, like that of married love itself, was influenced by Puritan thought. It is significant that Clementina falls in love with Sir Charles while he is tutoring her in English by reading *Paradise Lost*; such Edenic love is precisely the ideal embodied by sentimental love, which Clementina, like Harriet, feels for Sir Charles. On Miltonic ideals of love, see Hagstrum, *Sex and Sensibility*, chap. 2 and Turner, *One Flesh*, esp. chaps. 6 and 7. For Miltonic overtones in Grandison, see Harris, *Samuel Richardson*, chap. 8. Richardson might also have derived a model for sentimental love from Mlle de Scudéry's allegorical map of love, *La Carte de Tendre*. According to James S. Munro, de Scudéry's work points out serious moral distinctions between different kinds of love, despite the fact that it was widely misinterpreted in her time as an intellectual exercise in gallantry. For instance, she repeatedly distinguishes the 'pays de Tendre' from the 'pays d'Amour' and characterizes 'tendresse,' which depends on sympathetic identification with another – or sensibility – as 'the overriding aim of love as well as friendship.' *Mademoiselle de Scudéry*, 86–7. De Scudéry's ideal love is similar to Richardson's own because it is inspired by the virtue of the lovers. But despite affinities which are apparent to a reader today, Richardson nevertheless found de Scudéry's work lacking.

25 On Richardson's use of romance conventions, see Harris, *Samuel Richardson*, 162–3; Doody, *A Natural Passion*, 294, n. 1; and Flynn, *Samuel Richardson*, 100.

26 On sentiment as a blend of reason and passion, see Brissenden, *Virtue in Distress* chap. 2; Hagstrum, *Sex and Sensibility*, chap. 5; and John Mullan, *Sentiment and Sociability*, 57–8.

27 Mullan, *Sentiment and Sociability*, 61. On the physical basis of sentiment, see chap. 1, note 94. For a reading of the significance of the body in *Grandison*, see McMaster, '*Sir Charles Grandison*: Richardson on Body and Character.' McMaster claims that 'the drama and sensational interest that balance the overt moralizing of the novel is the felt presence of the body' (85).

28 In a letter to Hester Mulso, Richardson suggests the existence of a superior form of passion that comprises all other kinds of love. He writes, citing Miss Mulso, '"Cannot all the natural and right affections of the heart, ask you, subsist together?" They can.' Letter dated 30 September 1751 in *Selected Letters*, 192.

29 Margaret Doody points out that '[t]o crown all [the other types of love relationships in this novel], there is the ideal, the passionate yet reasonable love which finds its complete fulfillment in marriage, which we see in the case of Sir Charles and Harriet.' *A Natural Passion*, 294.

30 This comparison was first observed by Golden, *Richardson's Characters*, 97. On this point see also Flynn, *Samuel Richardson*, 231–4 and Gwilliam, 114, 137. For an analysis of polygamy in *Grandison*, see Doody, 'Identity,' 128–30.

31 Several critics have addressed the problem of Sir Charles's double love. Gwilliam sees it as signalling Sir Charles's 'superior sensibility' (*Samuel Richardson's Fictions of Gender*, 149). Harris observes that Richardson introduced Clementina, and hence Sir Charles's double love, to regain *Grandison*'s narrative momentum, which was somewhat stalled after Harriet's kidnapping and rescue. Richardson later made revisions in the seventh volume to placate readers who were uneasy about double heroines and a double love (as he promised Lady Bradsheigh he would do). See Harris's introduction to *Grandison* (ix, xii) and her article 'The Reviser Observed.' Doody suggests that the double love serves to articulate the balance between the aesthetic and moral imperatives of stability and variety: 'Identity,' 126.

32 Sir Charles's absence is noted by Doody, *A Natural Passion*, 274 and Duncan Eaves and Kimpel, *Samuel Richardson*.

33 For other readings of Sir Charles's absence see Case, *Plotting Women*, and Chaber, '"Sufficient to the Day."'

34 Todd, *Sensibility*, 74.

35 The concept of self-policing is expressed by Nancy Armstrong's 'self-surveillance' in *Desire and Domestic Fiction*; by Ellen Pollack's 'myth of passive womanhood' in *The Poetics of Sexual Myth*; and by Mary Poovey's 'proper lady' in *The Proper Lady and the Woman Writer*.

36 Gwilliam reads these moments of injury as metaphors for castration (*Samuel Richardson's Fictions of Gender*, 124, 127, 130).

37 Richardson, *Correspondence*, i, cxxvii–cxxix. Cited by Doody, *A Natural Passion*, 263.

38 Richardson, *Selected Letters*, 171. Richardson was actually reporting Cibber's reaction to the idea of male virginity in a different context, but the sentiment is certainly applicable to Richardson's own hero.

39 Locke, *Two Treatises of Government*, 284.
40 Richardson's condemnation of libertine attitudes towards women explains why he is sometimes taken for a feminist. See, for instance, Stevenson, '"A Geometry of His Own,"' 477. However, the progressiveness of endorsing Harriet's right to choose her husband is muted by the fact that her father is dead, and so there is no clear paternal authority in her family, and because her relatives have decided to allow her this privilege. Despite her claims to entitlement, her liberty is thus a privilege rather than a right. For a succint and convincing summary of Richardson's endorsement of 'patriarchal sovereignty,' see Beasley, *Richardson's Girls*, 35–52.
41 A baby is a doll or a puppet (Doody, *Sir Charles Grandison*, 678 n. 437). The association of women with dolls (usually the dolls girls play with) is a familiar trope of antifeminist writing.
42 See Staves, 'Pin Money,' and *Married Women's Separate Property*, chap. 5. Pin money evolved through economic haggling over marriage settlements. In order to deny wives their common law right of dower, which entitled a widow to a third of her husband's estate, husbands and their families often bargained for marriage settlements that provided jointure, a specified sum that was likely to be a lesser proportion. Pin money, as well as other forms of married women's separate property, was a concession made in order to gain this advantage. The husband would agree to relinquish control over some of his own money or his wife's property during his lifetime so that a greater proportion of his property would remain in the hands of his own family in the event of his death. Staves points out that 'continued complaint about settlements' which make a wife independent 'displaces responsibility onto women's demands and masks the dynastic motives and the interests of the husbands' families in these settlements.' Nevertheless, to counter the threat of female autonomy evoked by pin money, 'the law responded by developing idiosyncratic rules' (primarily in the form of conveyancing practice and equity opinions as opposed to new statutes) that 'minimized the possibility that such property could become a source of women's power or the material basis for equality between men and women.' 'Pin Money,' 79.
43 Astell, 'Reflections Upon Marriage,' 96.
44 Turner, 'Lovelace and the Paradoxes of Libertinism.'
45 Richardson elsewhere figures pregnancy as a form of female discipline: 'Childbed matronizes the giddiest Spirits, and brings them to reflection sooner than any other events.' *Familiar Letters on Important Occasions*, 170. Cited by Flynn, *Samuel Richardson*, 73. Lois A. Chaber notes that Charlotte and Pamela's experiences with maternity involve 'psychic mutilations that

entail loss of power and identity.' '"This Affecting Subject"' 238. Chaber discusses the theme of maternity in *Grandison* and *Pamela* with reference to the history and ideology of childbearing in the eighteenth century (71).

46 Chaber also reads Charlotte's breastfeeding as an acknowledgement of her subordination, which Charlotte recognizes as determined by sexual difference. '"This Affecting Subject,"' 245.

47 See, for instance, Charlotte's comments to Harriet on 3:518.

3. 'No small part of a woman's portion': Love, Duty, and Society in *Persuasion*

1 Austen, *Sense and Sensibility*, 378–9.

2 Cheryl L. Nixon observes that Brandon functions as a replacement for Willoughby in the context of arguing that in late twentieth-century films of Austen's novels, male protagonists prove their worth by meeting a demand for emotional display, our criteria for worth, rather than social restraint, the test of their worth in Austen's novels. 'Balancing the Courtship Hero,' 22–43. Along similar lines, Deborah Kaplan discusses the 'harlequinization' of *Sense and Sensibility* and other films of Austen's novels, which focus on romance and courtship at the expense of other topics. Kaplan notes that Brandon is handsome in the film but not in the book, where his plainness contributes to the novel's undermining of romance, and that the film emphasizes the 'romantic pleasures' of Marianne's marriage. 'Mass Marketing Jane Austen,' 171–85. Also commenting on the revision of Colonel Brandon, Devoney Looser observes that filmmakers have been influenced by ideals of masculinity promulgated by the feminist men's movement of the late twentieth century; filmmakers (screenwriters, directors, etc.) emphasize the sensitivity, emotional responsiveness, and nurturant qualities of their heroes rather than (as in the novels) their self-restraint. 'Jane Austen "Responds" to the Men's Movement,' 159–70. Versions of these last two articles appear in *Jane Austen and Hollywood*. Patrice Hannon notes that the film plays up the romanticism that the novel mocks and that Brandon is visually romanticized during Marianne's illness. 'Austen Novels and Austen Films: Incompatible Worlds?,' 24–32. As Rebecca Dixon observes, it is not only the men who are expected to be more passionate and emotional in Austen's films. The lesson of *Sense and Sensibility* (the film) is not that Marianne must learn to be more controlled but that Elinor must learn to be less repressed. 'Misrepresenting Jane Austen's Ladies,' 44–57.

3 Marianne's costume and bearing are also nearly identical in both scenes; she wears a white dress; she faces left, holding her body in much the same

posture; and, particularly noticeable, she wears the same ornate shoes, which protrude from her skirt. In her publication of the screenplay, Thompson includes stills from these two scenes, which clearly show their similarity. Thompson, *The Sense and Sensibility Screenplay and Diaries*, 17 and plate 14.

4 Thompson, *The Sense and Sensibility Screenplay*, 186. These lines are amended from the original, which reads: 'Ne is the earth the lesse, or loseth ought,/ For whatsoever from one place doth fall,/ Is with the tide unto an other brought:/ For there is nothing lost, that may be found, if sought.' Spenser, *The Faerie Queene*, V, canto xxxix, ll. 6–9.

5 Austen, *Sense and Sensibility*, 60.

6 For a discussion of contemporary use of the word 'persuasion,' see Moler, *Jane Austen's Art of Allusion*, 187–223.

7 Allestree, *The Ladies Calling*, 174, 176. The rules governing the marriage choice, including the child's right to veto, are staples of conduct literature. Compare similar pronouncements from two widely read conduct manuals: The father 'has always an undoubted Right to a Negative Voice, though not to a Compulsive One; as a Child is very justifiable in the Refusal of her Hand, even to the absolute Command of a Father, where her Heart cannot go with it; so is she extremely culpable, by giving it contrary to his Approbation.' Pennington, *An Unfortunate Mother's Advice*, 50; 'Your hearts indeed may be shut inflexibly and permanently against all the merit a man can possess. That may be your misfortune, but cannot be your fault. In such a situation, you would be equally unjust to yourself and your lover, if you gave him your hand when your heart revolted against him.' Gregory, *A Father's Legacy*, 103–4. Dr Gregory was a great favourite with Austen.

8 Fordyce, *Sermons To Young Women*, 2:173–4.

9 Ibid., 171.

10 On women and politics in the period, see Johnson, *Jane Austen: Women, Politics, and the Novel*. Johnson discusses the association of parental authority with anti-Jacobinism in conservative novels of the time (6, 10). Ronald Paulson discusses the ways in which sexuality was figured as revolution in *Representations of Revolution*, esp. chap. 7. Marilyn Butler points out that among conservatives in the 1790s, all strong feeling was suspect: 'sentimentalists came to be read as moral relativists who threatened to undermine established religion and society ... it was the absorption [of sentiment] ... in the conscious and unconscious mind which offended, because implicitly it put the individual before the group.' *Jane Austen and the War of Ideas*, 8. Warren Roberts observes that there was an 'inevitable connection in many minds between the feminist cause and political radicalism, which also opposed

traditional relationships, stood for sweeping social change and took the side of oppressed groups.' *Jane Austen and the French Revolution*, 155.

11 Fordyce, *Sermons to Young Women*, 2:174, 121.

12 Mary Poovey divides the lines of multiple plot differently, between what she calls a 'private' and a 'public' plot. *The Proper Lady and the Woman Writer*, 228.

13 Adela Pinch analogizes this retelling with reading rather than writing. This is a somewhat different but compatible emphasis; after all, the process of revision is always one of re-reading, and reading is always a 'writerly' activity, since we actively interpret in the process. *Strange Fits of Passion*, chap. 5.

14 On free indirect discourse see Roy Pascal, *The Dual Voice*. Focalization refers to the filtering of experience and perception through a given consciousness, whether this occurs through free indirect discourse or other formal means (e.g., one character reporting what another has said or done). See Genette, *Narrative Discourse*, 189–94. On focalization in *Persuasion*, see Warhol, 'The Look, the Body, and the Heroine,' 8. Warhol takes a 'gender-conscious look Austen's management of focalization, that is, her use of Anne Elliot as the central consciousness through which the story gets transmitted' (6).

15 Austen, *Northanger Abbey and Persuasion* (Oxford: Oxford University Press, 1983), 27. Subsequent references are to this edition and appear in the text.

16 There is disagreement among critics as to whether Austen should be viewed as a feminist or antifeminist. Critics have argued, for instance, that Austen is a feminist because she is a defender of women's rationality in the tradition of Wollstonecraft. Jane Kirkham, *Jane Austen*, xi–xvi and passim). Along similar lines, her work has been seen to echo that of Wollstonecraft (Auerbach, 'O Brave New World: Evolution and Revolution in *Persuasion*') and to articulate the 'themes of Wollstonecraftian revolution' (Sulloway, *Jane Austen*, 49). She is also said to be a feminist because she is an advocate of the view that women have 'rich and unapologetic senses of self-consequence,' characterizations which defy 'every [antifeminist] dictum about female propriety and deference propounded in the sermons and conduct books which have been thought to shape her opinions on all important matters' (Johnson, *Jane Austen: Women, Politics and the Novel*, xxiii) and because she associates the feminine focalization that relies on the heroine's viewpoint (rather than a male point of view) with the objectifying gaze (Warhol, 'The Look, The Body, and the Heroine,' 9). Those who doubt Austen's credentials as a feminist tend to see her as conflicted. David Monaghan contends that although 'she rejected many of her society's feminine stereotypes, ... Austen appears to have been almost entirely satisfied with

the restriction of women to domestic and polite functions' ('Jane Austen and the Position of Women,' 106–7). Mary Poovey argues that Austen betrays her feminist interrogation of patriarchal institutions through a conservative vision of the family. *The Proper Lady and the Woman Writer*, chaps. 6 and 7. Warren Roberts claims that Austen evinces a feminist consciousness in her first three novels and an antifeminist attitude in her last three, which were written when the conservative political reaction against all progressive ideas, including feminism, was in full force. The issue of determining Austen's attitudes is further complicated by the fact that feminists and their opponents held similar views on many issues. As Roberts points out, both Mary Wollstonecraft and Hannah More, '[t]he leading feminist and leading anti-feminist' of the time, despised superficial feminine 'accomplishments,' believed in cultivating women's reason through substantive education, and 'were in basic agreement in attacking the code of female gentility and standing for an ideal emphasising the development of the mind' (*Jane Austen*, 186). With Gary Kelly, I assume that 'feminism is always socially and historically particular, advancing the claims and rights of women within specific historical, social and cultural conditions' ('Jane Austen, Romantic Feminism, and Civil Society,' 19). A discourse or narrative can be considered to articulate a form of feminism if it argues for lifting restrictions and enlarging opportunities for women, or against the misogyny of the culture in any way. It is valid to assume that an author can express feminist positions without being consistently 'feminist.'

17 This and all subsequent definitions are taken from *The Shorter Oxford English Dictionary on Historical Principles* (*OED*). See 'natural,' definition I, 3.

18 *OED*, 'unnatural,' definition 1. Definition 3 is also appropriate: 'Outraging natural feeling or moral standards, monstrously cruel or wicked.'

19 Ibid., 'natural,' definition I, 1.

20 Ibid., 'sequel,' definition 7.

21 Ibid., 'romance,' definition II, 1–4.

22 Narratology distinguishes between plot and story. Story refers to the ordering of events in chronological time whereas plot refers to the positioning of narratives within a given text. While this distinction is not without problems, it nevertheless provides a useful way of discussing the formal structure of narratives as distinct from the order of events that we extrapolate.

23 Wollstonecraft, *A Vindication of the Rights of Women*, 185 and *passim*.

24 For a more extended discussion of Mrs Croft as a figure of feminism, see Johnson, *Jane Austen: Women, Politics and the Novel*, 152–4.

25 For discussions of the near impropriety of Anne's behaviour see Nardin,

Those Elegant Decorums, 14 and Reid-Walsh, '"She Learned Romance as She Grew Older,"' 220.

26 Jane Austen described her heroine Anne as being 'almost too good' for her in a letter to Fanny Knight, 23 March 1817. *Jane Austen's Letters to Her Sister Cassandra*, 142.

27 Jocelyn Harris points out that Austen alludes extensively to English literature in *Persuasion*, in the spirit of resistance rather than acceptance. 'Jane Austen and the Burden of the (Male) Past,' 96. Along similar lines, Sulloway notes, 'Anne Elliot's gentle objection to Captain Harville's ... clichés indicates how thoroughly Austen was aware of their prevalence in literature addressing the "woman question"' (*Jane Austen*, 32).

28 Tony Tanner observes, 'Wentworth at this critical moment has, however inadvertently, dropped (let go of, lost his grip on) that instrument which is at once a tool and a symbol of men's dominance over women ... It is as if he is open to a more equal (unscripted) relationship in which the old patterns of dominance and deference are abandoned, deleted, dropped.' *Jane Austen*, 241.

29 *OED*, 'morality,' definitions 3 and 3b.

30 Johnson, *Jane Austen*, xxiii–xxiv. Cf., Sulloway, *Jane Austen*, 4.

31 Despite the fact that Anne is older now, and probably wiser and more independent at twenty-eight than she was at nineteen, neither her family nor her society would necessarily have conceded her total freedom concerning the marriage choice. Dr Gregory assures his daughters that he will allow them to choose their own husbands completely independent of parental authority once they are fully adult, but he also points out that his liberal attitude differs from those of 'most parents': 'If I live till you arrive at that age when you shall be capable to judge for yourselves, and do not strangely alter my sentiments, I shall act towards you in *a very different manner from what most parents do*. My opinion has always been, that when that period arrives, the parental authority ceases' (*A Father's Legacy*, 111) [emphasis added]. Although Gregory wrote nearly fifty years before *Persuasion* was published, the narrator's description of Anne and Wentworth as ready to override opposition suggests that similar rules of conduct for daughters still apply. Moreover, the narrator casts Anne's two situations, past and present, as equivalent, and she imagines her succeeding through force, will, and independence rather than through a capitulation on the part of Lady Russell and her family.

32 Unsigned review, *British Critic*, March 1818, ix, 293–301. Reprinted in *Jane Austen: The Critical Heritage*, 84.

33 Derrida, *Of Grammatology*, 141–64.

34 There is no incontrovertible evidence that Austen was familiar with Hume's work; perhaps they only shared a common culture that directed their thinking in similar ways. Tony Tanner has also observed, in a different context, that Hume's philosophy provides an explanatory philosophical framework for reading Austen. See his 'Introduction,' *Pride and Prejudice*, 11.

35 Hume, *A Treatise of Human Nature* (1739–40; Oxford: Oxford University Press, 1981), 413. Subsequent references are to this edition and appear in the text.

36 Compare Lady Russell's opinion about Anne's engagement: 'Anne Elliot, with all her claims of birth, beauty, and mind, *to throw herself away* at nineteen ... ' (26) [emphasis added].

37 Mullan, *Sentiment and Sociability*, 30.

38 I discuss this controversy in my introduction.

39 This is a widely accepted premise of feminist political critiques of liberalism. Locke, Hobbes, and all major liberal theorists of rights exclude women from the legal and social entitlements guaranteed by the social contract by assuming the liberal subject to be a free, white male. Early on in the scholarship of feminist political theory, Susan Moller Okin analysed liberal theory for its gendered inequities. See *Women in Western Political Thought*. She extended and developed her criticism in *Justice, Gender and the Family*. A sampling of other studies that analyse the masculinist basis of classic liberalism include Brown, *States of Injury*, 135–65; Eisenstein, *The Color of Gender*, and Pateman, *The Sexual Contract*.

40 The literature on this subject is vast and originates from diverse disciplines (e.g., political theory, legal studies). But a sampling of representative texts includes Eisenstein, *Color of Gender*; Minow, *Making All the Difference*; and Okin, *Justice, Gender and the Family*. Brown has objected to such criticism on the basis that the recognition of difference often perpetuates the conceptualization of difference as inferiority.

41 Brown departs from many other feminist critics of liberalism by arguing that the very notion of rights depends on – not merely assumes – a subject who is masculine, whether or not this is biologically the case. That is to say, liberalism does not merely, and contingently, exclude the 'female subject'; rather, its very condition of possibility is such exclusion. The liberal subject is always masculine because his identity is 'premised upon a sexual division of labor and activities, a subject that persists even ... as it is detached from physiological correlates' (*States of Injury*, 152). Without deciding whether Brown's pessimism about liberal theory is correct, or whether liberalism can be rearticulated in the service of feminism, as other scholars

maintain, we can agree that the liberal subject is gendered within classic liberal theory.

42 Brown, *States of Injury*, 156.

43 John P. Zomchick analyses how Clarissa's grandfather's bequest transforms her into a juridical subject, against her will. She wishes to remain a family member with an 'affective' rather than legal identity with respect to her family. 'The criticism of abstract natural rights is the primary secular lesson of *Clarissa*.' *Family and the Law in Eighteenth-Century Fiction*, 58–80.

44 Whether or not they foreground this point, it is clear that critics of liberal theory ask that law and theory acknowledge that the distinction is a false one by demanding that rights take needs into account.

45 Gisborne, *An Enquiry into the Duties of the Female Sex*, 23. This extract appears in chapter 3, 'On the Peculiar Features By Which the Character of the Female Mind is Naturally Discriminated from That of the Other Sex.'

46 This association between feeling and women has remained prevalent within Anglo-American culture, even in feminist scholarship which is critical of masculinist assumptions. For instance, in one vein of contemporary feminism, the divide between rights and needs, thought and feeling, has been described in essentialist terms, most famously in the work of Carol Gilligan. Gilligan writes, 'This conception of morality [i.e., women's conception] as concerned with the activity of care centers moral development around the understanding of responsibility and relationships, just as the conception of morality as fairness ties moral development to the understanding of rights and rules.' Gilligan, *In a Different Voice*, 19. However sincerely Gilligan's formulation criticizes the liberal ethic of rights and seeks to create a more caring society, it also confirms the gendered construction of personality on which liberalism depends, and hence supports the very structures it seeks to challenge. Other scholars utilize these categories without affirming their essentially gendered nature.

47 As noted above, Wentworth betrays this propensity in his inflexibility towards Anne and women in general, at least until his reform.

48 Monica Cohen argues that *Persuasion* compares sailors with homemakers in order to make visible the affinities between professions such as the military, and domesticity, thereby defining women's work as a form of professional expertise. 'Persuading the Navy Home,' 363.

49 There was a debate within older Austen criticism as to whether or not the navy constituted a new economic and social class that challenged the hegemony of the aristocracy and gentry. This view was asserted by Mudrick, *Jane Austen*, 232; Duffy, Jr, 'Structure and Society in Jane Austen's Fiction'; Auerbach, 'O Brave New World'; Monaghan, *Jane Austen*, 143–4; and

Poovey, *'Persuasion* and the Promises of Love,' 152–79. But as R.W. Chapman pointed out early on, the naval officers were likely to have come from the landed classes, thereby undermining the idea that *Persuasion* is an allegory of class struggle. 'A Reply to Mr Duffy on "Persuasion,"' 154. On the fluidity of social mobility in Austen's fiction see Williams, *The Country and the City,* 113–14. Social mobility was a feature of Austen's social world. Tomalin, *Jane Austen: A Life,* 87–102. Although *Persuasion* emphasizes Wentworth's lack of social connection, this is to lend credibility to Lady Russell's aversion to him, rather than to identify him with a particular class. Daniel P. Gunn offers a somewhat different interpretation of *Persuasion* as representing class conflict. While he criticizes readings of the novel as simple class allegory, he nevertheless suggests that *Persuasion* contrasts an inherited code of aristocratic values with a code of ethics associated with the rise of capitalism and a newer middle-class ethic – in other words, we have class conflict once again, although represented by a war of ideologies rather than social groups. 'In the Vicinity of Winthrop: Ideological Rhetoric in Persuasion,' 403–18. I do not mean to suggest that class is not an issue in *Persuasion*, or that Austen is not criticizing the aristocracy, but rather that this is not the main objective of her criticism, which is organized by moral and not socio-economic categories. By 1818 the middle class had largely won the battle for ideological hegemony that Gunn describes, and Austen's representation of the aristocracy in *Persuasion* thus functions as shorthand for a retrograde moral position rather than as pointed criticism of a particular group.

50 Duckworth, *The Improvement of the Estate,* 184–8. The chapter on *Persuasion* is titled 'The Abandonment of the Estate.'

4. Feminism and Contract Theory in *He Knew He Was Right*

1 Thackeray, *The Newcomes* (London: Penguin Books, 1996), 291–2. Subsequent references are to this edition and appear in the text.

2 Carlyle, *Past and Present,* 148. For a selection of Victorian criticism of capitalism see *Critics of Capitalism,* ed. Jay and Jay.

3 Marx, *Capital, Volume One,* 168–9.

4 For a discussion of the colonizing momentum of capitalism, see Nunokawa, *The Afterlife of Property,* 3.

5 In *Capital* Marx defines use-value and exchange-value. 'The usefulness of a thing makes it a use-value' (126). That is to say, the purpose for which something may be used directly, with no alteration or mediation, constitutes its use-value. Conversely, '[e]xchange-value appears first of all as the

quantitative relation, the proportion, in which use-values of one kind exchange for use-values of another kind' (126). Exchange-value represents what something can be traded or exchanged for. I use these terms metaphorically: in a marriage for love, the affianced couple desire one another (use-value), whereas in the interested marriage, they desire what the other brings or represents (e.g., dowry, status, opportunity, and so forth). Capitalism depends upon exchange-value, and the production of commodities, 'the form products take when ... production is organized through exchange.' *A Dictionary of Marxist Thought*, ed. Bottomore et al. 86.

6 Despite his stringent critique of the ethos of capitalism, Dickens generally represents the most worthy kind of love as companionate love, the sort of elevated friendship we see between Little Dorrit and Clenham, as opposed to Clenham's earlier passion for Pet, or Pet's misguided passion for Gowan. In this sense, he departs from his contemporaries; romantic passion is not the antidote to materialism for Dickens as it is for Trollope and other novelists.

7 Trollope, *An Autobiography*, 294–5.

8 Anthony Trollope, *The Way We Live Now*, ed. and with an introduction by John Sutherland (Oxford: Oxford University Press, 1982), 77–8. Subsequent citations are to this edition and appear in the text. Cf., 'But the words [Fisker's account of the railway] had no reference at all to the future profits of the railway, or to the benefit which such means of communication would confer upon the world at large; but applied solely to the appetite for such stock as theirs, which might certainly be produced in the speculating world by a proper manipulation of the affairs.' *The Way We Live Now*, 1:88.

9 *Tom Jones* is, of course, the most famous exception, but the novel as a genre tended to follow Richardson's rather than Fielding's example, either creating exemplary suitors for its heroines or not inquiring too closely into the moral and sexual lives of prospective husbands.

10 See chap. 1, n. 58.

11 Before the seventeenth century, divorce was granted by ecclesiastical courts. There were two types. A divorce *a vinculo matrimonii* annulled a marriage, thereby enabling the parties to remarry but also rendering any children from the marriage illegitimate. A divorce *a mensa et thoro* could be granted to either party on three grounds: adultery, sodomy, or cruelty (almost always interpreted as physical abuse). Desertion was not a ground. In an annulment a woman regained her property rights, but in a divorce *a mensa et thoro* the laws governing property in marriage still obtained. The courts might also award a woman alimony, but since this was not a legal debt, it was impossible to enforce. In 1813, an act added the penalty of

imprisonment for failure to pay alimony, but in any case, alimony was only in effect during a husband's lifetime. It is obvious that divorce on these terms might easily impoverish women. In the seventeenth century, the practice of obtaining a divorce *a vinculo matrimonii* on ground of adultery through a private act of Parliament emerged. This involved first obtaining a divorce *a mensa et thoro* from the ecclesiastical courts, and if the husband was seeking a divorce, he had to charge another man with criminal conversation. Divorce by act of Parliament secured the legitimacy of children and settled property between the parties, usually including financial provision for the wife.

The expense involved in all these types of divorces made them available only to the wealthy. Moreover, women almost never obtained a divorce through Parliament. Holcombe notes that women successfully sued for divorce in only four cases during the eighteenth and nineteenth centuries before passage of the Divorce Act of 1857, and in each one, the woman pleaded bigamy or incest in addition to the husband's adultery (*Wives and Property*, 96). The Divorce and Matrimonial Causes Act of 1857 allowed separation (but not divorce) for women physically abused by their husbands and also granted women who obtained judicial separations or divorces, or who were deserted by their husbands, the property rights of single women. This was limited relief, however, for the determination of physical abuse was left to judges who were often biased, and in any case, poor women could not afford to apply to the divorce courts in London for separation orders, or to activate their independent status. The Matrimonial Causes Act of 1878 enabled a wife who was a victim of physical abuse to apply for a separation order from a local magistrate's court. But it was not until 1891 that the courts ruled that a man was not entitled to imprison his wife. See Holcombe, *Wives and Property*, chap. 5; Shanley, *Feminism, Marriage and the Law*, chap. 1; and Mary Lyndon Shanley, '"One Must Ride Behind."'

12 Staves, *Married Women's Separate Property*, chap. 5.

13 The other motive was to 'harmonize conflicting legal systems and to rationalize and modernize the country's judicial machinery.' Holcombe, *Wives and Property*, 46, 94. The first Married Women's Property Act (1870) allowed three kinds of property to be treated as separate: earnings, investments, and legacies of less than two hundred pounds. An earlier bill had been introduced in 1857, but was tabled in favour of the less radical Divorce Act of the same year. The Married Women's Property Act of 1882 allowed women to enter into contracts independently, and to will property to beneficiaries of their choice. Both property acts and the law of equity nevertheless recognized the rights of a wife's property rather than her personal rights. See

Holcombe, *Wives and Property*, chaps. 7 and 8; Shanley, *Feminism, Marriage and the Law*, chaps. 2 and 4.

14 Cobbe, 'Criminals, Idiots, Women and Minors: Is the Classification Sound?'
15 *Parliamentary Debates*, 3rd ser., vol. 192, 10 June 1868, col. 1353.
16 Ibid., col. 1364.
17 Ibid., col. 1355.
18 Ibid., col. 1358.
19 Hall, 'A Feminist in Spite of Himself.'
20 Mill was a member of Parliament and an activist for women's rights. He claimed that his close friend, later his wife, Harriet Taylor, collaborated in all his writings. For a discussion of their relationship, see Phyllis Rose, *Parallel Lives*. If it is true that Taylor collaborated on *The Subjection* it is ironic that her name does not appear on this most famous of Mill's writings on feminism. In this case, the failure to publicly credit her authorship reproduces the principle of coverture (the legal identification of a wife with her husband) of which the treatise is so critical.
21 Mill, 'The Subjection of Women' in John Stuart Mill and Harriet Taylor Mill, *Essays on Sex Equality*, ed. Alice S. Rossi (Chicago: University of Chicago Press, 1970), 168–9. Subsequent references are to this edition and appear in the text.
22 The view that women's rights were a necessary consequence of progress informed the arguments of other feminists as well. Cobbe, for instance, associates the progress of women's rights with the evolution of humankind: 'It is clear enough that we have reached one of those stages in human history which like a youth's attainment of his majority, makes some change in the arrangements of past time desirable if not imperative... [A]s the ages of force and violence have passed away and as more and more room has been left for the growth of gentler powers, women have gradually and slowly risen to a higher place' ('Criminals, Idiots, Women and Minors.' 791). Josephine Butler alludes to England's reform movements when she compares male activists for the reform of marriage law to 'men nobly born and possessing advantages of wealth and education [who] have fought the battles of poor men, and claimed and wrung from Parliaments an extension of privileges enjoyed by a few to classes of their brother-men who are toiling and suffering.' Introduction to *Woman's Work and Woman's Culture*, ed. Butler, xii–xiv. Francis Cornwallis recalls former 'insurrections and revolutions,' analogous to the feminist struggle, which are 'for the most part, nothing more than the consequences of the same obstinate perseverance in an old course, in spite of altered circumstances.' 'The Property of Married Women,' 340.

23 Anthony Trollope, *He Knew He Was Right* (Oxford: Oxford University Press, 1985), 30. Subsequent references are to this edition and appear in the text.

24 Until the nineteenth century, in cases of divorce or separation, fathers automatically received custody of the children, barring exceptional circumstances. The Infant Custody Act of 1839 allowed a woman separated from her husband to petition the equity courts for custody of her children under the age of seven, and for visitation rights thereafter. The next reform was the Infant Custody Act of 1873, which allowed a woman to petition for custody of children up to the age of sixteen. Since *He Knew He Was Right* was published in 1869, Emily would be subject to the 1839 law, which is referred to in the novel (581). But of course the courts could do nothing for Emily with respect to custody or any other issue, since the Trevelyans were not legally separated. Nor could a court grant them a legal separation, since neither had committed an offence to warrant it according to the existing law. The magistrate who advises Emily's father concludes that 'the husband had offered a home to his wife, and that in offering it he had attempted to impose no conditions which could be shewn to be cruel before a judge' (581).

25 *Four Lectures by Anthony Trollope,* 67–95.

26 *An Autobiography,* 266.

27 Robert Polhemus ventriloquizes Trevelyan's logic: 'If the role of woman is changing, and if a wife may disobey her husband and demand her rights, what will prevent her from going off the double standard and behaving with the promiscuity of a man? Nothing, according to Trevelyan, and he takes his paranoid suspicion for fact.' *The Changing World of Anthony Trollope,* 164.

28 *Parliamentary Debates,* 3rd ser., vol. 192, 21 June 1870, col. 604.

29 Simon Gatrell observes that in this novel, love is subversive of mastery. 'Jealousy, Mastery, Love and Madness,' 101. The assumption that love will obviate problems of authority within a good marriage is a staple of domestic ideology. We have seen how Lady L. preaches this dictum to her sister Charlotte in *Sir Charles Grandison.* This logic is implicit in arguments against changing marriage laws for 'exceptional cases' of marital discord, or for granting other women's rights. A conservative member of Parliament makes this clear, arguing that 'if the married women of England were appealed to they would be found opposed to it [married women's property]. They would prefer that spirit of mutual confidence, which was the great element of happiness in marriage, to the possession of unlimited

control over their property.' *Parliamentary Debates*, vol. 192, 10 June 1868, col. 1355.

30 Taylor was a seventeenth-century divine, whose works were popular with the Victorians. Most middle-class households possessed his sermons. On this point see Ruth apRoberts, 'Emily and Nora and Dorothy and Priscilla and Jemima and Carry,' 116.

31 Miller, 'The Novel as Usual: Trollope's *Barchester Towers*,' 107–45.

32 Showalter, *The Female Malady*, 55.

33 Andrew Dowling notes that the ubiquity of black clothing for men signalled the self-control, or what we would call repression, that was an indication of manliness in the Victorian era. *Manliness and the Male Novelist*, 13–14.

34 Peter K. Garrett observes the purpose of the significance of the 'interplay' between Trevelyan's story and the Stanbury subplot is 'to define Trevelyan's deficiencies.' *The Victorian Multiplot Novel*, 205.

35 Sutherland, notes to *He Knew He Was Right*, 935, n. 60.

36 Trollope, *An Autobiography*, 245.

37 Ibid.

5. Margaret Oliphant's Women Who Want Too Much

1 John Stuart Mill, 'The Subjection of Women,' in John Stuart Mill and Harriet Taylor Mill, *Essays on Sex Equality*, ed. Alice S. Rossi (Chicago: University of Chicago Press, 1970), 235. Subsequent references are to this edition and appear in the text.

2 Although the limited amount of criticism available on Oliphant tends to recognize the feminist implications of her novels, a biography written as recently as 1995 still concludes 'her opinions on the rights of women question seems to place her in what would now be labelled the anti-feminist camp.' Jay, *Mrs Oliphant*, 48.

3 Williams, 'Feminist or Antifeminist? Oliphant and the Woman Question,' 165.

4 'Her life is interrupted, broken up into morsels; now she can go forth, can work if it be needful, can use in any way that may be necessary the faculties that God has given her; and anon there comes a time in which all such labours must be suspended in consideration of something else which God has given her to do. But the man has no interruptions to his life.' Margaret Oliphant, 'Review of *The Subjection of Women* by John Stuart Mill and *Women's Work and Women's Culture: a Series of Essays*, edited by Josephine G.

Butler,' *Edinburgh Review* 130, Article XI (October 1869), 585. Subsequent citations to this article appear in the text. Although Mill believes that opportunities other than domestic life should be open to women, he agrees with Oliphant about the difficulty of combining family and career: 'Like a man when he chooses a profession, so, when a woman marries, it may in general be understood that she makes choice of the management of a household, and the bringing up of a family, as the first call upon her exertions, during as many years of her life as may be required for the purpose; and that she renounces, not all other objects and occupations, but all which are not consistent with the requirements of this.' However, he also maintains that there are exceptional women for whom 'there ought to be nothing to prevent faculties exceptionally adapted to any other pursuit, from obeying their vocation notwithstanding marriage: due provision being made for supplying otherwise any falling-short which might become inevitable, in her full performance of the ordinary functions of mistress of a family' (179–80). Mill has been criticized by feminist scholars for his acceptance of traditional ideas of gender and the family. See, for example, Annas, 'Mill and the Subjection of Women,' and Okin, *Women in Western Political Thought,* 197–230. But certainly Mill's contention elsewhere in *The Subjection* that it is difficult to know which institutions and beliefs are natural and which are culturally constructed conflicts with this easy acceptance of a woman's role. For an account of Mill that focuses on the more progressive aspects of his theory with respect to sex and gender, see Urbanati, 'J.S. Mill on Androgyny and Ideal Marriage.' Considerations of what is progressive, however, are open to question. In general, contemporary post-structuralist feminism and queer theory do not accept the distinction between the natural and the constructed.

5 Oliphant questioned the utility of the classical education for *both* men and women, and believed that attempting to educate girls in modern instead of classical languages would provide 'virgin soil' to test her proposed revision of the foreign language curriculum for boys ('Review,' 595).

6 This is so crucial a point of agreement – after all, the reform of marriage law is one of the primary goals of *The Subjection* – that it is worth quoting Oliphant at some length: 'For our own part, we agree with Mr Mill to a great extent as to the injustice of some existing laws which press very hardly upon women; and are perfectly disposed to accept the alterations he suggests, believing that they would furnish a real remedy for a distinct grievance. We believe that a great and universal injury – the injury of an insult – is done to all women by the present state of the marriage law in England. Were it universally – as it is in the vast majority of cases – a dead letter, it

would still outrage the sensibilities of one half of the race; and no end that is worth serving can be served by that. To say that a woman loses all rights, all property, all identity, as soon as she is married – although it is the merest legal fiction and idle breath – is in its actual words an insult to every woman' (579).

7 Margaret Oliphant, 'The Grievances of Women,' *Fraser's Magazine* 21 (May 1880), 699. Subsequent references to this article appear in the text.

8 Cf. Mill, 'The general opinion of men is supposed to be, that the natural vocation of a woman is that of a wife and mother. I say, is supposed to be, because, judging from acts – from the whole of the present constitution of society – one might infer that their opinion was the direct contrary. They might be supposed to think that the alleged natural vocation of women was of all things the most repugnant to their nature; insomuch that if they are free to do anything else – if any other means of living, or occupation of their time and faculties, is open, which has any chance of appearing desirable to them – there will not be enough of them who will be willing to accept the condition said to be natural to them. If this is the real opinion of men in general, it would be well that it should be spoken out. I should like to hear somebody openly enunciating the doctrine (it is already implied in much that is written on the subject) – "It is necessary to society that women should marry and produce children. They will not do so unless they are compelled. Therefore it is necessary to compel them"' (155).

9 Cf. 'A man's wife is considered to be his dependent, fed and clothed by him of his free will and bounty, and all the work that she does in fulfillment of the natural conditions of their marriage is considered as of no account whatever in the matter. He works, but she does not; he toils to maintain her, while she sits at home in ease and leisure, and enjoys the fruits of his labour, and gives him an ornamental compensation in smiles and pleasant-ness. This is the representation of married life which is universally accepted ... [T]he most liberal and the most generous men are often as much at fault as the coarsest. They will not allow the importance of the second part in the universal duet. They will give liberally and praise freely, but they will not acknowledge "My wife has as much to do as I have. Without her work mine would not have half its value; we are partners in the toil of living and she has earned the recompense of that toil as well as I."' 'Grievances,' 705–6.

10 Cobbe, 'What Shall We Do With Our Old Maids?'*Essays on the Pursuits of Women*, ed. Frances Power Cobbe (London: Emily Faithful, 1863), 594. Sub-sequent references to this article appear in the text.

11 Oliphant, *The Curate in Charge*, 193–4. Cited by Cohen, 'Maximizing Oli-

phant,' 111. Cohen sees this as a clear indication of Oliphant's feminism, arguing that although Oliphant claimed to dismiss this kind of ending on literary grounds, 'the imaginative (if not financial) impoverishment of the romance plot is, for Oliphant, no matter how she might pretend otherwise, a political and not an aesthetic question in so far as she consistently shakes her fist at the cultural conditions that presumably refuse its reinvention' (112).

12 Linda Peterson also analyses Oliphant's work as a revision of conventional narrative, averring that it is reworking of the *Bildungsroman*, which includes the marriage choice in some of her novels. Although this paradigm is important, the revision of the courtship plot is even more germane to Oliphant's work. Moreover, to view the novels as centred on the development of Oliphant's heroines misses an important point. Although her characters certainly learn in the course of their stories, a significant feature of all three heroines discussed is that they have already developed in unusual ways, independent and defiant of men's influence and guidance, by the time these novels begin. We do not so much witness the evolution of character, as in the traditional *Bildungsroman*, as the way in which a certain kind of character confronts a society that refuses to ratify its existence. Peterson, 'The Female Bildungsroman.'

13 Langland, *Nobody's Angels*, 1–23, and passim.

14 Arlene Young notes, 'the doggedness and energy with which Phoebe embarks on her mission to save Mr May's reputation suggest that her virtues are not the traditional feminine ones of tenderness and subservience, but the supposedly masculine ones of action and command.' *Culture, Class and Gender in the Victorian Novel*, 132.

15 Margaret Oliphant, *Phoebe Junior* (New York: Penguin Books, 1989), 80. Subsequent references are to this edition and appear in the text.

16 Within the many gradations in status between different strata of the middle class, there was a vast difference between being in trade and shopkeeping.

17 There is an implicit critique of Trollope's character Lily Dale in *The Small House at Allington* (1867) in the character of Sophia. Lily, jilted like Sophia, decides to remain single as a result of her experience, despite the repeated proposals and genuine love of Johnny Eames, and to the disappointment of Trollope's readership. There is something pure and romantic in Lily's refusals; like the heroines of old, she has loved once, truly and too well, and is unable to feel such sentiments again, or to commit herself when she cannot. Oliphant provides a reality check; a woman who has been jilted was unlikely to get a second chance. The difference in social position between

Lily and Sophia might account for their different reactions to some extent: Lily is not poor, but does live in a cottage, while Sophia is obviously one of the county gentry. Still, Trollope underplays the social ignominy that would have resulted from such an experience, and Oliphant implicitly corrects him.

18 The distinct social positions of Ursula and Northcote ensure that the reader knows that this is a love match. Northcote is well off, but he is also a Dissenter, and although he is a gentleman in appearance, behaviour, and education, he has not been produced by the system that officially denotes such gentlemanliness; he has not had an Oxbridge education. He is a gentleman of the industrial north, as his name indicates, produced by industrial wealth and an alternative system of gentility that is not quite the genuine article. His social origins offset the attractions of his wealth, so that Ursula's love must indeed be genuine to defy the snobbish opinion that would disapprove of such a marriage, especially since a woman takes on the social standing of her husband. The reverse is true for Northcote: he gains little in social status by marrying Ursula and nothing financially. His attentions to her are necessarily disinterested.

19 Margaret Oliphant, *Hester* (1883; New York: Penguin Books, Virago Press, 1985), 130, 135. Subsequent references are to this edition and appear in the text.

20 Hester's answer rejects his antifeminist ideology: 'Do you really think ... that the charm of inspiring, as you call it, is what any reasonable creature would prefer to doing? Women would need to be disinterested indeed if they like that best. I don't see it' (331).

21 Girárd, *Deceit, Desire, and the Novel*, 10.

22 Sedgwick, *Between Men*, 22.

23 Butler, *Bodies That Matter*, 89.

24 Margaret Oliphant, *Kirsteen: The Story of a Scotch Family Seventy Years Ago* (New York: Harper & Brothers, 1890), 34. Subsequent references appear in the text.

25 Peterson reads *Kirsteen* as a female *Bildungsroman*, but this is only part of its play on genre. Kirsteen does not need to learn or to develop to the same extent as the heroes in the novels I cite.

26 Romance: 'A fictitious narrative in prose of which the scene and incidents are very remote from those of ordinary life.' *OED*, definition II, 2.

27 Cf. Pip's journey on the road to London in *Great Expectations*.

28 For a different reading of Kirsteen's renunciation of her family name, see Jay, *Mrs Oliphant*, 62–3.

6. Liberalism and Feminism: The End of the Line

1 Oliphant, *The Autobiography*, 7.
2 Deirdre D'Albertis argues convincingly that the division established in passages such as this is a false one, and that Oliphant's life and work were 'complementary rather than competing realms.' Oliphant's difference from Eliot was due as much to her rejection of the latter's aesthetic of writing, which 'required great plumbing of depths or a contemplative sensibility' (823), as to practical factors. In this light, Oliphant's statement here becomes one more attempt at self-promotion rather than a rueful lament over unfulfilled potential. 'The Domestic Drone: Margaret Oliphant and a Political History of the Novel.'

Bibliography

Allestree, Richard. *The Ladies Calling, In Two Parts*. Oxford, 1720.

Althusser, Louis. 'Ideology and Ideological State Apparatuses (Notes towards an Investigation).' In *Lenin and Philosophy and Other Essays*, translated by Ben Brewster, 127–86. New York: Monthly Review Press, 1971.

Andrew, D.T. 'The Code of Honour and Its Critics: The Opposition to Duelling In England 1700–1850.' *Social History* 5 (1980): 416–20.

Annas, Julia. 'Mill and the Subjection of Women.' *Philosophy* 52 (1977): 179–94.

apRoberts, Ruth. 'Emily and Nora and Dorothy and Priscilla and Jemima and Carry.' In *The Victorian Experience: The Novelists*, edited by Richard A. Levine, 87–120. Columbus: Ohio University Press, 1976.

Armstrong, Nancy. *Desire and Domestic Fiction: A Political History of the Novel*. Oxford: Oxford University Press, 1987.

Armstrong, Nancy, and Leonard Tennenhouse, eds. *The Ideology of Conduct: Essays on Literature and the History of Sexuality*. London: Methuen, 1987.

Astell, Mary. 'Reflections Upon Marriage.' In *The First English Feminist: 'Reflections Upon Marriage' and Other Writings by Mary Astell*, edited by Bridget Hill, 67–132. New York: St Martin's Press, 1986.

Auerbach, Nina. 'O Brave New World: Evolution and Revolution in *Persuasion*.' *ELH* 39 (1972): 112–28.

Austen, Jane. *Jane Austen's Letters to Her Sister Cassandra and Others*. Edited by R.W. Chapman. Oxford: Oxford University Press, 1979.

– *Northanger Abbey and Persuasion*. Oxford: Oxford University Press, 1983.

– *Pride and Prejudice*. Oxford: Oxford University Press, 1983.

– *Sense and Sensibility*. Oxford: Oxford University Press, 1983.

Ballaster, Ros. *Seductive Forms: Women's Amatory Fiction from 1684 to 1740*. Oxford: Clarendon Press, 1992.

Bannet, Eve. *The Domestic Revolution: Enlightenment Feminisms and the Novel*. Baltimore, MD: Johns Hopkins University Press, 2000.

Barker, Gerald A. *Grandison's Heirs: The Paragon's Progress in the Late Eighteenth-Century Novel*. London: Associated University Presses, 1985.

Barker-Benfield, G.J. *The Culture of Sensibility: Sex and Society in Eighteenth-Century Britain*. Chicago: University of Chicago Press, 1992.

Beasley, Jerry C. 'Richardson's Girls: The Daughters of Patriarchy' in *Pamela, Clarissa*, and *Sir Charles Grandison.' New Essay on Samuel Richardson*, edited by Albert J. Rivero, 35–52. New York: St Martin's Press, 1996.

Beauty's Triumph: or, The Superiority of the Fair Sex Invincibly Proved. New Haven: Research Publications, Inc., 1975.

Behn, Aphra. *The Rover*. Lincoln: University of Nebraska Press, 1967.

Blackstone, Sir William. *Commentaries on the Laws of England*. 4 vols. Oxford: Clarendon Press, 1765.

Boone, Joseph Allen. *Tradition Counter Tradition: Love and the Form of Fiction*. Chicago: Chicago University Press, 1987.

Bottomore, Tom, Laurence Harris, V.G. Kiernan, and Ralph Miliband, eds. *A Dictionary of Marxist Thought*. Cambridge: Harvard University Press, 1983.

Bourdieu, Pierre. *Outline of a Theory of Practice*. Cambridge: Cambridge University Press, 1977.

Brathwaite, Richard. *The English Gentlewoman, drawne out to the full Body*. London, 1641.

Brent, Charles. *Persuasions to a Publick Spirit*. 1704.

Brissenden, R.G. *Virtue in Distress*. New York: Harper and Row, 1974.

Bronte, Charlotte. *Jane Eyre*. New York: Penguin, 1996.

Brown, Homer. *Institutions of the Novel from Defoe to Scott*. Philadelphia: University of Pennsylvania Press, 1997.

Brown, Laura. *English Dramatic Form, 1660–1760*. New Haven: Yale University Press, 1981.

– *Fables of Modernity: Literature and Culture in the English Eighteenth Century*. Ithaca, NY: Cornell University Press, 2001.

Brown, Wendy. *States of Injury: Power and Freedom in Late Modernity*. Princeton: Princeton University Press, 1995.

Browning, Elizabeth Barrett. *Aurora Leigh*. Edited by Margaret Reynolds. New York: W.W. Norton & Company, 1996.

Burke, Edmund. *Reflections on the Revolution in France*. Oxford: Oxford University Press, 1993.

Burn, W.L. *The Age of Equipoise: A Study of the Mid-Victorian Generation*. New York: W.W. Norton & Company, 1964.

Butler, Josephine. Introduction. In *Woman's Work and Woman's Culture: A Series of Essays*. Edited by Josephine Butler. London: Macmillan and Co., 1869.

Butler, Judith. *Bodies That Matter: On the Discursive Limits of Sex*. London: Routledge, 1993.

Butler, Marilyn. *Jane Austen and the War of Ideas*. Oxford: Clarendon Press, 1975.

Carlyle, Thomas. *Past and Present*. Boston: Houghton Mifflin Company, 1965.

Case, Alison. *Plotting Women: Gender and Narration in the Eighteenth- and Nineteenth- Century English Novel*. Charlottesville: University of Virginia Press, 1999.

Chaber, Lois A. '"Sufficient to the Day": Anxiety in *Sir Charles Grandison*.' In *Passion and Virtue: Essays on the Novels of Samuel Richardson*, edited by David Blewett, 268–94. Toronto: University of Toronto Press, 2001.

– '"This Affecting Subject": An "Interested" Reading of Childbearing in Two Novels by Samuel Richardson.' *Eighteenth-Century Fiction* 8, no. 2 (January 1996): 193–250.

Chapman, R.W. 'A Reply to Mr. Duffy on "Persuasion".' *Nineteenth-Century Fiction* 9 (1955): 1–20.

Cibber, Colley. *Love's Last Shift*. London, 1755.

Cleaver, Robert. *A Godly Forme of Household Government*. London: Thomas Man, 1603.

Cobbe, Frances Power. 'Criminals, Idiots, Women and Minors: Is the Classification Sound?' *Fraser's Magazine* 78 (1868): 777–94.

– 'What Shall We Do With Our Old Maids?' In *Essays on the Pursuits of Women*, edited by Frances Power Cobbe, 594–610. London: Emily Faithful, 1863.

Cohen, Monica. 'Maximizing Oliphant.' In *Victorian Women Writers and the Woman Question*, edited by Nicola Diane Thompson, 99–115. Cambridge: Cambridge University Press, 1999.

– 'Persuading the Navy Home: Austen and Married Women's Professional Property.' *Novel* (Spring 1996): 346–66.

Congreve, William. *The Way of the World*. Lincoln: University of Nebraska Press, 1965.

Cornwallis, Francis. 'The Property of Married Women: Report of the Personal Laws Committee (of the Law Amendment Society) on the Laws Relating to the Property of Married Women.' *Westminster Review* 66 (1856): 1–20.

Cott, Nancy. 'Passionlessness: An Interpretation of Victorian Sexual Ideology, 1790– 1850.' *Signs* (Winter 1978): 1–20.

Court of Good Counsell. 1607.

Crane, R.S. 'Suggestions toward a Genealogy of The Man of Feeling.' *ELH* 1 (December 1934): 228–9

Crittenden, Ann. *The Price of Motherhood: Why the Most Important Job in the World Is Still the Least Valued*. New York: Henry Holt and Company, 2001.

D'Albertis, Deirdre. 'The Domestic Drone: Margaret Oliphant and a Political History of the Novel.' *Studies in English Literature 1500–1900* (Autumn 1997): 805–29.

Davidoff, Leonore, and Catherine Hall. *Family Fortunes: Men and Women of the English Middle Class, 1780–1850.* Chicago: University of Chicago Press, 1987.

Davies, Kathleen M. 'Continuity and Change in Literary Advice on Marriage.' In *Marriage and Society: Studies in the Social History of Marriage,* edited by R.B. Outhwaite, 58–80. London: Europa, 1981.

– 'The Sacred Condition of Equality – How Original Were Puritan Doctrines of Marriage?' *Social History* 5 (May 1977): 663–80.

Defoe, Daniel. *Conjugal Lewdness; or, Matrimonial Whoredom. A Treatise Concerning the Use and Abuse of the Marriage Bed.* Gainsville, FL: Scholars' Facsimiles and Reprints, 1967.

– *Robinson Crusoe.* New York: Signet Books, 1961.

de la Barre, François Poulain. *De L'Égalité des deux Sexes.* Paris, 1673.

Derrida, Jacques. *Of Grammatology.* Translated by Gayatri Chakravorty Spivak. Baltimore, MD: Johns Hopkins University Press, 1976.

Dickens, Charles. *Great Expectations.* New York: W.W. Norton, 1999.

– *Little Dorrit.* Oxford: Oxford University Press, 1989.

Diderot. *Correspondance,* vol. 3. Paris: Les Éditions de Minuit, 1957.

Dixon, Rebecca. 'Misrepresenting Jane Austen's Ladies: Revising Texts (and History) to Sell Films.' In *Jane Austen in Hollywood,* edited by Linda Troost and Sayre Greenfield, 44–57. Lexington: University Press of Kentucky, 1998.

Doody, Margaret Anne. 'Identity and Character in Sir Charles Grandison.' In *Samuel Richardson: Tercentenary Essays,* edited by Margaret Anne Doody and Peter Sabor, 110–32. Cambridge: Cambridge University Press, 1989.

– *A Natural Passion.* Oxford: Clarendon Press, 1974.

Dowling, Andrew. *Manliness and the Male Novelist in Victorian Literature.* Aldershot, Hants.: Ashgate, 2001.

Duckworth, Alistair. *The Improvement of the Estate: A Study of Jane Austen's Novels.* Baltimore, MD: Johns Hopkins Press, 1971.

Duffy, Joseph M. Jr. 'Structure and Society in Jane Austen's Fiction.' *Nineteenth-Century Fiction* 8 (1954): 272–89.

Eagleton, Terry. *The Function of Criticism From The Spectator to Post-Structuralism.* London: Verso, 1984.

– *Ideology of the Aesthetic.* Oxford: Basil Blackwell 1990.

– *The Rape of Clarissa.* Minneapolis: University of Minnesota Press, 1982.

Earle, Peter. *The Making of the English Middle Class: Business, Society and Family Life in London, 1660–1730.* Berkeley and Los Angeles: University of California Press, 1989.

Eaves, T.C. Duncan, and Ben D. Kimpel. *Samuel Richardson*. Oxford: Oxford University Press, 1971.

Eisenstein, Zillah. *The Color of Gender: Reimaging Democracy*. Berkeley and Los Angeles: University of California Press, 1994.

– *Feminism and Sexual Equality: Crisis in Liberal America*. New York: Monthly Review Press, 1984.

– *The Radical Future of Liberal Feminism*. Boston: Northeastern University Press, 1981.

Eliot, George. *Middlemarch*. London: Penguin, 1994.

Essay on the New Species of Writing founded by Mr. Fielding: with a Word or Two upon the Modern State of Criticism. London: William Owen, 1751.

Ferguson, Moira, ed. *First Feminists: British Women Writers 1578–1799*. Bloomington: Indiana University Press, 1985.

Fielding, Henry. *The History of Tom Jones, a Foundling*. Middletown: Wesleyan University Press, 1975.

Filmer, Sir Robert. *Patriarcha and Other Writings*. Edited and with an introduction by Johann P. Somerville. Cambridge: Cambridge University Press, 1990.

Flint, Kate. *The Woman Reader, 1837–1914*. Oxford: Clarendon Press, 1993.

Flynn, Carol Houlihan. *Samuel Richardson: A Man of Letters*. Princeton: Princeton University Press, 1982.

Fordyce, James. *Sermons to Young Women*. 3rd American ed. from the 12th London ed. Philadelphia: M. Carey, 1809.

Foucault, Michel. *The History of Sexuality, Volume I: An Introduction*. Translated by Robert Hurley. New York: Vintage, 1980.

Galley, Henry. 'Some Considerations upon Clandestine Marriages.' In *The Marriage Act of 1753: Four Tracts*, edited by Randolph Trumbach, 1–164. New York: Garland Publishing, 1984.

Garrett, Peter K. *The Victorian Multiplot Novel: Studies in Dialogical Form*. New Haven: Yale University Press, 1985.

Gatrell, Simon. 'Jealousy, Mastery, Love and Madness: A Brief Reading of He Knew He Was Right.' In *Anthony Trollope*, edited by Tony Bareham, 95–115. New York: Barnes and Noble, 1980.

Gay, Peter. *The Bourgeois Experience, Victoria to Freud: The Tender Passion*. Oxford: Oxford University Press, 1986.

Genette, Gérard. *Narrative Discourse: An Essay in Method*. Ithaca, NY: Cornell University Press, 1980.

Gilligan, Carol. *In a Different Voice: Psychological Theory and Women's Development*. Cambridge: Harvard University Press, 1993.

Gillis, J.R. *For Better, For Worse: British Marriage 1600 to the Present*. Oxford: Oxford University Press, 1985.

Girard, René. *Deceit, Desire, and the Novel: Self and Other in Literary Structure*. Baltimore, MD: Johns Hopkins University Press, 1976.

Gisborne, Thomas. *An Enquiry into the Duties of the Female Sex*. London: T. Cadell jun. and W. Davies, 1798.

Golden, Morris. *Richardson's Characters*. Ann Arbor: University of Michigan Press, 1963.

Gonda, Danielle. *Reading Daughters' Fictions 1709–1834*. Cambridge: Cambridge University Press, 1996.

Gramsci, Antonio. *Selections from the Prison Notebooks*. Edited and translated by Quintin and Geoffrey Nowell Smith. New York: International Publishers, 1971.

Gregory, John. *A Father's Legacy to his Daughters*. London, 1775.

Grossmith, George, and Weedon Grossmith. *Diary of a Nobody*. London: Penguin Books, 1985.

Gunn, Daniel P. 'In the Vicinity of Winthrop: Ideological Rhetoric in Persuasion.' *Nineteenth-Century Literature* 41, no. 4 (March 1987): 403–18.

Gwilliam, Tassie. *Samuel Richardson's Fictions of Gender*. Stanford: Stanford University Press, 1993.

Habakkuk, H.J. 'Marriage Settlements in the Eighteenth Century.' *Transactions of the Royal Historical Society*, 4th ser. 32 (1950): 15–30.

Hagstrum, Jean H. *Sex and Sensibility: Ideal and Erotic Love From Milton to Mozart*. Chicago: University of Chicago Press, 1980.

Hall, N. John. 'A Feminist in Spite of Himself.' *Trollopiana: The Journal of the Trollope Society* 10 (August 1990): 13–19.

Hammerton, A. James. *Cruelty and Companionship*. London: Routledge, 1992.

Hampton, Jean. 'Feminist Contractarianism.' In *A Mind of One's Own: Feminist Essays on Reason and Objectivity*, edited by Louise M. Antony and Charlotte E. Witt, 337–68. Cambridge: Westview, 2002.

Hannon, Patrice. 'Austen Novels and Austen Films: Incompatible Worlds?' *Persuasions: Journal of the Jane Austen Society of North America* 18 (December 1996): 24–32.

Harris, Jocelyn. 'Introduction.' In *Sir Charles Grandison*, edited by Jocelyn Harris, vii–xxiv. London: Oxford University Press, 1972.

– 'Jane Austen and the Burden of the (Male) Past.' In *Jane Austen and Discourses of Feminism*, edited by Devoney Looser, 87–100. New York: St Martin's Press, 1995.

– *Jane Austen's Art of Memory*. Cambridge: Cambridge University Press, 1989.

– 'The Reviser Observed: The Last Volume of *Sir Charles Grandison*.' *Studies in Bibliography* 29 (1976): 1–31.

– *Samuel Richardson*. Cambridge: Cambridge University Press, 1987.

Harstock, Nancy. *Money, Sex, and Power: Toward a Feminist Historical Materialism*. New York: Longman, 1983.

Harth, Erica. 'The Virtue of Love: Lord Hardwicke's Marriage Act.' *Cultural Critique* (Spring 1988): 123–54.

Helsinger, Elizabeth K., Robin Lauterbach Sheets, and William Veeder. *The Woman Question: Society and Literature in Britain and America 1837–1883*, vol. 1. Chicago: University of Chicago Press, 1983.

Hill, Bridget, ed. *Eighteenth-Century Women: An Anthology*. Boston: Unwin and Allen, 1984.

Hirschman, Nancy. *Rethinking Obligation*. Ithaca, NY: Cornell University Press, 1992.

Holcombe, Lee. *Wives and Property: Reform of the Married Women's Property Law in Nineteenth-Century England*. Toronto: University of Toronto Press, 1983.

Honan, Park. 'Richardson's Influence on Jane Austen.' In *Samuel Richardson: Passion and Prudence*, edited by Valerie Grosvenor Myer. Totowa, NJ: Barnes and Noble, 1986.

Hughes, Thomas. *The Manliness of Christ*. Boston: Riverside Press, 1880.

Hume, David. *A Treatise of Human Nature*. Oxford: Oxford University Press, 1981.

Hunter, J. Paul. *Before Novels: The Cultural Contexts of Eighteenth-Century English Fiction*. New York: Norton, 1990.

Jagger, Alison. *Feminist Politics and Human Nature*. Totowa, NJ: Rowman and Allenheld, 1983.

Jay, Elisabeth. *Mrs. Oliphant: A Fiction to Herself: A Literary Life*. Oxford: Clarendon Press, 1995.

Jay, Elisabeth, and Richard Jay, eds. *Critics of Capitalism: Victorian Reactions to 'Political Economy.'* Cambridge: Cambridge University Press, 1986.

Johnson, Claudia L. *Equivocal Beings: Politics, Gender, and Sentimentality in the 1790s*. Chicago: University of Chicago Press, 1995.

– *Jane Austen: Women, Politics and the Novel*. Chicago: University of Chicago Press, 1988.

Johnson, Samuel. *Journal of a Tour to the Hebrides*. Edited by Allen Wendt. Boston: Houghton Mifflin/Riverside, 1965.

– 'Rambler 4, Saturday, March 31, 1750.' In *Samuel Johnson: Rasselas, Poems and Selected Prose*, edited by Bertrand H. Bronson, 67–72. New York: Rinehart and Winston, Inc. 1971.

Jones, Vivien. 'Introduction.' *The Young Lady's Pocket Library, or Parental Monitor*. Bristol: Thoemmes Press, 1995.

Kahn, Victoria. 'Margaret Cavendish and the Romance of Contract.' *Renaissance Quarterly* 50 (1997): 526–66.

Kaplan, Deborah. 'Mass Marketing Jane Austen: Men, Women, and Courtship in Two of the Recent Films.' *Persuasions: Journal of the Jane Austen Society of North America* 18 (December 1996): 171–85.

Kay, Carol. *Political Constructions: Defoe, Richardson and Sterne in Relation to Hobbes, Hume, and Burke.* Ithaca, NY: Cornell University Press, 1988.

Kelly, Gary. 'Jane Austen, Romantic Feminism, and Civil Society.' In *Jane Austen and Discourses of Feminism,* edited by Devoney Looser, 19–34. New York: St Martin's Press, 1995.

Kidder, Richard. *Charity Directed.* 1676.

Kiernan, V.G. *The Duel in European History: Honour and the Reign of Aristocracy.* Oxford: Oxford University Press, 1988.

Kirkham, Jane. *Jane Austen, Feminism and Fiction.* Totowa, NJ: Barnes and Noble, 1983.

La Calprenède, Gaultier de Coste. *Cassandra.* London, 1737.

Laclau, Ernesto, and Chantal Mouffe. *Hegemony and Socialist Strategy: Towards a Radical Democratic Politics.* London: Verso, 2001.

La Fayette, Madame de. *The Princess of Cleves.* New York: New Directions Publishing Corporation, 1988.

Langbauer, Laurie. *Women and Romance: The Consolations of Gender in the English Novel.* Ithaca, NY: Cornell University Press, 1990.

Langford, Paul. *A Polite and Commercial People.* Oxford: Clarendon Press, 1989.

Langland, Elizabeth. *Nobody's Angels: Middle-Class Women and Domestic Ideology in Victorian Culture.* Ithaca, NY: Cornell University Press, 1995.

Laqueur, Thomas. *Making Sex: Body and Gender From the Greeks to Freud.* Cambridge: Harvard University Press, 1990.

Lennox, Charlotte. *The Female Quixote.* London: Pandora Press, 1986.

A Letter to the Public: Containing The Substance of what hath been offered in the late Debates upon the Subject of the Act of Parliament, For the better preventing of Clandestine Marriages. In *The Marriage Act of 1753: Four Tracts,* edited by Randolph Trumbach, 1–56. New York: Garland Publishing, 1984.

Lewis, Sarah. *Woman's Mission.* London: John W. Parker, 1839.

Lloyd, Genevieve. *The Man of Reason: Male and Female in Western Philosophy.* Minneapolis: University of Minnesota Press, 1984.

Locke, John. *An Essay Concerning Human Understanding.* Edited by Peter H. Nidditch. Oxford: Clarendon Press, 1985.

– *Two Treatises of Government.* Edited and with an introduction by Peter Laslett. Cambridge: Cambridge University Press, 1988.

Lonsdale, Roger, ed. *Eighteenth-Century Women Poets: An Oxford Anthology.* Oxford: Oxford University Press, 1989.

Looser, Devoney. 'Jane Austen "Responds" to the Men's Movement.' *Persuasions: Journal of the Jane Austen Society of North America* 18 (December 1996): 159–70.

Mackenzie, Henry. *The Man of Feeling.* New York: Oxford University Press, 1972.

MacKinnon, Catherine A. *Toward a Feminist Theory of the State.* Cambridge: Harvard University Press, 1989.

Macpherson, C.B. *The Political Theory of Possessive Individualism: Hobbes to Locke.* Oxford: Oxford University Press, 1979.

Manley, Delarivier. *New Atalantis.* London: Pickering and Chatto, 1991.

Markley, Robert. 'Sentimentality As Performance: Shaftesbury, Sterne, and the Theatrics of Virtue.' In *The New Eighteenth Century,* edited by Laura Brown and Felicity Nussbaum, 210–30. New York: Methuen, 1987.

Marks, Sylvia Kasey. *Sir Charles Grandison: The Compleat Conduct Book.* Lewisburg: Bucknell University Press, 1986.

Martineau, Harriet. *Household Education.* London: E. Moxon, 1849.

Marx, Karl. *Capital, Volume One.* Translated by Ben Fowkes. New York: Vintage Books, 1977.

Massinger, Philip. *A New Way To Pay Old Debts.* Oxford: Clarendon Press, 1926.

Maurer, Shawn Lisa. *Proposing Men: Dialectics of Gender and Class in the Eighteenth-Century English Periodical.* Stanford: Stanford University Press, 1998.

Mayer, Robert. 'Did You Say Middle Class? The Question of Taste and the Rise of the Novel.' *Eighteenth-Century Fiction* 12 (January–April, 2000): 1–20.

McKeon, Michael. *The Origins of the English Novel, 1600–1740.* Baltimore, MD: Johns Hopkins University Press, 1987.

McMaster, Juliet. '*Sir Charles Grandison*: Richardson on Body and Character.' *Eighteenth-Century Fiction* 1 (January 1989): 83–102.

Mermin, Dorothy. *Godiva's Ride: Women of Letters in England, 1830–1880.* Bloomington and Indianapolis: Indiana University Press, 1993.

Mill, John Stuart. 'The Subjection of Women.' In *Essays on Sex Equality,* edited by Alice S. Rossi. Chicago: University of Chicago Press, 1970.

Miller, D.A. *The Novel and the Police.* Berkeley and Los Angeles: University of California Press, 1988.

Milton, John. 'The Doctrine and Discipline of Divorce.' *Complete Prose Works of John Milton,* vol. 2, edited by Ernest Sirluck, 234–356. New Haven: Yale University Press and Oxford: Oxford University Press, 1959.

– *Paradise Lost.* Edited by Alastair Fowler. London: Longman, 1971.

Minow, Martha. *Making All the Difference: Inclusion, Exclusion, and American Law*. Ithaca, NY: Cornell University Press, 1990.

Moler, Kenneth. *Jane Austen's Art of Allusion*. Lincoln: University of Nebraska Press, 1968.

Monaghan, David. 'Jane Austen and the Position of Women.' In *Jane Austen in a Social Context*, edited by David Monaghan, 105–21. Totowa, NJ: Barnes and Noble, 1981.

− *Jane Austen: Structure and Social Vision*. London: Macmillan Press, 1980.

More, Hannah. *Strictures on the Modern System of Female Education*. Oxford: Woodstock Books, 1995.

Morgenstern, Naomi. 'The Afterlife of Coverture: Contract and Gift in *The Ballad of the Sad Cafe*.' Forthcoming in *differences: A Journal of Feminist Cultural Studies*.

Mudrick, Marvin. *Jane Austen: Irony as Defense and Discovery*. Princeton: Princeton University Press, 1952.

Mullan, John. *Sentiment and Sociability: The Language of Feeling in the Eighteenth Century*. Oxford: Clarendon Press, 1988.

Munro, James S. *Mademoiselle de Scudery and the Carte de Tendre*. Durham: Durham University Press, 1986.

Mylne, Margaret. 'Woman and her Social Position.' *Westminster Review* 35 (January 1841): 1–20.

Nardin, Jane. *Those Elegant Decorums*. Albany: State University of New York Press, 1973.

Nixon, Cheryl L. 'Balancing the Courtship Hero: Masculine Emotional Display in Film Adaptations of Austen's Novels. In *Jane Austen in Hollywood*, edited by Linda Troost and Sayre Greenfield, 22–43. Lexington: University Press of Kentucky, 1998.

Noddings, Nel. *Caring: A Feminine Approach to Ethics and Moral Education*. Berkeley: University of California Press, 1984.

Norton, Caroline. *Selected Writings of Caroline Norton: Facsimile Reproductions*. Introduction and Notes by James O. Hoge and Jane Marcus. Delmar, NY: Scholars' Facsimiles and Reprints, 1978.

Nunokawa, Jeff. *The Afterlife of Property: Domestic Security and the Victorian Novel*. Princeton: Princeton University Press, 1994.

Nussbaum, Martha. *Sex and Social Justice*. Oxford: Oxford University Press, 1999.

Okin, Susan Moller. *Justice, Gender and the Family*. New York: Basic Books, 1989.

− 'Patriarchy and Married Women's Property in England: Questions on Some Current Views.' *Eighteenth-Century Studies* 17 (Winter 1983/4): 121–38.

– Women and the Making of the Sentimental Family.' *Philosophy and Public Affairs* 11, no. 1 (1981): 65–88.
– *Women in Western Political Thought*. Princeton: Princeton University Press, 1979.
Oliphant, Margaret. *The Autobiography*. Chicago: University of Chicago Press, 1988.
– *The Curate in Charge*. Stroud, Gloucs.: Alan Sutton, 1985.
– 'The Grievances of Women.' *Fraser's Magazine* 21 (May 1880): 1–20.
– *Hester*. New York: Penguin Books, 1985.
– *Kirsteen: The Story of a Scotch Family Seventy Years Ago*. New York: Harper & Brothers, 1890.
– *Phoebe Junior*. New York: Penguin Books, 1989.
– 'Review of *The Subjection of Women* by John Stuart Mill and *Women's Work and Women's Culture: a Series of Essays*, edited by Josephine G. Butler.' *Edinburgh Review* 130 (October 1869): 1–20.
Parker, Henry. *Jus Populi*. London, 1644.
Parker, Todd C. *Sexing the Text: The Rhetoric of Sexual Difference in British Literature*. Albany: State University of New York Press, 2000.
Parliamentary Debates, 3rd ser. vol. 192 (1868–70).
The Parliamentary History of England from the Earliest Period to the Year 1803, vol. 15. London: Hansard, 1813.
Pascal, Roy. *The Daul Voice: Free Indirect Speech and Its Functioning in the Nineteenth-Century Novel*. Totowa, NJ: Roman and Littlefield, 1977.
Pateman, Carole. 'Equality, Difference, Subordination: The Politics of Motherhood and Women's Citizenship.' In *Beyond Equality and Difference: Citizenship, Feminist Politics and Female Subjectivity*, edited by Gisela Bock and Susan James. London: Routledge, 1992.
– *The Problem of Political Obligation: A Critique of Liberal Theory*. Berkeley: University of California Press, 1979.
– *The Sexual Contract*. Stanford: Stanford University Press, 1988.
Pateman, Carole, and Elizabeth Grosz, eds. *Feminist Challenges: Social and Political Theory*. Boston: Northeastern University Press, 1986.
Paulson, Ronald. *Representations of Revolution, 1789–1820*. New Haven: Yale University Press, 1983.
Pearson, Jacqueline. *Women's Reading in Britain, 1750–1835: A Dangerous Recreation*. Manchester: University of Manchester Press, 1999.
Pennington, Sarah. *An Unfortunate Mother's Advice to Her Absent Daughters, In a Letter to Miss Pennington*. London, 1761.
Perkin, Harold. *The Origins of Modern English Society 1780–1880*. London: Routledge and Kegan Paul, 1969.

Perry, Ruth. 'Mary Astell and the Feminist Critique of Possessive Individual-
ism.' *Eighteenth-Century Studies: The Politics of Difference* (Summer 1990):
444–57.
– 'Women in Families.' In *Women and Literature in Britain 1700–1800*, edited by
Vivien Jones, 111–31. Cambridge: Cambridge University Press, 2000.
Peterson, Linda. 'The Female Bildungsroman: Tradition and Subversion in
Oliphant's Fiction.' In *Margaret Oliphant: Critical Essays on a Gentle Subversive*,
edited by D.J. Trela, 66–89. London: Associated University Presses, 1995.
Pinch, Adela. *Strange Fits of Passion: Epistemologies of Emotion, Hume to Austen*.
Stanford: Stanford University Press, 1996.
Polhemus, Robert. *The Changing World of Anthony Trollope*. Berkeley and Los
Angeles: University of California Press, 1968.
Pollak, Ellen. *The Poetics of Sexual Myth: Gender and Ideology in the Verse of Swift
and Pope*. Chicago: University of Chicago Press, 1985.
Poovey, Mary. '*Persuasion* and the Promises of Love.' In *The Representation of
Women in Fiction*,' edited by Carolyn G. Heilbrun and Margaret R. Higonnet,
152–79. Baltimore, MD: Johns Hopkins University Press, 1983.
– *The Proper Lady and the Woman Writer: Ideology as Style in the Works of Mary
Wollstonecraft, Mary Shelley, and Jane Austen*. Chicago: University of Chicago
Press, 1984.
– *Uneven Developments: The Ideological Work of Gender in Mid-Victorian England*.
Chicago: University of Chicago Press, 1988.
Reid, Marion. *A Plea for Woman*. Edinburgh, 1843.
Reid-Walsh, Jacqueline. '"She Learned Romance as She Grew Older": From
Conduct Book Propriety to Romance in *Persuasion*.' *Persuasions: Journal of the
Jane Austen Society of North America* (December 1993): 216–25.
Rendall, Jane. *The Origins of Modern Feminism: Women In Britain, France and the
United States, 1780–1860*. London: Macmillan, 1985.
Richardson, Samuel. *Clarissa or The History of a Young Lady*. Harmondsworth:
Penguin, 1985.
– *The Correspondence of Samuel Richardson, Author of Pamela, Clarissa, and Sir
Charles Grandison, Selected from the Original Manuscripts, Bequeathed by Him to
His Family. To which are prefixed, A Biographical Account of that Author and
Observations on His Writings*. Edited by Anna Laetitia Barbauld. 6 vols. New
York: AMS Press, Inc., 1966.
– *Familiar Letters on Important Occasions*. Edited by Brian W. Downs. London:
George Routledge and Sons, Ltd., 1928.
– *Pamela, or, Virtue Rewarded*. Oxford: Oxford University Press, 2001.
– *Selected Letters of Samuel Richardson*. Edited by John Carroll. Oxford: Claren-
don Press, 1964.

– *Sir Charles Grandison.* Edited and with an introduction by Jocelyn Harris. London: Oxford University Press, 1972.

Richetti, John. *Popular Fiction Before Richardson: Narrative Patterns 1700–1739.* Oxford: Clarendon Press, 1969.

Rivero, Albert J. 'Representing Clementina: "Unnatural" Romance and the binding of *Sir Charles Grandison.*' In *New Essays on Samuel Richardson*, edited by Albert J. Rivero, 193–223. New York: St Martin's Press, 1996.

– '"Unnatural" Romance and the Ending of *Sir Charles Grandison.*' New Essays on Samuel Richardson. Edited by Albert J. Rivero. New York: St Martin's Press, 1996.

Roberts, Warren. *Jane Austen and the French Revolution.* New York: St Martin's Press, 1979.

Rose, Phyllis. *Parallel Lives: Five Victorian Marriages.* New York: Alfred Knopf, 1983.

Rousseau, Jean Jacques. *Émile.* Translated by Barbara Foxley. New York: Dutton, 1969.

– *Julie ou La Nouvelle Héloïse: Lettres de deux amants habitants d'une petite ville au pied des Alpes recueilles et publiées par J.-J. Rousseau.* Paris: Gallimard, 2002.

Savile, George, Marquis of Halifax. 'The Lady's New-year's Gift: or, Advice to a Daughter.' In *The Works of George Savile Marquis of Halifax*, edited by Mark N. Brown, 2: 363–406. Oxford: Clarendon Press, 1989.

Sedgwick, Eve Kosofsky. *Between Men: English Literature and Male Homosocial Desire.* New York: Columbia University Press, 1992.

Selections from The Tatler and The Spectator of Steele and Addison. Harmondsworth: Penguin Books, 1982.

Shakespeare, William. 'As You Like It.' *The Riverside Shakespeare.* Boston: Houghton Mifflin Company, 1974.

– A Midsummer Night's Dream. *The Riverside Shakespeare.* Boston: Houghton Mifflin Company, 1974.

Shanley, Mary Lyndon. *Feminism, Marriage and the Law in Victorian England: 1850–1895.* Princeton: Princeton University Press, 1990.

– 'Marriage Contract and Social Contract.' *Western Political Quarterly* 32 (March 1979): 79–91.

– '"One Must Ride Behind": Married Women's Rights and The Divorce Act of 1857.' *Victorian Studies* 25 (Spring 1982): 255–76.

Shaw, Harry E. *Narrating Reality: Austen, Scott, Eliot.* Ithaca, NY: Cornell University Press, 1999.

Shevelow, Kate. *Women and Print Culture: The Construction of Femininity in the Early Periodical.* London: Routledge, 1989.

Showalter, Elaine. *The Female Malady.* New York: Penguin, 1987.

Skinner, Gillian. 'Women's Status as Legal and Civic Subjects.' In *Women and Literature in Britain, 1700–1800*, edited by Vivien Jones, 91–110. Cambridge: Cambridge University Press, 2000.

Smith, Adam. *The Theory of Moral Sentiments*. Edited by D.D. Raphael and A.L. MacFie. Indianapolis: Liberty Press, 1982.

Snawsel, Robert. *A Looking Glass for Married Folk*. London, 1610.

Southam, B.C., ed., *Jane Austen: The Critical Heritage*, vol. 1. London: Routledge, & Kegan Paul, 1968.

The Spectator. Edited by and with an introduction and notes by Donald F. Bond. Oxford: Clarendon Press, 1965.

Spencer, Jane. *The Rise of the Woman Novelist: From Aphra Behn to Jane Austen*. Oxford: Basil Blackwell, 1986.

Spenser, Edmund. *The Faerie Queen*. Harmondsworth: Penguin, 1978.

Staves, Susan. *Married Women's Separate Property in England, 1660–1833*. Cambridge: Harvard University Press, 1990.

– 'Pin Money.' *Studies in Eighteenth-Century Culture* 14 (1985): 47–77.

– 'Where Is History But in Texts? Reading the History of Marriage.' In *The Golden and the Brazen World: Papers in Literature and History, 1650–1800*, edited by John M. Wallace, 125–43. Berkeley: University of California Press, 1985.

Stebbing, Henry. 'An Enquiry into the Force and Operation of the Annulling Clauses in a late Act for the better preventing of Clandestine Marriages, With Respect to Conscience.' In *The Marriage Act of 1753: Four Tracts*, edited by Randolph Trumbach, 1–55. New York: Garland Publishing, 1984.

Steele, Richard. *The Christian Hero*. Oxford: Oxford University Press, 1932.

– *The Conscious Lovers*. Lincoln: University of Nebraska Press, 1960.

Stevenson, John Allen. '"A Geometry of His Own": Richardson and the Marriage Ending.' *Studies in English Literature* (1986): 469–83.

Stone, Lawrence. *The Family, Sex and Marriage in England 1500–1800*. New York: Harper and Row, 1977.

Stone, Lawrence, and Jeanne Fawtier Stone. *An Open Elite? England 1540–1880*. Oxford: Clarendon Press, 1984.

Sulloway, Alison. *Jane Austen and the Province of Womanhood*. Philadelphia: University of Pennsylvania Press, 1989.

Tanner, Tony. 'Introduction.' *Pride and Prejudice*. New York: Penguin Books, 1985.

– *Jane Austen*. Cambridge: Harvard University Press, 1986.

Taylor, Jenny Bourne, and Sally Shuttleworth. *Embodied Selves: An Anthology of Psychological Texts 1830–1890*. Oxford: Oxford University Press.

Taylor, John Tinon. *Early Opposition to the English Novel: The Popular Reaction from 1760 to 1830*. New York: King's Crown Press, 1943.

Temple, Kathryn. *Scandal Nation: Law and Authorship in Britain, 1750–1832*. Ithaca, NY: Cornell University Press, 2003.

Temple, Sir William. *An Essay on Popular Discontents. Miscellanea. The Third Part*. London, 1701.

Thackeray, William Makepeace. *The Newcomes*. London: Penguin Books, 1996.

Thompson, Emma. *The Sense and Sensibility Screenplay and Diaries: Bringing Jane Austen's Novel to Film*. New York: Newmarket Press, 1995.

Thompson, William. *Appeal of One Half of the Human Race, Women, Against the Pretensions of the Other Half, Men, To Retain Them in Political, and Thence in Civil and Domestic Slavery: in Reply to Mr. [James] Mill's Celebrated 'Article on Government.'* New York: Source Book Press, 1970.

Tilney, Edmund. *The Flower of Friendship: A Renaissance Dialogue Contesting Marriage*. Edited and with an introduction by Valerie Wayne. Ithaca, NY: Cornell University Press, 1992.

Todd, Janet. *Sensibility: An Introduction*. London and New York: Methuen, 1986.

Todd, Margo. *Christian Humanism and the Puritan Social Order*. Cambridge: Cambridge University Press, 1987.

Tomalin, Claire. *Jane Austen: A Life*. London: Penguin, 2000.

Tosh, John. *A Man's Place: Masculinity and the Middle-Class Home*. New Haven: Yale University Press, 1999.

Trollope, Anthony. *An Autobiography*. Berkeley and Los Angeles: University of California Press, 1947.

– *Can You Forgive Her?* Oxford: Oxford University Press, 1982.

– *Four Lectures by Anthony Trollope*. Toronto: Macmillan Company, 1938.

– *He Knew He Was Right*. Edited and with an introduction by John Sutherland. Oxford: Oxford University Press, 1985.

– *The Small House at Allington*. Oxford: Oxford University Press, 1986.

– *The Way We Live Now*. Oxford: Oxford University Press, 1982.

Tronto, Joan. *Moral Boundaries*. New York: Routledge, 1993.

Trumbach, Randolph. *The Rise of the Egalitarian Family*. New York: Academic Press, 1978.

Tucker, Irene. *A Probable State*. Chicago: University of Chicago Press, 2000.

Turner, James Grantham. 'Lovelace and the Paradoxes of Libertinism.' In *Tercentenary Essays*, edited by Margaret Doody and Peter Sabor, 70–88. Cambridge: Cambridge University Press, 1989.

– *One Flesh: Paradisal Marriage and Sexual Relations in the Age of Milton*. Oxford: Clarendon Press, 1993.

Urbanati, Nadia. 'J.S. Mill on Androgyny and Ideal Marriage.' *Political Theory* 19 (1991): 627–49.

Van Brugh, Sir John. *The Provok'd Wife*. Lincoln: University of Nebraska Press, 1989.

– 'The Relapse.' *Four Comedies*. Harmondsworth: Penguin, 1989.
Van Sant, Jessie Ann. *Eighteenth-Century Sensibility and the Novel*. Cambridge: Cambridge University Press, 1993.
Vickery, Amanda. *The Gentleman's Daughter*. New Haven: Yale University Press, 1998.
– 'Golden Age to Separate Spheres? A Review of the Categories and Chronology of English Women's History.' *Historical Journal* 36, no. 2 (1993): 383–414.
Wahrman, Dror. *Imagining the Middle Class: The Political Representation of Class in Britain, c. 1780–1840*. Cambridge: Cambridge University Press, 1995.
Warburton, Richard, and Hugh Blair. *On Fictitious History*. 1726.
Warhol, Robyn. 'The Look, the Body, and the Heroine: A Feminist-Narratological Reading of *Persuasion*.' *Novel: A Forum on Fiction* 26(1) (Fall 1992): 5–19.
Warner, William B. *Licensing Entertainment: The Elevation of Novel Reading in Britain, 1648–1750*. Berkeley and Los Angeles: University of California Press, 1998.
Watt, Ian. *The Rise of the Novel*. Berkeley and Los Angeles: University of California Press, 1957.
Whatley, William. *A Bride Bush, or a Wedding Sermon*. 1619.
Williams, Ioan, ed. *Novel and Romance 1700–1800: A Documentary Record*. London: Routledge and Kegan Paul, 1970.
Williams, Merryn. 'Feminist or Antifeminist? Oliphant and the Woman Question.' In *Margaret Oliphant: Critical Essays on a Gentle Subversive*, edited by D.J. Trela, 165–80. London: Associated University Presses, 1995.
Williams, Raymond. *The Country and the City*. New York: Oxford University Press, 1973.
– *Marxism and Literature*. Oxford: Oxford University Press, 1977.
Wollstonecraft, Mary. *A Vindication of the Rights of Woman*. New York: Penguin Books, 1992.
Young, Arlene. *Culture, Class and Gender in the Victorian Novel: Gentlemen, Gents and Working Women*. London: Macmillan Press Ltd., 1999.
Zomchick, John P. *Family and the Law in Eighteenth-Century Fiction*. Cambridge: Cambridge University Press, 1993.

Index